The Sociology of Good Works

Joseph H. Fichter
✳
The Sociology of Good Works
Research in Catholic America
✳
Foreword by Paul M. Roman

A Campion Book

Loyola University Press
Chicago

Loyola University Press
3441 North Ashland Avenue
Chicago, Illinois 60657

Cover and interior design by Nancy Gruenke.
Cover art by Nancy Gruenke and Robert Voigts.

Library of Congress Cataloging-in-Publication Data
Fichter, Joseph Henry, 1908–
    The sociology of good works: research in Catholic America/
by Joseph H. Fichter.
      p. cm.
    Includes bibliographical references and index.
    ISBN 0-8294-0751-0
    1. Catholic Church—United States—History—1965–
2. Sociology. Christian (Catholic) 3. Fichter, Joseph Henry, 1908– .
4. Catholic Church—United States—Clergy—Biography.
5. Sociologists—United States—Biography. I. Title.
BX1406.2F514 1993
282'.73'09047—dc20
                                    93-19779
                                          CIP

Contents

✷✷

Foreword

✷❈✷

I should like to think of myself as having played a tiny part in getting this book written, but I may be wrong. As is well known, Father Fichter published his professional autobiography *One-Man Research* in 1973. Starting several years ago, in a half-joking manner, I repeatedly reminded him that his autobiography was "out of date" and that a sequel was needed to update it. Upon reflection, this seems a rare and perhaps even singular event. There is no indication in the earlier publication that he planned to retire (perish the thought) or even consider slowing down. Thus, this second volume of professional reflections may have been planned all along. In any event, it is most welcome.

An important set of observations emerges while looking at these new chapters as well as in reflecting on the earlier volume of this research odyssey. Father Fichter's work demonstrates all the ironies of the insider-outsider dilemma in conducting social research. Let me describe my version of it. To collect and analyze data objectively one needs to have a degree of "outsideness" for at least two reasons. First, outsideness usually offers assurance that one will really see what is going on and not confuse personal experience and bias with empirical reality. Second, one must feel free to report what one sees, blemishes and all. With a degree of outsideness it is likely that such reportage will be objective.

Studying aspects of one's home place risks bias by making things look good. I think, however, we can rest assured that Father Fichter calls them as he sees them. Not only does his research include descriptions of the "warts," it also reports the censorship and other meddling with his data collection and research reports by Church superiors and bureaucrats. Thus, the book contains a strong dose of objectivity—what Alcoholics Anonymous would call tough love.

The other aspect of the dilemma is "insideness." To be able to collect data effectively one has to have intimate knowledge of a particular research site as well as rapport with the people at that site. Further, one has to know the issues and the argot in order to grasp fully what may be going on during the research process. Finally, one needs to have enough intimacy to avoid being conned or bluffed by the research subjects. In studying the Church, its activities, and many of its personnel, Father Fichter is the consummate insider. This is certainly reflected in the range and diversity of projects he has handled. More often than not good research is blocked by the researcher's inability to gain access to the site where the data lie. This has not been a problem for Father Fichter.

The Sociology of Good Works provides valuable insights of the insider-outsider dilemma. Father Fichter has resolved this dilemma in most of his research by reporting what he observes, even at the risk, through his honesty, of alienating himself from important brothers and sisters in the Church. He is a master at playing the role of the critical insider.

I remember distinctly my first encounter with Father Joe after he had returned from Harvard in the early 1970s. It occurred in the New Orleans living room of a mutual friend, Dr. Manuel Carballo, now researcher and administrator with the World Health Organization in Geneva. While I was not trained in the sociology of religion, my mentors at Cornell University were closely connected to Harvard and the same doctoral program Joe had completed in the 1940s. He was remembered there also for having given a lecture to the Peace Corps trainees on the day President Kennedy was killed. Thus his name was well known to me. As a junior sociologist on the Tulane faculty I remember I was quite overwhelmed by being in his famous presence. That feeling dissolved quickly as my twenty-year-plus friendship with him began.

Joe and I saw each other frequently at professional events. Occasionally my wife and I would invite him to our home for dinner or host a meal at one of the many fine eateries in New Orleans. We were honored guests when the *National Catholic Reporter* hosted a birthday dinner for him at the Pontchartrain Hotel. It is only by reading this book that I learned the remarkable story of the evolution of that periodical and Joe's role in it. A few years later I prepared a dinner of grillades and grits to celebrate his birthday with him and several of his closest New Orleans friends.

My contact with Joe decreased after I moved in 1986 from Tulane University to the University of Georgia. I greatly miss that socializing, for it always featured some new set of ideas that Joe was pursuing in his research and writing. Most of these issues were centered on some aspect of change within the Roman Catholic Church and the alternatives that the processes of change presented. Then and now I have always tried to play the devil's advocate on the thin border between my own High Church Anglicanism and the Church of Rome.

My direct involvement in the series of good works reported here was quite minimal. As Joe emphasizes in this and the previous volume, he does "one-man research." Beyond our long-term friendship, our professional contact began with Joe's interest in alcoholism, which is my own research specialty. I may have spurred this interest slightly, but it developed quite independently of anything I had to offer. There were background discussions that may have helped him make some conceptual distinctions, but Father Fichter's extensive study of "ardent spirits subdued" had relatively little input from me.

In 1981 Father Joe was invited to speak at a symposium, sponsored by Eagleville Hospital in Pennsylvania, on alcohol and drugs in the workplace. Very much by coincidence, I was invited to be one of the plenary speakers at the same conference. The other speaker was an international expert on burnout in the workplace. Perhaps needless to say (and as documented by this book), Father Fichter had little patience with the concept of burnout, particularly as this speaker presented it as a condition created by intense involvement in work and career. Father Joe's remarks essentially suggested that burnout is nothing less than an excuse for

sloth and laziness, hardly worthy of designation as a psychiatric syndrome. I wish I had a recording of that talk, for it was
the height of my suspicion that Father Fichter must be directly
descended from the inventors of the Protestant work ethic,
which is indeed closely linked to his German heritage.

Another anecdote of interest took place in Atlanta in 1987
during Father Fichter's research of the Episcopal priests who
were "crossing the Tiber." Because of my own commitments I
had a mixed set of feelings about the Vatican's "Pastoral
Provisions" for the transfer of these priests and their implications. Joe came to Atlanta to attend the meetings of the
Southern Sociological Society, arriving early to spend time
with my wife and me. We discussed the possibility of interviewing some Episcopal priests about their attitude toward
clerical colleagues who were being accepted into the Roman
Catholic Church. My wife and I had been attending two different parish churches, both some distance from our home, and
I casually suggested that these rectors might be good subjects
for interviews.

At the first church, the rector could not fit us into his
schedule but cordially referred us to his associate rector, who
he said might be able to help us even though in my introduction I was very vague about the topic of conversation. I sat in
on Father Joe's interview with the associate rector, who was
forthright and interesting but seemed oddly strained. I was
not able to be present for the second interview, which
occurred the next day with the rector of another parish, but
Joe told me that it went well. The punch line to this story is
that by total coincidence, both of these interviewees turned
out to be priests who would eventually leave the Episcopal
Church and be accepted as married priests within the Roman
Catholic Church! Such intentions must have existed at the time
of the interviews. Even so, the first priest in particular mentioned how amazed he was that he had been chosen for an
interview on this subject. I must say that such movements by
the Holy Spirit seem to have occurred throughout the time I
have spent with Joe both as a friend and colleague.

I would not be honest if these words did not include a bit
of loving criticism of my dear friend's research work. Some
of us needle him about his involvement with the "Moonies,"
but this is not serious criticism; his work with the Unification
Church has been a tremendous sociological contribution. But

there is something else: criticism not of this fast-moving priest-researcher but of his slow-moving Church. While his work has covered a broad range of issues of equity and equality, I recognize one Roman Catholic issue that seems to remain insoluble: the Church's refusal to allow women entry to Holy Orders at all levels of ministry.

As is well documented in Joe's own research and writing, the Episcopal Church has experienced tremendous upheaval and painful division over its somewhat quick decision to ordain women into the priesthood. The reverberations and aftershocks of the decision continue to this day. At a personal level I initially wanted to avoid this issue because it was troublesome. It meant that traditions with which I had grown up would be disrupted. The vision of a woman conducting any part of the liturgy was an uncomfortable idea. But in all honesty I was not, at the time of the change, in a diocese where women were ordained, so the issue was out of sight and out of mind.

It was actually through a professional colleague, a mutual friend of Father Fichter and myself, that I became aware of the genuinely sinful nature of my attitudes. The epiphany occurred during a conversation with a woman whom we both knew as a highly competent and respected sociologist. That she had been ordained a priest was an utter surprise to me. Perhaps it was in this context that I had already accepted and respected the professional character of this woman that the correctness of women's ordination finally became clear to me.

In conclusion, this volume is a compelling set of stories on the one hand and a set of studies on the other. As an occupational study it describes an incredible fit between a man and the work he has chosen to pursue. Father Fichter's enthusiasm and gusto for his research and writing are almost overwhelming. *The Sociology of Good Works* is about the life calling of a sociologist and of a priest, two very special forms of the Lord's work. It is a loving privilege to have been invited to share these pages with this man of God, a vital giant of a human being.

Paul M. Roman
Research Professor of Sociology
University of Georgia
Athens, Georgia
July 1993

Introduction

✻✻✻

In 1973 I was brash enough to publish a book subtitled *Reminiscences of a Catholic Sociologist*[1] that gave an account of five research projects for which I received heavy blame and criticism. I conducted these sociological studies over the two decades between 1948 and 1968. As the dust jacket of the book revealed, I chronicled "five research projects, showing how each originated and developed in reaction to unforeseen and intrusive elements. While the projects' subject matter varied greatly (parish sociology, the politics of racism, police behavior, ecclesiastical politics, and school problems), all were initiated in an attempt to improve group relations, and in varying degrees were planned and executed in the face of opposition from people who felt threatened by the study."

During the 1970s and 1980s, I became involved in another series of academic episodes that also dealt with live issues that were sometimes controversial but seldom "threatening" to anyone. All of the groups and programs I experienced are manifestations of the kind of "good works" that are common among church people. As a veteran sociologist I analyzed these activities as objectively as possible, but I was not an "outsider." I was not "value free," either as observer or participant. While social scientists are not expected to "promote" the programs of the groups under study, there should be no reluctance to tell the truth about them.

Some of the data from these studies revealed what people do not know. The establishment of a Professorship of Roman Catholic Studies in the reputedly bigoted Protestant Harvard Divinity School called for empirical exploration. In each of these personal experiences I was on the search for knowledge, and sometimes the findings were unexpected. For instance, many people concerned about the rehabilitation of clergy alcoholics were surprised to learn that only one in twenty Catholic priests is addicted to alcohol. In my health survey of Catholic priests, the hierarchy was skeptical at the disclosure that American priests are the healthiest men in the country. The upbeat report on four comparative hospital systems attracted very little notice and seems to have disappeared into the archives of government documents where federally-funded studies are consigned.

The Catholic Pentecostals cooperated cheerfully with my study of the charismatic renewal but were not too happy when I described the movement as a cult. The more devout among them wondered why I did not become a member. My dealings with the Sisters of the Holy Family were more edifying. They were deeply devoted to the care of the sick, the needy, and the elderly. Participating on the advisory board of St. John Berchmans Manor and on the historical commission for the canonization of Mother Henriette Delille was a benefit that transcended sociological research. Consorting with the controversial Moonies was an interfaith experience of international proportions. It aroused the conventional *miramur*[2] from church authorities and counterattacks from religious bigots.

My investigation of the moral and social values of students in Jesuit schools was fully approved by the authorities in these schools, who were, nevertheless, not happy with the research findings. The high academic achievement of the students, however, was not matched with a satisfactory moral and religious development. Even so, Jesuit liberal education is praised by the successful graduates of the sytem. Another liberal expression of Catholic culture is the *National Catholic Reporter (NCR),* with which I was closely associated for twenty years. The paper has had a colorful history, surviving several financial, editorial, and organizational crises. It has never been called a conservative paper.

The research studies that I directed to the Catholic priest-hood during these two decades addressed the controversial option between celibacy and marriage. The center of contro-versy was, of course, the status of women in relation to the sacraments of matrimony and holy orders. My investigations went much deeper than the contemporary discussions of the time and emerged in my book *Wives of Catholic Clergy.*[3] Most permanent deacons are married, and wives are expected to share in their ministry. Married priests who converted from other denominations are relatively few in number but have, with their wives, willingly cooperated in my research. The most vigorous proponents of clergy marriage are the members of Corp of Reserve Priests United for Service (CORPUS), who have since organized the National Association for a Married Priesthood (NAMP). The members and their wives whom I interviewed and studied are a small proportion of many thou-sand married priests about whom we have no information.

The Sociology of Good Works demonstrates that I continued along the road of "one-man research," conducting these stud-ies quite independent of sociological colleagues. A distinct dif-ference, however, from my earlier research is that institutional church doors are now open for sociological investigation. Church authorities are even sometimes willing to provide modest funds for research studies and are ready to accept the data. An overview of the chapters in this book will indicate the direction of one sociologist's quarter-century of investigation.

Chapter 1

One of the best demonstrations of Catholic-Protestant ecu-menism was the healing of the long-standing rift between "the Loyolas and the Cabots."[4] The centuries-old anti-Catholic big-otry exhibited by the New England Puritans had its most eru-dite expression in the annual Dudlean lectures, the fourth of which centered on the Roman papacy, or the "whore of Baby-lon." The belated Feeney countermovement, just outside the walls of the Harvard Yard, exhibited an equally bigoted anti-Protestantism.

The Charles Chauncey Stillman Chair of Roman Catholic Studies was endowed by an alumnus who had converted to Catholicism. As a Catholic sociologist I was appointed to this chair at the time when the ecumenical *aggiornamento* of the Second Vatican Council was widely heralded. The courses I taught at Harvard Divinity School and in the Harvard Yard were informed by the sixteen documents of the council. A whole range of contemporary social problems was discussed under this variety of constitutions and decrees.

The period from 1965 to 1970 was a time of discontent and rebellion among college youth, who protested against the draft, the ROTC, and the Vietnam War. The free speech movement was expressed in a general antiauthoritarian attitude culminating in a campuswide student strike demanding the removal of ROTC. The divinity students were in strong moral support of conscientious objectors and gave sanctuary to AWOLs and draft dodgers.

Chapter 2

One of the clearest examples of openness to research is the changed approach of Church leaders, bishops, and religious provincials to the study of alcoholic clergy. What had once been scandalous conduct, shameful and guilt-ridden, was now recognized as an illness, open to treatment and rehabilitation. The managers of treatment facilities, such as Guest House in Michigan and Southdown in Toronto, no longer needed to "tone down" the specifics of their therapeutic ministry. Their willingness to invite "outsiders" to visit the facilities and examine their results indicated confidence in objective research.

The changed attitudes of Church officials toward the long hidden problems of clergy alcoholism were noted in the willingness of the Bishops' Committee on Priestly Life and Ministry to sponsor a research study. I enjoyed full confidence and cooperation from bishops and provincials when I interviewed them about their problem-drinking priests. For the first time I was able to collect reliable data to demonstrate that the rate of clergy alcoholism is about 5 percent of all Catholic priests—half of what was commonly assumed. Diocesan and religious administrators were made aware of the "health program" devised by the members of the National Clergy Conference on Alcoholism, most of them recovering alcoholics. Extensive research described also for the first time the entire therapeutic routine: identifying the alcoholics, getting them into treatment, and following them through medical, psychological, and spiritual procedures to recovery. Most of the sick alcoholics have been returned to a busy and zealous pastoral ministry.

Chapter 3

The secretary of the Bishops' Committee on Priestly Life and Ministry, Monsignor Colin MacDonald, called on me for another research project when the bishops were widely decrying the declining health of the clergy. They thought that the physical health of priests was "one of the most critical issues facing the Church today." I had already conducted a survey of the health and life-style of the Southern Jesuits when the monsignor asked me to research the physical health of American priests. An earlier report, *The Priest and Stress,* which was published in 1982 and sponsored by the same committee, had told a disturbing story of their psychological ailments. The clergy were said to be overworked, emotionally distressed, and on the verge of burnout.

The findings of my national survey of the physical health of American priests revealed a very different diagnosis and seemed to take the bishops by surprise. They found it hard to believe that a majority (84 percent) said their current state of health was good or excellent. Hardly any (13 percent) had been hospitalized during that particular year; most had not even had severe headaches (64 percent); and a majority had not been sick enough to spend a day in bed (64 percent).

The facts are that priests generally live longer than men in other professions, have fewer accidents, and experience less illnesses. They tend also to grow old in better mental and psychological health than other males. When my research report was published by the National Conference of Catholic Bishops in 1984, it contained an extraordinary preface that I had not written and that essentially repudiated its contents. In a sense, it was a warning to the reader that priests do not tell the truth when you ask them about their state of health. According to the preface, these priests represent the "mystique of the strong male," who overestimates his personal well-being. In spite of such peculiar misinterpretation of priestly truthfulness, the findings of this survey provided the first comprehensive study of the healthy American Catholic clergy.

While the physical and mental aspects of health care were subject to research studies, I was interested also in the spiritual dimension that health professionals brought to their patients. The inquiry I described in my book *Religion and Pain* was answered by 692 health professionals in three hundred Catholic hospitals and demonstrated that the holistic approach to health care has to incorporate the spiritual dimension. I pursued this theme in a series of conversations with health-care professionals, who appreciated both advanced medical technology and the beneficial effects that religion can have on patients. A selection of these interviews was published in my book *Healing Ministries.*

Chapter 4

Research in the area of health and healing led me to a comparative study of four nonprofit hospitals. It also renewed my contact with the management of the Center for Applied Research in the Apostolate (CARA), an independent Catholic research institute in Washington, D.C. They had previously analyzed, edited, and published my research study for the diocese of Peoria, Illinois, entitled "Parents' Attitudes on Church Vocations." Paul Besanceny, one of the directors of CARA, explained that their contract with the Department of Health, Education, and Welfare (HEW) investigated the manner in which these hospitals achieved the national health priorities set by the United States Congress in Public Law 93–641.

A committee of health-care experts had been assembled to assess and nominate the hospitals most likely to fit the congressional qualifications. The research study entailed a week-long visit to each of the four chosen locations: Santa Rosa in San Antonio, Presbyterian in Albuquerque, Greenville in South Carolina, and Mid-Maine in Waterville. These hospitals enjoyed a national reputation for providing excellent health care among knowledgeable experts. With the competent cooperation of Suzanne Ahern, project assistant, I was able to verify this.

We could discover no "hidden agenda" in these hospitals, and we were impressed with the humane philosophy expressed by the management and exemplified at all levels of employment. While the medical professionals, surgeons, and physicians formed the functional core of these institutions, they were not the owners. The distinguishing feature at each hospital was available health care for people of limited income. Associated with this concern for the poor and needy was, in every case, a genuine appreciation for pastoral ministry.[5] It was a wholesome and humane sociological experience to investigate these "islands" of socially conscious health professionals in a society that seems incapable of providing an adequate health system for all its citizens.

Chapter 5

There was another significant "healing ministry" to which I paid considerable research attention and out of which emerged my book *The Catholic Cult of the Paraclete*. The Catholic charismatic movement was a strange socioreligious phenomenon for me when I first encountered it at Loyola University. The members had a special and enthusiastic devotion to the Paraclete, the Holy Spirit, in whose name they experienced baptismal renewal. Speaking in tongues (*glossolalia*) was a shared experience that seemed to identify a cult-like community. I participated in prayer meetings and Eucharistic services as an observer with a ready tape recorder. I interviewed numerous members—leaders and followers, cleric and laic—and distributed questionnaires to 744 members in 155 prayer groups.

The renewal movement had overtones of Pentecostal enthusiasm, inspired by Protestant clergy, such as David Wilkerson, David du Plessis, Graham Pulkingham, and Vinson Synon. A priestly supporter of the renewals, Father Edward O'Connor, said that some members seemed to suffer from the affliction of "charismania."[6] From the perspective of conventional American Catholicism, it is exceptional not only in its liturgical practices but also in its relative independence of clergy dominance. It was originated by laypersons and continues to be governed by the laity. The charismatic movement focuses on personal piety and a close relationship with God. It has little interest in organized social reform. I witnessed the charismatics' enormous enthusiasm, and I was an invited speaker in 1973 at both their state convention in Louisiana and their national conference at the University of Notre Dame.

The general trend among the respondents was traditional and conservative. They accepted the subordinate status of women within the Church and the family, and they did not support feminist liberation or the ordination of women into the priesthood. They tended to accept prophetic witness in anticipation of the Second Coming and the end of time. Many have become ardent promoters of the pilgrimage to Medjugorje, while others are hesitant to accept the Marian apparitions. This disagreement suggests a growing rift, a kind of "power struggle," setting the doomsayers apart from others. The movement now boasts a center of higher education at the Franciscan University of Steubenville, Ohio, under the dynamic influence of Father Michael Scanlan.

Chapter 6

The noisy piety of the Catholic Pentecostals contrasted sharply with the quiet spirituality of the Sisters of the Holy Family. My friendship with these nuns and my appreciation for their apostolic ministry goes back to the early 1950s, when I was deeply involved with the desegregation of all Catholic facilities. I thought we could start the process by admitting black students to Loyola University. After two sisters were enrolled as part-time students, I began to learn more about the history of this congregation of nuns, which was established in New Orleans in 1842. Some of the older sisters claimed that Loyola University had granted academic credits to their sisters back in the 1920s. The historical records of this unusual interracial enterprise could not be found in the archives of either Loyola University or the Holy Family motherhouse. Instead, I discovered these records, complete and detailed, in the archives of the Sisters of Charity at Seton Hill College in Greensburg, Pennsylvania. The Sisters of Charity taught summer school to young Holy Family sisters receiving college credit from Loyola University.[7]

I was involved in two other ongoing ventures with the sisters. The first was the study of their ambitious program of high-rise residences for the elderly poor. I was elected to the advisory board of the first of these residences, St. John Berchmans Manor, which went into operation in 1982. Another and smaller residence is the Delille Inn, named after the Mother Founder Henriette Delille, and dedicated in 1988. Adjacent to the inn is the Lafon Nursing Home, which was built in two sections. One wing was completed in 1973, the other in 1978. The sisters proved themselves adept in financing these projects. They received aid from Hill-Burton funds as well as substantial grants from the Department of Housing and Urban Development.

Research is now under way in the cause for the canonization of Henriette Delille, born in 1812 as a "free person of color." She appears to be representative of a distinctive category of persons of mixed racial ancestry who were Catholics, reared to French culture and language. Their ancestors had been slaves, but their "freedom" did not allow them entrance to white society. Further, they have been the subject of fictionalized and romanticized accounts that need to be disentangled through historical research. I was appointed by Archbishop Francis Schulte to the historical commission charged with the task of searching out the truth of Mother Henriette's life and works.

Chapter 7

The search for truth was a sociological motive for my study of the controversial Unification Church, which resulted in an equally controversial book, *The Holy Family of Father Moon*. The Moonies have been slandered and their revered founder vilified and unjustly sentenced to prison. My religious ideology condemns not only racism and sexism but also the kind of religious bigotry that assaults the Unificationists. The God-centered family is the sociological and theological underpinning of Unification church solidarity. My article on this topic, "Marriage, Family and Sun Myung Moon," generated severe criticism on both myself and the magazine's editors.

While I could not accept the eclectic theology of the Unificationists, I greatly admired their patterns of personal behavior and their extraordinary programs of social welfare. I have seen first hand the munificence of the founder and the generosity of the members in sponsoring programs for the needy. I participated in the annual International Conference on the Unity of Science (ICUS), the several Assemblies of the World's Religions, and numerous ecumenical programs of study and discussion. I functioned as group moderator in programs that invited scholars and clergy from around the world to learn about the Unification Church. These three- or four-day assemblies were held in the United States and Europe as well as in Mexico, Japan, and Korea.

Such far-flung meetings were not held for the purpose of recruiting new members since the structure for conversion to the Unification Church is completely different from the academic and sociological programs in which I participated. Even so, I watched carefully for evidence of thought control, brainwashing, and other devious methods of entrapping young persons to the movement. In talking with ex-Catholics who were active in the Unification Church, I was sensitive to any kind of delusion, seduction, or trickery. I published a sampling of the converts in *Autobiographies of Conversion* and found no hint of coercion.

Chapter 8

I searched the Jesuit educational system for the spiritual and moral influence we are said to have over our students. Having spent most of my professional life in the classroom I assumed that the vocation of the teacher is aimed at more than measurable academic results. Although I had much personal experience as a teacher—briefly at the high school level but also many long years on the college campus—I suffered a vague uncertainty and uneasiness about the vaunted reputation of Jesuit education. I was nudged to make an inquiry by the leaders of the Committee on Jesuit Secondary Education in the 1960s and instigated my own investigation of college students in the 1980s.

Surveys of ethics and religion among college students have been recorded since World War I and have consistently revealed that college experience secularizes students. My fellow Jesuits do not seem to be disturbed by this fact. They rationalize it along two lines: The first explanation is that such conduct lies in the "time of life" when you expect behavior to change, and the second is that the moral effects of this excellent religious teaching occur somewhat later, when the alumnus has settled down and begun to start a family. Another theory bypasses both these explanations altogether, with the assertion that "values" are not measurable.[8]

The dilemma is unsatisfactory on both sides; that is, the assertion that it is not the fault of the school if the student tends to delinquency and the problematic contention that moral and religious values cannot be measured. In either case the Jesuit educator escapes blame. Of course, there is always the humble suggestion that "others can do it better." There had always been the assumption that church-related schools are better than secular and public schools in the production of morally upright graduates. It is sometimes suggested that Catholic colleges—even Jesuit schools—are inevitably going the way of the nationally famous church-founded colleges and universities that are now admittedly secular. The simple fact is that in four carefully conducted surveys—two among high school students and two among college students—I could not identify the moral, ethical, and religious improvements that the Jesuit system was created to produce.

Chapter 9

While I was searching for the transmission of social and moral values in the Jesuit educational system I participated for twenty years in a Catholic communications enterprise: the *National Catholic Reporter.* This weekly newspaper was greeted with enthusiasm by readers who were, at the same time, praising the *aggiornamento* of the Second Vatican Council. Founding editor Robert Hoyt set standards for Catholic journalism and was ready to publish and evaluate the activities of bishops and clergy as well as events involving prominent laity. Donald Thorman was its organizing force, maintaining its existence through the paper's critical years, until his untimely death in 1977.

At its peak of readership in 1969, *NCR* had "scooped" other news sources with important stories, such as my survey of clergy celibacy[9] and the preliminary report of the papal commission on birth control. When subscriptions declined and finances became precarious, and "there was no hope for the future of *NCR*," three board members—Dan Herr, Bob Burns, and Martin Marty—resigned. When the founding editor failed to "turn the tide" of subscriptions, he was dismissed. A series of new people joined the board over the years, starting with Monsignor Jack Egan, businessman John Caron, theologian

Albert Outler, social activist Rose Lucy, and Sisters Francis Borgia Rothluebber and Joan Chittister.

Don Thorman had hired Arthur Jones as editor, with the frequent reminder that the Jones family did not like living in Kansas City and that Jones had tempting offers for newspaper jobs in his native England. He did resign to go home in 1980 but was soon back and reemployed. During his editorship, the *NCR* began to feature the sexual escapades of the Catholic clergy. Despite my remonstrances, this trend continued under the new editor, Tom Fox, who sent out investigative reporters for stories on clerical pedophilia and homosexuality. I brought this problem to the attention of the board, with a motion that the *NCR* board exercise its obligation of moral overview and express its disapproval of such stories and articles. When no agreement was forthcoming I knew it was time for me to resign.

Chapter 10

The occasional resignation of a priest in the years before the Second Vatican Council had been seen as a personal problem of spiritual failure or psychological imbalance. The avalanche of priestly departures in later years, however, has gained the attention of sociologists who see it as a social movement organized first as the National Association for Pastoral Renewal (NAPR) and later as CORPUS, which eventually changed its name to the National Association for a Married Priesthood. One of my research projects, *America's Forgotten Priests,* emphasized the theme of "optional marriage." A later project, *The Pastoral Provisions: Married Catholic Priests,* focused on "actual marriage" and the family of priests.

In almost every conversation about married Catholic priests, the problem of the "double standard" is raised. This is especially pertinent among the relatives and friends of the priests who have resigned to marry. The answer is always a moral judgment: the ones who left did wrong; the ones who joined did right. Hardly anyone asks whether and when the Church will ordain women. Everyone knows that for many centuries the Catholic Church embraced a married clergy: deacons, priests, bishops, and popes. There is wide confidence among both laity and clergy that a married priesthood must eventually be returned to Roman Catholicism.

Meanwhile, the influx of married clergy from non-Catholic denominations continues at a slow rate and makes only a minimal impression on the increasing shortage of Catholic priests. The exodus of priests who resign to marry seems to have diminished, but the Vatican has given no sign of inviting their return to active ministry. While the laity is widely receptive of these married resigned priests, the bishops are only gradually recognizing this large category of trained and ordained talent. Job opportunities for church work are slowly opening for laity in the dioceses where priestless parishes need help.

The research reports I released on my study of resigned priests and their wives seemed to fit the experiences of the women who read them. A strong criticism, however, came from Ann Bukovchik, the only woman elected to the board of CORPUS, who claimed that I did not "ask the right questions." We had frequent discussions about the questionnaires she had distributed to over six hundred wives, all of whom were members of CORPUS. She presented her survey findings at the fourth national conference in New York in June 1991, where a panel of young people discussed my article "The Children of Resigned Priests."[10] Although the yearly rate of priestly resignations seems to be slowing down, most of those who do leave get married and have families. Their wives and children are still out of favor with the hierarchy.

Chapter 11

The sociological problem of sexism, or gender inequality, has been my concern for many decades, and it is logical that I look at the rapidly expanding category of deacons' wives. I recognize their status as different from the wives of convert priests and the wives of noncanonical priests. I am a dues-paying member of the Women's Ordination Conference (WOC) and an active member of Sociologists for Women in Society (SWS). In my research studies I actually conducted more interviews with the wives than with the clergy husbands. After all, they are the novelty in the midst of the celibate tradition.

As women move closer to parity within the Catholic Church, they are gradually permitted to participate in more and more activities—cultural, educational, administrative, and liturgical. Their personal relations with the clergy become more meaningful in marriage with deacons and priests. Yet the American bishops were not able to complete their much-discussed pastoral. Oddly enough, the strongest critic of my research on married priests is the married convert priest, Father James Parker, Cardinal Bernard Law's assistant, who was "displeased" that I interviewed these women "without permission." Nevertheless, their stories are available in my two books: *Pastoral Provisions: Married Catholic Priests* and *The Wives of Catholic Clergy*.

✳✥✳✥✳✥✳✥✳✥✳

The "manifestation" of these good works is in the actual performance of the many individuals involved in them. That they are "doing" good works must be manifest to everyone around them and to the reader. While I have been an objective observer—and sometimes a participant—I cannot pretend to be the detached researcher of social science. The fact that I have described and analyzed these organized activities, I too have made them "manifest." It remains for the reader to judge in what ways and to what extent these activities are genuine "good works."

1

The Stillman Chair

✳✦✳

When I arrived in Cambridge in 1945 to begin doctoral studies in sociology at Harvard University, I made an early courtesy call at St. Benedict Catholic Center to greet my fellow Jesuit, Father Leonard Feeney. I detected a chill in the short conversation I had with Catherine Clarke, founder of the center. After my brief words with her, Father Feeney emerged from behind a partition where he had been listening. Without shaking hands, he gruffly informed me that he did not want this place "cluttered up" with priests who were students at Harvard. Later I heard from Catholic graduate students who had also been forbidden access to his Catholic center. They were in a "state of mortal sin" as long as they attended the heretical Protestant campus of Harvard University. A defense of the center and the story of Father Feeney's ultimate dismissal from the priesthood was told later by Catherine Clarke in *The Loyolas and the Cabots.*

Father Feeney's Irish Catholic animosity against Protestant Harvard was by this time out-of-date, but it was a throwback to a much earlier period when suspicion and distrust were official Catholic policy. Thirty years or so earlier, in 1914, after the German invasion of Belgium, President R. Lawrence Lowell and the faculty of the Harvard Divinity School offered asylum to the great Jesuit Bolandist, Father Hippolyte

Delehaye, offering him a faculty position until he could return to postwar academic work in Belgium. Boston's William Cardinal O'Connell and Jesuit Provincial Father Anthony Maas refused to approve the Harvard proposal even when President Lowell subsequently suggested a joint appointment with Jesuit Boston College.

This Catholic repudiation of Lowell's conciliatory gesture probably reflected the long memory of Harvard's 150 years of antipopery. The so-called Dudlean lectures instituted in 1757 consisted of a cycle of four conferences delivered in rotation. Reverend Protestant scholars were invited to discourse on natural religion, revealed religion, the errors of popery, and the validity of nonepiscopal ordinations. Every four years Harvard students listened to lectures that deliberately discredited Roman Catholicism and kept alive an attitude of bigotry. The third lecture of the cycle was terminated in 1909, when it no longer served any purpose. "The lecture's incongruity and intolerance at Harvard could itself no longer be tolerated."[1]

The Harvard Yard gradually became more accessible to the Boston Irish and to Catholics generally, who also enrolled more readily in the graduate schools. At the end of World War II many Catholic veterans took advantage of the G.I. Bill of Rights, which provided previously unavailable financial support. Positions on the faculties became available for Catholic scholars. Meanwhile, Father Feeney's challenge, "no salvation outside the Church," continued to be shouted by his followers in and around Harvard Square.

Religious bigotry dies hard on both sides. In January 1958, when Chauncey Stillman, an alumnus and devout convert to Catholicism, gave an endowment of $400,000 for a chair in Roman Catholic studies, Professor Paul Tillich opposed the offer. So did the Preacher to the University, George Buttrick, who felt that the chair would jeopardize the school's "nonsectarian" independence. Letters arrived from concerned alumni of the Divinity School who were certain that the scholarship would be contaminated by papal influence. These intolerant complaints were disregarded in the final decision by the Harvard president and fellows.

Since there is no department of religion at the Harvard undergraduate level, it had been Chauncey Stillman's hope to establish the professorship in the Harvard Yard. In the end he conceded that "the Charles Chauncey Stillman Professorship of Catholic theological studies will be assigned to the Faculty of Theology, that is, the faculty of the Harvard Divinity School. If at some future date Harvard College should establish a Department of Religion or similar administrative unit or program in the Department of Arts and Sciences, this chair may be transferred to the said Faculty of Arts and Sciences, if, in the opinion of the President and Fellows of Harvard College, the purpose of this endowment can be more effectively accomplished by such a transfer."

My postwar years as a graduate sociology student had been spent mainly in and around Emerson Hall, then headquarters of the Department of Social Relations, where I took courses from brilliant social scientists, such as Gordon Allport, Clyde Kluckhohn, Talcott Parsons, and Pitirim Sorokin. I learned later that the Divinity School was then struggling for its very existence. In the early 1940s, President James Conant had threatened to close it down or sell it. Indeed, we were hardly aware of its existence. My only visit to the Divinity School had been in April 1947, when Jesuit John LaFarge presented a Dudlean lecture entitled "Two World Concepts."

The fortunes of the Divinity School began to revive in 1953 when the newly elected president, Nathan Pusey, gave it first priority and encouraged the growth of the endowment. Then, with the appointment of English convert and church historian, Christopher Dawson, to the Stillman Chair in 1958, ecumenical relations began to flourish. When the Second Vatican Council opened, professors George Williams and James Adams were invited to Rome as observers. In 1963, Augustin Cardinal Bea was the featured speaker at the Divinity School's Catholic-Protestant symposium. In the following year ecumenical outreach included Judaism in a colloquium entitled "Church and Synagogue in Boston Renewal."

It was this ecumenical colloquium that renewed my contact with Harvard University, this time with the Divinity School. In January 1964, I accepted an invitation from Professor James Adams to discuss my sociological research of urban parishes. I delivered a paper entitled "The Integrative Factors of Metropolitan Religion" to the dean and full faculty and many of the seminarians. The paper was later published in the *Harvard Divinity Bulletin*.[2] It was only in retrospect that I realized that this was the kind of "trial lecture" usually expected of prospective faculty appointees. Two months later, Samuel Miller, dean of the Divinity School, asked if I was interested in an invitation to join the divinity faculty in the chair of the Chauncey Stillman Professorship. He was ready to propose my name for this position to the president and the fellows of Harvard University.

It was an offer that I was eager to accept, but I had to postpone it because of a previous commitment to spend a year at the Department of Sociology at the University of Chicago. On the recommendation of Father Andrew Greeley, I was invited by Peter Rossi to work at the National Opinion Research Center of the university, starting in the fall of 1964. The postponement proved acceptable to Dean Miller who, in June 1964, requested to place my name "in nomination for the Charles Chauncey Stillman Professorship of Roman Catholic Studies, for a term of three years, beginning July 1, 1965."

During the summer session of 1964 I conducted a course in the sociology of religion at George Williams University in Montreal where I shared an office with Robin Williams, professor of sociology at Cornell University. At George Williams, a church-related urban campus, I taught the six-week summer session, followed by the annual convention of the American Catholic Sociological Society in August. Before moving on to Chicago I participated in the annual meeting of the American Sociological Society in Montreal.

By the time the Harvard Divinity School announced my appointment to the Stillman Chair on November 5, I was well settled at NORC. The academic year, 1964–65, at the University of Chicago was a period of sociological research, with only occasional lectures, seminars, and conferences. I worked closely with Professor Peter Rossi, director of NORC, analyzing the research data collected from a national sample of black college students, which was conducted under government contract. My report was belatedly accepted and approved in Washington, D.C., but was not published until 1967 under the title *Graduates of Predominantly Negro Colleges*. For some unexplained reason, the much larger parallel study of students at predominantly white colleges was never published by the Government Printing Office.

Another research project that occupied my time while at the University of Chicago was a survey of graduates of forty-four Jesuit high schools in the United States for 1965. Bernard Dooley, secretary of the Jesuit Secondary School Association, which distributed the survey in April 1965, assisted me with the composition of the questionnaire. My analysis was reported to the Association Workshop that summer at Loyola University of Los Angeles.[3] I remained at the University of Chicago until September 14, when I arrived at Cambridge to take over my duties at the Harvard Divinity School.

It was Chauncey Stillman's wish that "the incumbent be not only a distinguished scholar but also an inspiring teacher" with the unstated expectation, of course, that the professor also be a believing and practicing Catholic of high moral integrity. The first person to match these characteristics was the celebrated English historian Christopher Dawson, who was on the verge of retirement from his faculty position. He was appointed to the Harvard Chair with the blessing of Richard Cardinal Cushing in 1958 (who complained, by the way, that "he speaks so quietly you can hardly hear him"). It was also Stillman's wish that his professor be appointed for a period that would normally be of not less than three, or more than five, years.

In any event, Dawson remained in the chair for four years before returning to England in 1962. He was followed by a Belgian medievalist, Professor Astrik Gabriel, who stayed for one year, and by Dominican Father Roland DeVaux, director of the Ecole Biblique in Jerusalem, who filled the academic year, 1963–64. Since no appointment was made to the Stillman Chair for the following academic year, 1964–65, funds from the Stillman endowment were used to defray the costs of the much-publicized ecumenical Cardinal Bea Conference held while the Vatican Council was in full session.

While the official preliminary correspondence about the Stillman position came from Dean Samuel Miller, my preparatory academic exchange was with James Luther Adams, in whose Department of Church and Ethics I was slated to give my courses. He had been an observer at the council and was in full agreement that I should base my lectures on "The Church in the Modern World."[4] This document, *Gaudium et Spes*, was still under discussion at the council but not yet available in printed form. Still it was contemporary headline news that appeared daily in the *New York Times* and, together with background materials provided by Xavier Rynne in the pages of the *New Yorker*, essentially functioned as my text-book. Thus, the final session of the Vatican Council, which ended in December 1965, served as an up-to-date source of information for my first semester in the Stillman Chair. Members of the faculty, and a growing number of students, appreciated that my academic area of research and teaching was the sociology of religion.

In response to a query from Jesuits in higher education, I explained that "the Harvard Divinity School is neither a secular campus nor a seminary in the way that Catholics seem to understand these terms. It is an inter-faith professional and graduate school of divinity. The faculty and student body represent about twenty different religious affiliations. Most of the faculty are ordained clergymen, and the majority of students will eventually go into some form of church ministry. The emphasis is on a high level preparation for the professional career."

The school has no direct link with the ordination of its students, nor is the curriculum controlled by any denomination or group of denominations. Although there is a broad faculty consensus on the areas of knowledge in which students should be prepared and in which they have to pass final examinations, no one tells professors how to teach their courses. Whether and when students are ready for ordination to the ministry is a question not even discussed by the faculty. It is decided in some manner by their own church or denomination.

Early in my first semester at the Divinity School I spelled out for my fellow Jesuits my role as Chauncey Stillman Professor. "In general it is the same as that of any other faculty members here: it is the serious, impartial, and unbiased investigation of truth in the field of religion. Less generally, and as a sociologist of religion, my effort is to bring a contemporary and empirical approach to religious studies that have been largely handled in a historical and abstract manner. Thirdly, as a Christian, I am interested in the contemporary parallels of structural and functional problems among the larger American churches. Finally, as a Catholic, I want to share, and receive, knowledge that is of value to the understanding of the changing Church in the contemporary world."[5]

When I arrived at Cambridge in the middle of September 1965, the first scheduled meeting I attended was the annual "retreat" of Divinity School faculty, held at the Framingham

Congregational Center. This meeting featured a faculty panel discussion of Harvey Cox's newly published book, *The Secular City*. Under the circumstances I had expected a gentle, polite, and kindly critique, but Professor Herbert Richardson delivered a resoundingly negative criticism. Harvey Cox's calm and reasoned response seemed quite adequate. It was my first experience of the intellectual and academic "exchange" between Divinity School professors.

Early in the fall I made a courtesy call to Richard Cardinal Cushing, who received me at his residence in his usual cordial and cheerful manner. He expressed personal friendship with President Nathan Pusey and more than ecumenical appreciation for Dean Samuel Miller. He felt that the Divinity School Library should stock books that would be most useful for the Stillman Professor and showed his concern with an annual donation of $5,000 to be used toward this literary purpose. The ecumenical spirit of the Cardinal and his friendly cooperation with me and all of the Divinity School continued during the five years I spent there.

Professor James Luther Adams served as chairman of the Department of Theology and Ethics, which tended to focus on the contemporary Church, its progress and problems. The spirit of *aggiornamento*, so aroused by the Second Vatican Council, had gained attention throughout the Christian world. In the fall of 1965, I presented a course on the Church in the modern world and conducted a seminar on the problems of Church organization. For the spring semester of 1966, I developed one course on ecumenism and another on institutional organization of modern Christian churches. The content of these courses was in keeping with a suggestion I had made by letter in November 1964 to James Adams: my intended focus at Harvard will be, I wrote, "contemporary American Sociology of Religion, an area in which I have done most of my research and writing."

At the end of my first academic year in the Stillman Chair, the president and fellows of Harvard University voted to delete the word *guest* from the title of the professorship. As Dean Miller informed me on May 11, 1966, this change now raised me to a "full voting member" of the faculty. At the same time, the dean gave me a thousand-dollar raise. My sense of belonging changed to a feeling of permanency when

Jim Adams invited me to membership in the Ministers' Club of Greater Boston. The club, which meets seven times a year for an intellectual and culinary gathering, was founded in 1870 as an exclusively Protestant association. In addition to myself, another Catholic, a monsignor, was a member.

Every Monday during the semester the Divinity School faculty gathered for a luncheon discussion at which professors took turns presenting a problem from current research or study. This was the kind of informal fellowship that encouraged mutual exchange of knowledge and ideas. Another regular function I had was preaching at the morning service in the Appleton Chapel. Although the university called itself nondenominational (while the Divinity School proclaimed itself Protestant) an officially-appointed Preacher to the University, Dr. Charles Price, scheduled a daily religious service of fifteen minutes at 8:45 a.m. He invited speakers from any faculty of the university, and I took my occasional turn.

In preparing courses for the 1966–67 academic year, I suggested to Dean Miller and Professor Adams that we schedule a course on religion and women. They agreed that while the Divinity School was modern and progressive on Christian social issues it was still fairly conservative on the "woman question." An exception was Professor Krister Stendahl who, in an early dissertation entitled "The Bible and the Role of Women," had supported women's ordination. Nevertheless, for the first time the Divinity School offered a formal semester course on the status and role of women in organized religion. One of the papers submitted was by a coed who deplored the fact that no women had been admitted to the House of Deputies at the PECUSA General Convention in 1964.[6] She devised a strategy for admission of women to the next convention in 1967 and submitted it to her bishop. Occasionally I invited academic women to address the class. Dr. Mary Daly came to talk about a book she was writing, *The Church and the Second Sex*, for which I eventually provided a dust jacket recommendation.

The Divinity School's concern about the religious needs of women came to the attention of leaders in the American Association of Women Ministers, from whom I received an invitation to address their forty-seventh annual assembly at Jordan Hall in Ocean Park, Maine. In her introduction the reverend president of the organization remarked that it was fitting that the first Roman Catholic priest ever to address their group should be from Harvard because Harvard was a pioneer among divinity schools by establishing a Chair of Roman Catholic Studies.

Women students had always been a minority at the Harvard Divinity School but after the introduction of my course on women and religion to the schedule, women expressed interest in the other courses I presented. In a minor key, there was a sort of "popular" demand that I again do a formal treatment of the topic. It was around this time that the National Organization for Women (NOW) had been founded in Milwaukee, and shortly thereafter the women's liberation movement came to life in Chicago and elsewhere. In the fall of 1969 a dozen graduate students (seven women and five men) signed up for a research seminar on the subject to which I invited guest lecturers.

The lecturers ranged from a religious sister in campus ministry to an African-American scholar in the religion of the Congo. The topics included "The Role of Women in Judaism," "The Grail and Religious Liberation," and "Professional Women on Theological Faculties." In other words, the three major American religious traditions—Catholic, Protestant, and Jewish—were represented. From a liberationist perspective the most challenging lecture was given by Dr. Mary Daly, who later proclaimed herself a "post-Christian" and exhorted women to reject the Church as hopelessly sexist.[7]

Most of the students who took my courses were male or mature seminarians preparing for a career in organized religion. I was curious enough about their background that I suggested a questionnaire survey, similar to studies I had made in Catholic seminaries. The B.D. (Bachelor of Divinity) students reported a strong religious upbringing, although less than one out of twenty was a "preacher's kid." They represented more than twenty different denominations, the largest being Roman Catholic, followed by Presbyterian, Baptist, and Methodist. Most had attended private or church-related colleges, where they majored in religion, history, languages, or philosophy.

We held the common assumption that the main purpose of the Divinity School was to prepare its students for professional ministry in the Church. The fact is that the Divinity

School had also gained a reputation as a seat of higher scholarship attractive to men who were interested mainly in academic graduate studies. Although six out of ten (57 percent) said they definitely sought ordination to the ministry, they were among a large majority (78 percent) who intended to do graduate studies beyond the B.D. degree. The relatively large minority (43 percent) who did not anticipate pursuing ordination led to the decision to institute a new two-year program leading to the degree, Master of Theological Studies (M.T.S.), which began in the fall of 1967. We opined at the time that "the B.D. program will continue to provide learned ministers for the Church, while the M.T.S. curriculum will also serve the church by providing a theological education for those who do not seek ordination."

In the spring of 1967, Professor Robert Bellah telephoned me to say that he had accepted an offer to teach at the University of California at Berkeley. He asked if I could arrange to give his course on the sociology of religion that he and Talcott Parsons had been team-teaching, a course that I had often taught elsewhere. Dean Miller agreed with the sociology chairman that it could be cross-listed for both Harvard Yard and the Divinity School. I presented this course for the next three years to larger than average attendance, including coeds from Radcliffe College and students from the Boston Theological Consortium.

From then on, I had one foot in the Harvard Yard and one in the Divinity School. Each year, in the spring semester, I was asked to conduct another cross-listed course—this time on religion and race relations. The number of coed students was growing in both schools and for both courses, but there was only a small increase of black students. While this arrangement doubled my teaching burden and the amount of student contact, I was fortunate to have an excellent teaching fellow, a full-time personal secretary, and a part-time research assistant.

My original contract for the Stillman professorship was three years, subject to a two-year extension. The president and fellows of Harvard University took due notice of this formality and notified me, through Dean Samuel Miller, that my term would be an additional two years, ending in July of 1970. I was therefore the first incumbent to complete the full five-year term and, incidentally, the only American and the only sociologist to hold the chair.

Dean Miller made his announcement of the renewed contract and a raise in salary on March 18, 1968. Two nights later, after attending the Boston Symphony with his wife, Molly, and the Gordon Allports, he suddenly expired in his sleep. This, of course, came as a deep shock to friends and associates—he was held in the highest regard by all who knew him. Professor Krister Stendahl was soon named as his successor.

In my five years in the Stillman Chair, I presented courses and seminars that were rooted mainly in the sociological research that I had conducted in the American Catholic social system. My seminar, "Religion and Education," for example, emerged from research I had conducted on parochial schools, secondary Jesuit schools, and college students. The seminar, "Religion as an Occupation," owed much to an earlier book I had published under the same title. Similarly, I had taught an annual course on social problems as a basis for another seminar that viewed such problems from the perspective of organized religion. The "Church as an Institution" seminar had its foundations in both the "Sociology of Religion" and the "Documents of the Second Vatican Council" courses. In other words, the academic intent of the Stillman professorship was not limited to theology and Scripture.

The Harvard undergraduates and the Radcliffe coeds who took my sociology course in the Yard were younger by several years than the seminarians and graduate students at the Divinity School. But they seemed to respond at about the same level to the general student unrest of the period. The Harvard Divinity School was not a self-centered island set apart from the large American youth culture. The five years of my tenure as Stillman professor were a time of turmoil with mounting opposition to the Vietnam War. Discontent was exhibited in the free speech movement, women's liberation, the 1965 Watts riot, and the burning of the ghettos in Detroit, Newark, and elsewhere in the summer of 1967. The murder of Martin Luther King, Jr., in April 1968 and Robert F. Kennedy in June of that year were followed by the Chicago police riot at the Democratic National Convention.

It was not surprising then that the Students for a Democratic Society (SDS) gradually gained membership among the Harvard and Radcliffe students. The divinity students were especially sensitive to the burning of draft cards and to the plight of conscientious objectors. On more than one occasion they offered "sanctuary" to draft evaders in the Divinity School chapel. The collective discontent, aroused by SDS, focused on the removal of ROTC from the campus. In December 1968, SDS staged an anti-ROTC sit-in at Paine Hall. In February 1969, the faculty voted to withdraw academic credit from ROTC courses, but the more radical students were still not satisfied. In March, they kept the protest alive by systematically invading and disrupting the lectures of certain professors. I was not the target of this embarrassment.

The scheduled meetings of the Arts and Science faculties, which were usually sparsely attended, now began to draw large numbers and had to be transferred to the Loeb Theater. Some of the more outspoken professors took the side of the student protest and criticized the administration. It was my feeling that none of the professors expected the students to go on strike. This might happen—and it did—at Columbia, Wisconsin, Michigan, Cornell, and elsewhere, but it was unthinkable at Harvard. I had often remarked that "here at Harvard we settle disputes in rational discourse."

All attempts at rational discourse between SDS and the administration were of no avail, however. On the morning of Wednesday, April 9, 1969, a group of students occupied the dining room of the Harvard Faculty Club but left before the lunch hour. I missed this excitement because I was at the Marsh Chapel of Boston University delivering the fourth of the Lowell Institute Lectures. In my absence, a large group of SDS members broke into University Hall, removed the administrators and staff, and took possession of the building. They had already issued a list of six "un-negotiable" demands, the first of which was "Abolish ROTC immediately by breaking all existing contracts and not entering any new ones."

The number of demonstrators grew until more than four hundred were inside the building, among them the president of the Divinity School Student Association who supported the sit-in with the words, "Let us share this issue in the spirit of Martin Luther King and Jesus Christ." Meanwhile, President Pusey met with the deans and other administrators and made a conciliatory offer to discuss a settlement but was rebuffed throughout the afternoon and evening. President Pusey told me later that he sought counsel from five university presidents who had experienced takeovers on their campus. From all of them he received the same advice: "Get them out of the building right away."

The somber decision was made to summon police for the removal of the demonstrators at daybreak. A combined force of more than two hundred state troopers, one hundred Cambridge police, and almost as many from Boston and the Metropolitan District Commission assembled at Memorial Hall to discuss strategy. Robert Tonis, chief of the university campus security, did not allow campus police to participate in the raid. His advice to the assembled "outside" officers was to "preserve the peace" and avoid all unnecessary roughness. The police broke into University Hall, used their clubs on resisting students, and arrested 145 of them, all of whom later pleaded not guilty to charges of criminal trespass.[8]

The SDS promptly began a rally in Harvard Yard that ended in a mass gathering of over two thousand students in the Memorial Church. In the midst of confusing and contradictory demands, they voted to declare a student strike: "A three-day strike must take place, effective tomorrow, with a convocation Monday evening to decide whether to continue it." The Divinity School faculty met informally at the dean's home on Thursday night, April 10, and with the Arts and Science faculties on Friday at the Loeb Theatre. The strike did not "close down" the university, but the more radical SDS students heckled the instructors in several regularly scheduled classes. In the ensuing two weeks there was plenty of activity: thousands attended two mass rallies at the stadium, the faculties held emergency sessions twice a week, and colloquia on all phases of university life and governance were held.

I resumed my own classes on Wednesday, April 16, and continued regularly until the reading period began at the end of the month. The divinity students were generally favorable to the demands of the SDS. For the most part they were pacifists, opposed to the war in Vietnam, and sympathetic toward students who resisted the draft (as seminarians they were exempt from the draft). In our class discussions and our informal conversations, they remarked that they wanted Harvard to discontinue formal relations with the military and to cancel all activities of the ROTC.

When I returned after the summer vacation to begin the final year of my tenure, the divinity students seemed to be in a more subdued mood. John Bethell, former editor of the *Harvard Bulletin*, wrote that "Many students who underwent temporary radicalization last April returned deradicalized in September." But there was more to come. This time it was the complaint of the black students. On Friday, December 5, they took over University Hall and occupied it for six hours. The protesting black students were represented by the Organization for Black Unity (OBU), a university-wide coalition. It was not a protest against the war or the ROTC nor was it arguing for students' rights. Their attention was focused on the rights of black workers on the campus and on the construction sites of the university. The goal was the hiring of 20 percent of black workers on each project. On December 11, they closed down the Gund construction site, then occupied the dining room of the Faculty Club, requesting guests and personnel to leave. At noon, they left the club and crossed the Yard to University Hall, and took it over. Late in the afternoon a sheriff arrived to serve a temporary restraining order. About ninety occupiers then marched out singing "Power to the People. Black Power to the African People."[9]

On December 15, OBU proclaimed that black students would boycott classes during the five days remaining before the Christmas holidays, which meant that two-thirds of Harvard's six hundred black students participated.

One of the "fringe benefits" of the Stillman Chair was that it provided the opportunity for a three-week pilgrimage to the Holy Land. On a brief tour I visited holy places such as Nazareth and Capernaum and was privileged to celebrate midnight Mass in Bethlehem at Christmas. At the same time I discussed the hypothetical question of theocracy in Israel: what was the significance of "established religion" in a parliamentary democracy under Hebrew law and custom? Although the Torah is held sacred and high holy days are observed, my interviews with Jewish professors and other well-placed citizens left me with the impression that Israel is a Westernized secular society.

During the final year of my term in the Stillman Chair, Dean Stendahl began his search for a successor. Stillman himself was concerned about the candidates under consideration. When I was asked to quietly "check out" two men whose names had been submitted, I found that one had just left the priesthood and another was on the verge of doing so. Early in the year a "search committee" of five students (none of them Catholic) had been appointed by the student council, who preferred a "revolutionary priest from the Third World," a choice that would have horrified the conservative Mr. Stillman.

As early as November 1969, I had sent my "reflections" about the Stillman professorship to Dean Stendahl. I said that "from the repeated comments of Mr. Stillman, it appears that the appointee should be a practicing Catholic, even a 'solid' Catholic, who is in 'good standing' with the Church." I also pointed out that the appointees had consisted of two historians—one biblical scholar and one sociologist. My suggestion was that consideration be given to the appointment of a scholarly Catholic theologian.

The dean then extended the search to include European Catholic scholars. In March 1970, the professorial committee of the Divinity School faculty recommended the appointment of Father Otto Pesch, O.P., a German scholar and expert on both Aquinas and Luther. He had received his doctorate in fundamental theology at the University of Munich. Father Pesch accepted the invitation to a two-year appointment and arrived in mid-September 1970. Around Christmas, he announced his engagement to his German fiancée, whom he married at the end of the academic year, in June 1971. Most of the Divinity School professors were probably indifferent to the marriage of a Catholic priest. Officially, however, Dean Stendahl had to be sensitive to the incongruity of the situation in which Mr. Stillman's basic principles were being flaunted.

My five years as a Catholic priest-professor in Harvard's Divinity School involved more than the presence of a Catholic on a largely Protestant faculty. It represented the full manifestation of Roman Catholic ecumenism that had emerged from the Second Vatican Council. After all, my "Catholic" courses were sociological rather than scriptural and theological in nature. I later presented them at the Illif School of Theology at the University of Denver, the Divinity School of Princeton University, and Unification Theology Seminary in Barrytown. I then held a one-year appointment during 1974–75 to the Favrot Chair of Human Relations at Tulane University, where I taught the sociology of religion.

2

Alcoholic Clergy

During my childhood there were no "drunks" in my family, or among my relatives, although we heard occasionally that my mother's Uncle Mike, long since dead, had been known as a "souse." I never heard of any scandalous alcoholic priest until I was in the seminary, when the provincial once told us about a man he had to dismiss because of heavy drinking. Everyone knew that this fine Jesuit pastor was a gifted preacher and a zealous minister to his people, but he "just couldn't get off the booze, no matter how often he took the pledge." He was accepted into a diocese by a friendly bishop but never entered a recovery program.

Our seminary professors, even those who taught courses on ethics and moral behavior, apparently knew nothing about Alcoholics Anonymous. To stop overindulgence in liquor, they said, you followed the example of Matt Talbot, a pious alcoholic layman, who prayed a great deal and visited the Church frequently.[1] In our future ministry, they told us to preach against intemperance and administer the pledge to refrain from liquor but limit it to one or two months. Some of the seminarians wore the pin of the Irish Temperance Society. Beer and wine were not served on the menu of the seminary, but we were able to get a drink of liquor at a small cafe down the road.

It was many years later, after I had completed my formal academic studies, that I chanced across Jack Alexander's article about Bill Wilson, cofounder of Alcoholics Anonymous, in the *Saturday Evening Post*. In February 1949, Father Ralph Pfau, founder in 1949 of the National Clergy Council on Alcoholism, came to New Orleans for a lecture at the Notre Dame Seminary, exclusively for the clergy and by invitation only. In 1958, under the pseudonym Father John Doe, he published (with the assistance of Al Hirshberg) *Prodigal Shepherd*.[2] This brought to my attention for the first time the "problem" of clergy alcoholism. On the Jesuit faculty of Loyola a popular professor of ethics became known among the students as the "booze priest." He raided the cabinet for altar wine when he ran out of the "hard stuff" and carelessly tossed whiskey bottles onto the lawn outside his window. He finally was forced to retire from the lecture hall, transferred to another Jesuit community, and died an alcoholic.

In the early years of my teaching—after World War II— there were no treatment facilities for alcoholics in Orleans Parish County. The ordinary drunk was picked up by the police and left to "dry out" overnight in a cell and then released. Others were admitted to a hospital by physicians who had no "remedy" for alcoholics—did not consider alcoholism a sickness—and treated them for other illnesses. Meanwhile, and in a very secret fashion, members of Alcoholics Anonymous began to meet privately and encouraged one another to remain sober. They were little discussed among the clergy, except an occasional snide remark about "holy rollers, who make public confessions." After all, they were modeled on the Protestant "Oxford Group," who were held in low repute by many priests.

Father Ralph Pfau gained sobriety through Alcoholics Anonymous, the association of recovering addicts. He stopped drinking in 1943 and quietly established in Indianapolis the National Clergy Conference on Alcoholism, which allowed no "outsiders" to its annual convention. In 1956 he encouraged Austin Ripley, himself a recovering alcoholic, to establish in Michigan the Guest House treatment facility exclusively for alcoholic priests. Gradually, the secrecy was removed from the Church response to clergy alcoholism. Guest House advertised widely, but discreetly, within the Catholic Church, targeting specifically bishops and religious provincials. Josephite Father William Clancy, chairman of the board of NCCA as well as an alumnus and active supporter of Guest House, opened a kind of halfway house for recovering alcoholics in New Orleans. He kept close contact with Arthur Baker, director of Guest House, whom he advised to contact me, which he did, in late 1973. This conversation initiated for me an intensive study of the systematic treatment of clergy alcoholics.

Like other treatment centers, Guest House endeavored to maintain relations with its graduates, specifically for assurance that they were staying sober. In 1968 they conducted an extensive survey of their alumni, inquiring of their health conditions and pastoral activities. This gave them a clue to their "success rate" of maintaining sobriety. Dr. Russell Smith, himself a recovering alcoholic, was the research "specialist" for Guest House and was confident of the high rate of recovery of his patients, but he wanted "outside" evidence gathered by an independent researcher. Smith obtained a grant from the De Rance Foundation of Milwaukee and solicited research proposals from two companies that conducted opinion polls but could not come to terms with them. He and his colleagues decided on a sociological study of the treatment needs of nine hundred Guest House graduates. They wanted the research done by a Catholic sociologist, preferably a priest, to survey their alumni and to analyze the data.

Father Clancy brought the Guest House administrators, Arthur Baker and Russell Smith, to New Orleans on March 23, 1974, to deliver their "sales pitch" to the assembled rectors of the Southern Jesuit communities. Smith told hilarious stories about his own escapades, of drinking his way through medical school while in an alcoholic haze. He is representative of the articulate "showmen" who have often told their story at A.A. meetings. Through repetition, the tales keep getting better and funnier and considerably lighten the burden of this serious illness.

Nevertheless, he was proud of Guest House's successful program of rehabilitation and was willing to allow "independent" outside appraisal of its reputation. In this way, I made my first professional contact with the world of clergy alcoholism. The Guest House management was aware of my two national surveys of the American Catholic priesthood that were published in the 1960s. In my earlier study *Priest and People* in 1965, I had focused on the relations between the parish priest and his "best" parishioners. The second study *America's Forgotten Priests* in 1968 investigated the role and status of parish curates and made some special reference to optional celibacy for priests. In neither survey had I delved into questions of health and illness.

The administrators of Guest House were looking for something else. They wanted to test their own judgment against that of the priests who had completed the alcohol recovery program. The information, therefore, had to come from the alumni, of whom I was to ask all the pertinent questions. On that Saturday in March 1974 in New Orleans we sat through a long lunch, working out the details of the research program and focusing our attention on the key questions that had to be asked. One of the points I insisted on was the inclusion of a "control group" of priests who were considered nonalcoholic.

It was my suggestion that we ought to "match" the background and vital statistics of the two sets of priests: those who had undergone the Guest House treatment and those who were not alcoholic. Of course, Guest House was specifically concerned about their own graduates. I was interested also in discovering whether there were any biographical factors involved in the process of becoming an alcoholic that were absent from other priests. The sample I derived from the *Kenedy Official Catholic Directory* was only an approximation of a "match" with the Guest House men.

When we began to plan the research study of clergy graduates of Guest House, we thought we should look for both the differences and the similarities between alcoholic and nonalcoholic priests. We decided to take a matching sample of supposedly nonalcoholic priests from the Catholic directory. Most of the items on the questionnaire—which was titled "Clergy Life Style Project"—were the same for both categories of priests. We hypothesized that if the answers showed a marked dissimilarity, we could then construct a sociological profile of the alcoholic that would be quite different from the nonalcoholic. By and large, this failed. Clergy who become alcoholics are pretty much the same as clergy who do not.

Anonymity is a sacred word among alcoholics, and I had no intention—or opportunity—to make direct inquiry among the graduates of Guest House. After we worked out the details of the questionnaire, I composed a cover letter using Guest House stationery, with the request that they send their anonymous response to me at the Sociology Department of Loyola. On May 21, 1974, the inquiry was distributed from Guest House to 628 alumni, of whom 403 returned usable questionnaires before the deadline of September 1. The most important question was, of course, "when did you have your last drink?" Our definition of the sober alcoholic refers to the person who has not had a drink since leaving the treatment center and/or during the previous four years. After all, this was the criterion by which Guest House measured success. The report I compiled on the assembled data was ready for publication in early 1975, but Guest House decided to publish only chapters 9 to 11, under the title of *The Guest House Experience, 1956–1974*.

The matter of abstinence allowed us to discuss three categories of respondents: those who were completely "dry" (74 percent), those who experienced some lapses (15 percent), and those who simply continued to drink (11 percent). Comparative responses revealed that the patients' enthusiasm for the treatment roughly correlated with the degree of success they had since ending the treatment. The majority who were completely dry were much more likely than the minority who were still drinking to give a high rating to the Guest House program.

The research findings indicated that the therapy program is not universally successful in spite of the highest professional competence available to all patients. Recovery begins in the admission that one is an addicted drinker. There are some instances of priests who "fight" the treatment and are unwilling to accept the diagnosis ("I was in and out of hospitals. I was detoxed six times before I was thirty-one"). One priest, in particular, has probably set a record in having been in "more than twenty places; three times at Harrison; twice in State mental hospitals, and at the Institute of Living where they do therapeutic dancing." Only two out of five (42 percent) priests in the study who continued to drink were ready to admit that they were afflicted with alcoholism. These are probably the same patients who "comply" with the requirements of the program but never come to "surrender" to the admission that they are "powerless over alcohol" and that their life "had become unmanageable."[3]

Although alcoholic priests are well treated in the therapy centers of Southdown and Tower Hill, the alumni of Guest House are convinced that their treatment is exceptional. It was Austin Ripley who originally conceived the idea that sick alcoholic priests needed "a dignified, exclusive retreat, free of stigmatic and punitive overtones, where there would be sufficient time and competent professional guidance to enable them to understand and accept the diagnosis of alcoholism, and to learn and apply the proven dynamics of recovery."

Many of the alumni of Guest House continue their association in a kind of informal fellowship, contributing messages about their continuing sobriety and ministerial activities. They attend the annual homecoming and compete in the alumni golf tournament. I had come to know some of the alumni in southern Louisiana, with whom I discussed the research findings. At the homecoming in August 1975, at Pontiac, Michigan, I presented a paper about the research and was inducted with a certificate of honorary alumnus. This led also to membership in the National Clergy Council on Alcoholism, to which most alumni were close adherents.

In January 1974, I attended the twenty-sixth annual national conference at Barry College in Miami and presented a copy of the official alcoholism policy of the Southern Province of Jesuits. I was the dinner guest of ten Guest House alumni, who insisted that I take martinis to accompany the stone crab delicacy. At the twenty-eighth annual convention, I gave a paper on the findings of the Guest House survey and compared it with a sample of nonalcoholic priests selected from the Catholic directory.

I continued research and publication on the problem of clergy alcoholism from 1976 to 1978 and I published six articles in 1976, four in 1977, and three in 1978, all of which came out of a continuing series of investigations I made through personal contact with people in the field of alcohol therapy. Starting at the Miami conference in 1974, I taped interviews with recovering alcoholics, with their sponsors and superiors, and with directors and therapists in treatment centers.

While I did not pretend that the Guest House alumni were an adequate sample of American recovering alcoholic clergy, I interviewed enough of them and their therapists to conclude that the rate of clergy alcoholism was being widely exaggerated. Data presented at the National Clergy Council on Alcoholism (NCCA) conference in 1976 showed a lower rate of clergy alcoholism, but the "program notes" insisted that the rate was 10 percent for priests and brothers and that 12 percent of sisters are addicted to either alcohol or medication, or both.[4] In late 1975 I received a telephone call from an old friend, Monsignor Colin MacDonald, of the Bishops' Committee on Priestly Life and Ministry, suggesting I consider a survey of clergy alcoholism. I was invited to a meeting of this committee in Milwaukee to assess the episcopal request.

This study was not an inquiry among alcoholic priests themselves. The cover letter sent by Archbishop Raymond Hunthausen in March 1976 was directed to all the dioceses and religious orders of men in the United States. Of the 165 dioceses listed in the 1975 Catholic directory, I had a response rate of 84 percent. Responses came from 110 congregations of religious men. The archbishop's memorandum mentioned the "alarming situation concerning alcoholism among our American clergy." The questionnaires were delivered to the Washington, D.C., office of the U. S. Catholic Conference and then rerouted to the Sociology Department at Loyola University in New Orleans. The replies came from 138 dioceses with a membership of 27,815 priests and from 110 religious congregations with 22,958 members.

We asked these diocesan officials and religious superiors whether they considered clergy alcoholism a serious problem and whether it was increasing among the priests. Hardly any (1.6 percent) considered it a severe problem while half (49.6 percent) felt that it was minimal or even nonexistent. We asked also for an opinion about the drinking "trend" among priests and found that one-tenth (9.8 percent) thought that alcoholism was on the increase while about one quarter (26 percent) gave the opposite opinion. The majority, however, thought that there was hardly any change. When we later asked this same question of a national sample of recovering clergy, three out of ten (31 percent) believed that clergy alcoholism was on the increase and only 12 percent said that it was declining. Such divergence of opinion indicates that estimates of the size of the problem must be compared with hard data.

We were on safer ground when we inquired about the number of men who are known to be alcoholics in the dioceses and religious orders. I asked how many have actually entered alcohol treatment centers. Answers provided what is unquestionably the most accurate information of the entire survey. There are, of course, some men who sought sobriety exclusively in the A.A. fraternity, but we have no information about them. The low proportion of priests (2.9 percent) who went to treatment was the same for both diocesan and religious priests while the rate of recovery was slightly higher for religious (74 percent) than for diocesan priests (71 percent).

Aside from the priests who were actually sent for alcohol treatment, I asked how many were active alcoholics who should be considered for rehabilitation. We found that approximately the same number as those who had gone for treatment still needed therapy. In other words, the alcoholics identified consisted of those who were recovering and those who needed treatment. If we combine these statistics we have reliable data that allow us to say with some confidence that the rate of Catholic clergy alcoholism is approximately 5 percent. This estimate contradicts the inaccurate guesswork of commentators, such as the sociologist who speculates that "because of the loneliness and isolation they feel, the alcoholism rate is just enormous."[5]

In this same survey, I asked who in the diocese or religious order "handles" the problem drinker and found that in the majority of instances it is done by the bishop himself (56 percent) or by the religious superior (73 percent). I found too that in most instances the recovering alcoholic is returned to the same or a similar ministerial post that he previously held. Approximately one-third of them do not regularly attend A.A. group meetings. I asked whether the NCCA program was used in the diocese or order and found only one out of six (16 percent) answered affirmatively. About three out of ten (28 percent) said that they had no need for this program. Six out of ten preferred to send their men to treatment facilities (61 percent) designed exclusively for clergy (such as Guest House, Paracletes, and Southdown), while one quarter (24 percent) preferred a center mainly for laity.

The report of this study was completed in November 1976, and sent to Monsignor MacDonald and his committee. With a brief introduction, provided by the members of the Bishops' Committee on Priestly Life and Ministry, it was published and distributed in 1977. The report included "practical principles of rehabilitation in regard to alcoholic priests."[6]

While the inquiry among Church leaders was providing interesting and important information, I was determined to do further research in a personal interview type of study. With an adequate grant from the Jesuit Council on Theological Reflection, I spent the summer of 1976 on a twofold mission: to visit treatment centers that had included clergy among their patients and to interview Church officials about the prevalence of alcoholism in their dioceses and congregations. For three months, June to August, I drove over seven thousand miles, visiting twenty-four rehabilitation centers and tape-recording interviews with forty-three of the staff personnel. I also interviewed twenty-four Church officials who were in a position to discuss the alcohol problems of their priests.

The wider research program was not simply a matter of finding data to compare with the achievements of the Guest House alumni or with the experiences of Church officials. I was looking for a sample of clergy alcoholics across ecumenical lines and, thus, asked at each facility whether they had treated any clergy in the past five years. The fact is that half of these centers had not had any clergy patients, which was an informal indication that the rate of clergy alcoholism may not have been severe. I was not simply looking for statistics but rather for experiences they may have shared with clergy.

Visiting the treatment centers brought me into contact with a category of exceptional people—therapists who pursued their vocation with the zeal of the evangelist. Virtually all are recovering alcoholics themselves, whose mission is to restore the alcoholic to sobriety. They all agreed that it could be done with "tough love." The therapist with the toughest approach was the owner of the Alina Lodge in New Jersey. Almost all of her "students," as she called them, had been treated elsewhere, usually several times. She claimed to succeed where others had failed. Her strict rules governed every aspect of their behavior, and they had to continue residence until she decided they were ready to leave.

Patients who were priests received no privileges from her. They were not permitted to celebrate Mass, for example. "I tell them they have to earn the right to be a priest again. To say Mass is a privilege which you have destroyed because you loved alcohol more than you love your Church and your God." The alcoholics are not patients; they are ambulatory. They are not guests, because, she remarked, "I did not invite them." In the field of alcohol treatment she has the reputation of being the toughest but also the most successful. She does not, however, want her name officially attached to this report.

Another "hard" therapist was a recovering alcoholic and a former religious brother (who also wants to remain anonymous). He treated priest patients with "creative distrust" that was determined by what they did, not what they said. "Clergy are used to being coddled and getting preferential treatment," he remarked. He disagreed with the Guest House philosophy of deep respect for men simply because they are priests. "I put them right in there with everybody else, truck drivers, lawyers, housewives." Although not all therapists are recovering alcoholics, those who are in the recovery stage tend to insist that "only" a recovering alcoholic really knows how to treat other alcoholics.

The experience of having been a "drunk" is also seen by some to be a helpful preparation for physicians who are successful in treating alcoholics; otherwise, "doctors don't know what they are talking about." One of my first doctor interviewees was a physician in Miami who had been adviser to recovery centers. He insisted that alcoholism is not a sickness but that it led to sickness. He felt it a subterfuge to call it illness. It was, he claimed, the most obvious manifestation of human disregard for others. A profound selfishness is one of the strongest predisposing factors of alcoholism. "The alcoholic demands more of your time than any other kind of patient, and you cannot treat him as you would a sick person. Alcoholics Anonymous puts too much emphasis on the fallacy of sickness," he noted. This doctor—who shall remain anonymous—has given much assistance to a priest who runs a halfway house in Miami for recovering alcoholics.

Most of the recovering alcoholics with whom I spoke had very little use for physicians or, indeed, for the medical profession. They had been in and out of hospitals, usually with little more benefit than temporary detoxification. The treatment centers I visited were seldom located in hospitals. One large and important exception was Lutheran General Hospital in Park Ridge, Illinois, where Sister Theresa Golden was director of therapy for women alcoholics. In Milwaukee, the DePaul Hospital had a recovery section under the care of Dr. Bela Maroti. St. Vincent Hospital in Cleveland has an elderly nun in charge of operations. She is considered the successor to the famous Sister Ignatia, who was the first to admit Bill Wilson's alcoholic friends for treatment in Akron.[7]

Alcoholic treatment centers, for the most part, are established separately from hospitals and virtually never have physicians in charge. The administrators I interviewed at the larger centers were not medical doctors. One of the better known, and successful, facilities is Hazelden in Center City, Minnesota, under the direction of Dr. Daniel Anderson. Guest House has two facilities, Lake Orion, Michigan and Rochester, Minnesota, and treats only clergy alcoholics, as do Southdown in Toronto, and Tower Hill in St. Louis. Some of the addiction centers eschew hospital titles and use imaginative names, such as Livengrin in Maryland, Second Chance in Connecticut, Valley Hope in Kansas, Chit Chat Farms in Pennsylvania, and La Hacienda in Texas.

While I learned a great deal about alcoholism and its treatment among these expert therapists, my central concern was for alcoholic clergy. How does the alcoholic priest differ from the "ordinary drunk"? How does he get into the treatment facility? Is he harder to deal with than the layperson? Is he better off in an exclusively clerical center, such as Guest House, Southdown, and Tower Hill, or should he mingle with others? All these queries were preparation for the actual distribution of the survey questionnaire.

Another preliminary, but important, source of information about the treatment of alcoholic clergy lay with the bishops and provincials who were personally concerned about the alcoholic priests under their charge. Some of the bishops in the smaller dioceses had few problem drinkers but were close to them. I interviewed Church officials in the summer of 1976 after I had completed the Guest House survey. One of the more cooperative prelates was Bishop Charles Helmsing, of Kansas City, Missouri, who said he had kept the pledge until he became bishop. He did not allude to the fact that I was on the board of the *National Catholic Reporter*, which he had severely reprimanded a decade earlier.[8] He had access to a smoothly functioning health panel of A.A. priests as well as a joint working arrangement with the Episcopal Bishop Arthur Vogel.

In the smaller diocese of Mobile, Alabama, Bishop John May had not established the NCCA policy and program and handled two recent cases by sending the men to the Benedictine Abbey, under the care of Abbott Hilary Dreaper. The bishop was concerned and displeased about the "false loyalty" shown by priests who "cover" for their alcoholic priest friends.

Handling the problem of drinking priests is more personal and immediate for the bishop of a small diocese who "knows everybody." Bishop Edward O'Rourke spoke about the men in Peoria, Illinois, where "the drinker soon complains that he doesn't have enough money. Also, you hear complaints of improper functioning, even if he covers it up. In other words, here is a guy who used to be very efficient in sending in his marriage papers, all in good order. Now they are sloppy, and they are late. We can tell. Just give me a month, and I'll tell you who has been hitting the bottle. Now, these guys who hit the bottle and then reform, or maybe hadn't touched it at all, then got on it. I knew it before anyone else had told me. Two main things begin to surface here: A good chancery office is kind of like a nerve center, and you can sense a problem even before the fellow himself knows the problem. When a very efficient orderly priest begins to be in disorder, it's time to talk to him." This accords with the expertise of Sister Theresa Golden, who says, "you don't wait till you see bloodshot eyes and a staggering gait. You first look for changes in behavior, carelessness, lack of punctuality. Soon you know it comes from heavy drinking."

Perhaps the best NCCA program and policy of any diocese was in Chicago, where John Cardinal Cody placed the entire procedure in the hands of the diocesan health committee. My anonymous priestly informant said, "when I asked permission to take training in alcohol therapy, he did not know I was an alcoholic until I told him. Cardinal Cody was not available for an interview, and he turns over all such requests to Monsignor Ignatius McDermott." Other large dioceses had different approaches to the problem of clergy alcoholics. In the archdiocese of Philadelphia, there was no official recognition of the NCCA program. On the other hand, the archdiocese of

Boston had a very active program, promoted mainly by the A.A. priests themselves.

The experience I had with members of the Guest House survey team, and among the many recovered alcoholic priests with whom I had conferred since the summer of 1975, provided the questions I had asked the Church officials the following year. In November 1975, I was ready to send packets of questionnaires to the cooperative treatment centers. Like the survey of Guest House alumni, these were addressed individually and sent by the management of each treatment center. The respondents remained completely anonymous to the researchers. I supplied 1,300 questionnaires to the cooperative administrators but could not discover how many they actually sent to the clergy alumni. Thus, the 677 respondents are obviously not a "representative sample" of alcoholic clergy alumni.

From the substantive data gathered in these interviews, with both alcoholics and nonalcoholics, I was able to formulate the most meaningful items for a questionnaire to the recovered alcoholic clergy themselves. This survey was under constant revision during the months of interviewing, and it resulted in a series of questions that had strong spiritual, moral, and theological overtones. I began to appreciate the remark made by Southdown director Mark Eveson that alcoholism is a "mysterious" illness. I was impressed by recovering alcoholics, who insisted that "it is in some respect a 'spiritual' illness, and that efforts to overcome the addiction require some kind of relationship with God."[9]

At the treatment facilities I visited I was careful to speak only to administrators and therapists. On several occasions I was approached by patients and asked if I would accept the Fifth Step (admitting the exact nature of our wrongs). I had no experience in this and had been told that the patients must distinguish between confessions and the Fourth Step (taking a moral inventory of ourselves) and that even clergy should not make the Step with a priest or minister. In the larger facilities, like Hazelden and the Johnson Institute, regular pastoral counselors were available. John Fraunces, a staff member of Chit Chat Farms, remarked that "we discourage priests from playing a priestly role while in treatment. They are there to be helped, not to help others. Priests need contact with non-clergy, as here; otherwise, they tend to get isolated and aloof."[10]

Great varieties of experiences and opinions were presented. Professor Paul Roman pointed out that—unlike the ecclesiatical counterpart—the secular employer is interested in job performance, not in the employee's private life. Sociologist Paul Chalfant notes that A.A. attempts to "medicalize deviance" and adds that accidental deviance is more acceptable than deliberate deviance. Father Peter Girardin thinks that A.A. is the "finest school of spirituality" and that "recovering alcoholics form the greatest pool of ascetics and of potential saints in this country." Father Joseph O'Donnell is V.A. chaplain in Houston, where the Navy sends its alcoholics for treatment, regardless of rank. At Houston, they continue to wear their uniform and are on a first-name basis.

Despite the populist democratic ideology of Alcoholics Anonymous, the recovering alcoholics tend to group according to occupation and social status. Thus, lawyers gather for their weekly luncheon, "uptown" alcoholics do not mingle with "lower-class" alcoholics, and many recovering clergy hesitate to associate at the so-called normal A.A. lay group. Opinions are sharply divided regarding the benefit of "open" centers, such as Hazelden and Chit Chat, rather than centers that are exclusively for clergy, such as Guest House and Southdown. Obviously, the "best" treatment center is the one at which the alcoholic regains sobriety, although it may take several attempts before finding the suitable center.

One of the repeated questions asked in the survey dealt with trends and the age differences of priest alcoholics. The "veterans" among the recovering alcoholics felt that the junior clergy drank much less than their elders, who had been accustomed to all-night poker games that were usually accompanied by heavy alcohol consumption. Younger priests tended to socialize among the laity and were more cautious about overdrinking. There was also much "wise" talk about the "enablers" of alcoholic clergy—from housekeepers and secretaries to parishioners and fellow priests—all of whom wanted to "protect" their clergy friend. Indeed, friends of the alcoholic priest sometimes mistrusted the stated intentions of superiors. Father Ed Healey, of Columbus, Ohio, had introduced the policy and program from the 1975 NCCA meeting to his diocese, but his fellow priests turned it down because they thought it smacked of a "spy system." This mistrust of authority seems to have been a result of bad experiences with their previous bishop, John Carberry, who had sinced moved to St. Louis.

In Baltimore, Father Tom Baumgartner works with an ecumenical committee on alcoholism, but it is separate from the diocesan personnel board. The board, in turn, operates independently from the clergy senate. These separate committees, each with its own function and membership, tend to act as a buffer from charges of spying.

Father Jake Powderly calls Washington, D.C., the "drinking capital" of the country, a title also claimed by Father Ed Gannon of Scranton and Father Terry Richey of Los Angeles. They all agree about the typical assessment: that the busy monsignor drinks because he is under pressure, but the ordinary curate is just the rectory drunk. There are still some A.A. old-timers around who scoff at the rehabilitation centers, but all of them—of any age—have a low opinion of physicians and hospitals. Father James O'Dea, in Hartford, prefers A.A. groups who have a strong connection to the laity and have a simple faith in turning their life over to God. He says the pledge is absolutely meaningless for an active alcoholic, although it might work for people who are not addicted.

Matt Kane, S.J., notes that the Philadelphia diocese does not have the NCCA program and policy or, indeed, any committee on alcoholism. The problem is handled by the chancery. Unfortunately, the chancery has closed down Padua House, which earned the nickname of "ecclesiastical prison" by the priests. Rather than being sent to Guest House, the priests were dispatched to a psychiatric hospital, St. John Vianney, in Downington, a center for emotionally disturbed priests and religious located twenty-five miles west of Philadelphia. Calvin Adams, at Chit Chat, remarked that no pastoral counseling was given there. Father John Fraunces, another Chit Chat staffer, worked as a therapist, not as a priest. The Fourth Step is not an exam of conscience; the Fifth Step not a confession. The patient is considered to be just another "drunk" and no attention is paid to his occupation or social status. Father Ed Gannon at Scranton, however, says that Guest House respects the dignity of the priesthood and does not attempt to debase or "de-priest" the clergy patient.

Edward Semko, director of the Straight and Narrow treatment center in Newark, New Jersey, mentioned that the center was started in 1948 by Monsignor William Wall of the Mount

Carmel Guild. Its capacity is fifty men, run by four psychologists and four social workers. Newark has a good diocesan network, with a six-month program for hard-core alcoholics. Therapist Jack Waldron thinks that religion has compounded the problem by making people feel guilty for their alcoholism. Monsignor Andrew Cusack, of Bridgeport, Connecticut, thinks that laypeople are more forgiving of priests' drinking problems than their sexual faults. The immorality lies with the threat of scandal rather than the drunkenness. There are many professionals among Fairfield County's A.A. membership, and most priest alcoholics are comfortable with them. However, Scotty Mertin, the owner of Second Chance, located near Bridgeport, Connecticut, claims that A.A. is not professional. He argues that "[p]sychiatry, religion, medicine, don't work, but A.A. does. Seven out of ten in any A.A. group never had professional therapy. They just walked in off the street into the A.A. meeting and gained sobriety."

Father Fred Harkins, of Holy Cross College, reports that the Worcester, Massachusetts, diocese has no program for recovering alcoholics. Rather the auxiliary bishop handles each case personally. The Boston archdiocese and the New England Jesuit province both have well-tried and excellent programs for alcoholic clergy. Jerry O'Brien manages the Gavin House in Boston, called AWOL (A Way of Life), which holds classes, lectures, and meetings for both clerics and laity. The question was raised whether the sponsor of the clergy alcoholic should be a priest or a layperson. Austin Ripley, for example, thought the sponsor should, at best, be a layman—he did not have a chaplain at Guest House. He also believed there should be no such thing as a priests' A.A. group, arguing that there is no "special" ecclesiastical type of alcoholism.

Father Peter Young reports that the Albany diocese has a good working program, endorsed by the bishop but not run by him. The men are sent mainly to Southdown, but occasionally also to Chit Chat, Sterling, and Guest House. Some priests, like other professionals, prefer to have their own A.A. group. They claim that clinicians and therapists lose interest in them. When there is Twelve-step work to be done—that is, to apply the principles of A.A. in daily life—they are not available, and the A.A.'s often have to do it themselves. They insist that alcoholism is not a symptom of a mental disorder. Further, these particular priests are annoyed with the expensive House of Affirmation, a nearby rehabilitation center, which, they insist, is not successful.

Monsignor William Taylor, in Syracuse, also dislikes psychiatrists, having gone unsuccessfully to two of them before treatment at Guest House. Unlike others, however, he thinks alcoholic priests should have priest sponsors. On the other hand, Vincent Collins, in Rochester, who says he was called "liquor vicar" under Bishop Fulton Sheen, says priests will listen more to a layman sponsor rather than a priest. His working formula consists of three meetings per week for three months. Recovering clerics, he notes, fear scandal and stigma and attend A.A. meetings in street clothes.

Vincent Enright, in Erie, says it's no mystery why priests get addicted. Too much is expected of them. Then, in middle life they get depressed and turn to drink. Older men are difficult to work with, he says, and young men are too smart to listen. At the same time, he finds that younger priests do not seem to drink as much as older men. They tend to be serious about ministry and desire a simpler life. Anthony Pilla, now bishop in Cleveland, supervised about twenty "reformed" priests who attended their own A.A. meeting every Thursday night. They also attended open A.A. meetings. They were very supportive of each other and were ready to do the Twelfth Step. Some went to Guest House, some to Southdown, some to Tower Hill Paracletes but only *after* Hazelden or Edgewood. In contrast, the St. Louis Paracletes seem to *add* spirituality training *after* men have had "regular" treatment at other places. Therapist Tim Conway says Rosary Hall, in Cleveland, is a continuation of Sister Ignatia's Hospital in Akron, where she started to take in alcoholics. There a quiet older sister, successor of the Akron sister, talked with us but not "for the tape." "Most alkie priests," she said, "have alkie sponsors."

In New Orleans, Father John Favalora, now bishop of St. Petersburg, Florida, says there is no official policy or program, but Bill Clancy, also in New Orleans, ran a center for addicts, called CARE, for which he sought funds from Archbishop Philip Hannon. Bill died in December 1974, but his influence was carried on through the work of his assistant John Harvey. The archbishop did sponsor a dinner meeting at the Fairmont Hotel in December 1975, at which Richard Paddock of Guest

House and the late Josephite Hugh Henneberry spoke, but it raised relatively little money. The CARE center attended to the needs of lay alcoholics more than clergy addicts. In an attempt to do more in the fight against drugs, the archbishop in 1976 appointed a nun to head the Catholic Office for Drug Education. Two years later, he appointed Father Anthony White to the Alcoholic Counseling Ministry of the Archdiocese.

The information I gathered satisfied me that the questionnaire covered all the essential aspects of the alcoholic clergy treatment. I had obtained promises of cooperation from thirteen of the centers and gave sufficient copies of the questionnaires to them. I had no control over their distribution, however, and I found that only nine treatment facilities had succeeded in eliciting clergy responses for me. My best estimate is that 1,279 questionnaires had been distributed by the treatment centers. At my Loyola University office I received 677 replies, a return rate of 53 percent. The report on the study was published in 1982 by the Human Sciences Press under the title *Rehabilitation of Clergy Alcoholics: Ardent Spirits Subdued*. The generalizations I present here are summarized from the book:

1) There is no reliable profile, sociological or psychological, to explain why the great majority of clergy are *not* alcoholics or why those who are addicts often continue to drink. The allergy hypothesis traces chemical dependence to a physiological predisposition that is triggered by the ingestion of alcohol.

   The sick role of the clergy alcoholic places him at the peculiar level of permanent convalescence. His behavioral deviance has been medicalized and his recovery from the illness goes beyond simple abstinence to quality sobriety.

2) The Church official tends to have a familial rather than an economic relationship with his subordinates. He expresses concern not only for the work performance of the clergy but also for their personal and private lives and their spiritual well-being.

   Although the structured program for alcohol rehabilitation needs the support of Church officials, the actual procedures are carried out by a subsidiary group, a health board, or panel, which includes some recovering alcoholic clergy.

3) The deviant alcoholic clergy tend to be protected by colleagues, associates, and friends and are seldom reported to Church officials by their physicians. A kind of loyalty exists within the clergy fraternity to cover up for wayward priests, but telephone hotlines and other recovering alcoholics are increasingly coming into play.

   Very few genuine alcoholics, including clergy, can achieve spontaneous remission. Depending on the gravity of their affliction, some are persuaded to attend meetings of A.A. and to follow the A.A. program. There appears to be considerable ambivalence on the part of Church officials to encourage participation, and some delay in insisting on therapy.

4) The period of inpatient treatment appears to be longer for alcoholic clergy than for alcoholic laity and is more than twice as long, on the average, in facilities exclusively for clergy. The longer the stay the more successful the treatment, as measured by frequency of posttreatment lapses in drinking.

   The complexity of alcohol addiction defies any single modality of treatment. The rehabilitation centers employ a multidiscipline team approach to recovery. The healing process aims not only at abstinence but also at the physical, psychological, spiritual, and social renewal of the whole person.

5) The personal fraternal bonds existing within the religious community continue to apply while the religious alcoholic is undergoing therapy and even after he returns from the treatment center. More than in the case of the diocesan clergy, his fellow clergy know where he is, keep in contact, and show confidence in him when he returns home.

   Both diocesan and religious clergy achieve about the same level of abstention as a result of alcohol treatment. Both groups also match approximately a similar improved quality of ministry and express a similar level of satisfaction about their current assignment and their ongoing clergy career.

6) Regular members of A.A. tend to show great concern for fellow alcoholics, responding to their need in Twelfth Step visits, listening to them in Fifth Step accounts, and acting as sponsors in the fellowship. The fact that they themselves had sponsors immediately after graduation from treatment helps to account for their close involvement with the A.A. group.

   The spirituality of the clergy alcoholic appears to be strengthened by his continued association with members of A.A. He is much more likely than the A.A. nonmember to experience a spiritual renewal in the rehabilitation process and to manifest this renewal in his habits of prayer.

7) The alleged contradiction between spirituality and religiosity does not appear in this survey. Those who have the lowest regard for the Church also rank the lowest in spirituality. Those who are high on spirituality are also high on religiosity.

   Approximately the same proportion of complete abstainers is found in both types of recovering alcoholic clergy. This finding seriously questions the generalization that the maintenance of sobriety depends essentially on a high degree of spirituality. It appears, however, that quality sobriety is achieved by those clerics who are high on both spirituality and religiosity.

8) Spiritual conversion is no firm guarantee of permanent sobriety, but it does seem to help. Those who have had this experience are much less likely to report a relapse. When we look separately at the minority (14 percent) of "backsliders," we found that they were in trouble on every measure of comparison. They tended to be tense, nervous, lonely, worried, and depressed.

   While the spiritual awakening may be seen as a very personal experience, it is greatly sustained in the company of fellow converts. It is characteristic of the fellowship that divine support for the maintenance of sobriety is enhanced by group support. Recovered alcoholics seek out a home base in which they can feel most comfortable.

3

Healthy American Priests

❊❊

In early 1985, a news reporter called me from New York inquiring about the "contradiction" in my book *The Health of American Catholic Priests*. He asked, "Why does your preface deny what your study reveals?" This observation would have embarrassed me had I authored it. The anonymous writer of the preface, who could have been one of nine bishops or one of eleven priests who formed the Bishops' Committee on Priestly Life and Ministry, said, in essence, that you can't believe priests when they tell you how they feel. "They tend to minimize their needs, failings, physical state, and weakness." Everybody knows that "the mystique of the strong male, free from sickness or difficulty, is the self-perception that continues to dominate American men."[1]

No one had found a contradiction of this kind in the study report, *The Priest and Stress*, sponsored by the same bishops' committee in 1982. Here the findings were in full agreement with the expectations of the hierarchy: advancing age, a shortage of priests, and multiple demands of the priesthood were subjecting the clergy to tension and stress, even to the point of burnout. In other words, the earlier report on *The Priest and Stress* fulfilled the conventional stereotype of the overworked and harassed pastor and raised an alarm about the emotional, mental, and psychological health of priests.

The bishops then expressed similar alarm about the physical health of priests as a matter of immediate and intense concern in the same priest and stress study. "We consider the physical health of priests to be one of the most critical issues facing the Church today. We also recognize that much more data are needed on this question." Accordingly, in early January 1982, Bishop Francis Kelly of Baltimore asked if I were interested in studying the physical health of the Catholic clergy. As chairman of the NCCB's Subcommittee on Priestly Affirmation and Support, he officially invited me to conduct the survey. The first meeting to discuss the details of this research project was planned for February 25 at the Ramada-O'Hare Inn in Chicago.

My research services had been recommended by Monsignor Colin MacDonald, for whose Bishops' Committee on Priestly Life and Ministry I had conducted an inquiry about alcoholism among Catholic clergy in 1977. In gathering data for the alcoholism study I did not directly contact the alcoholic priests, either active or recovering. The information for that study came from administrators and superiors in 138 dioceses and 110 religious congregations of men. In the long run, the accuracy and reliability of the findings rested on the knowledge of the Church authorities rather than on the drinking priests themselves.

From the perspective of research protocol among the Catholic clergy, it seems worthwhile to note that the request for information about clergy drinking came in a cover letter from Archbishop Raymond Hunthausen on behalf of the Bishops' Subcommittee on Priestly Affirmation and Support. In the Catholic ecclesiastical structure the researcher probably gets faster and more thorough responses from the clergy when the request comes through the hierarchy. Of course, there are no Church rules requiring such episcopal intervention, but every once in a while a priest wants to know whether this or that questionnaire has the approval of the bishop. In any case, I had excellent cooperation from Church authorities in gathering data for the alcoholic clergy study.

I had a vague speculation that I might similarly go to the "authorities" in the health professions to obtain basic information about sick clergy. I contacted the medical record directors of eighteen hospitals in the Sisters of Mercy Health Corporation in Michigan and learned that their computers do not list patients by occupation or profession. Since most dioceses and religious orders are covered by group insurance, I requested information from Blue Cross and the Pan American Life Center but received the same negative reply. I looked also to polling organizations like Gallup, Harris, and Roper and learned again that they do not have separate categories for clergy.

I came to the conclusion that I had better ask the priests themselves about the state of their health but thought it would be best to reach them through the authority of the local bishop. The members of the Episcopal Committee on Priestly Life and Ministry revealed that they personally knew enough bishops who were willing to cooperate. This casual approach to survey sampling had to be modified to obtain a fairly representative distribution of clergy respondents around the country. Colin MacDonald and I exchanged diocesan listings and compared the relative percentages of clergy in each diocese.

We finally selected 21 of the 174 dioceses on record in the 1982 edition of the Catholic directory. These dioceses contained 8,042 Catholic priests, or 14 percent of all American priests. They were physically distributed into four large regions. In the Northeast: the dioceses of Brooklyn, New York; Manchester, New Hampshire; Pittsburgh, Pennsylvania; and Providence, Rhode Island; North Central: Fargo, North Dakota; Kansas City, Missouri; Lafayette, Indiana; Milwaukee, Wisconsin; Rockford, Illinois; and St. Paul, Minnesota; Southern: Baltimore, Maryland; Covington, Kentucky; Fort Worth, Texas; New Orleans, Louisiana; and St. Augustine, Florida; and Far West: Baker, Oregon; Great Falls, Montana; Oakland, California; Pueblo, New Mexico; Sacramento, California; and Yakima, Washington. In September, committee chairman Bishop Justin A. Driscoll wrote personally to ask cooperation from the twenty-one diocesan bishops. A priest was designated in each diocese to supervise the distribution of questionnaires, and Bishop Driscoll personally encouraged these contact men to comply with the study.

The assurance of cooperation from the respondents was strengthened by the fact that every chancery office regularly makes a mailing to each priest in the diocese, active and retired, healthy and sick, young and old, religious and secular. This made it possible to reach the total clergy population in these dioceses. The questionnaires were sent in bulk from the NCCB headquarters in Washington, D.C., according to the enumeration provided in each diocese. To facilitate anonymous response, the questionnaires were introduced by a cover letter from the local bishop and were accompanied by a postpaid envelope addressed to the NCCB Committee in Washington, D.C. From a total of 8,042 priests in 21 dioceses came 4,660 usable responses, a satisfactory 58 percent rate of return. They were then repackaged by the committee staff in Washington, D.C. Since the survey was anonymous and the research funds limited, I did not ask the chancery offices to send a second wave of questionnaires.

In formulating the content of the questionnaire I had decided to call it the "National Survey of the Health, Work and Quality of Life of Catholic Priests." I had conducted a similar survey in 1974 of the Jesuit priests in the Southern Province. Nevertheless, I wanted the committee members to be satisfied that the content was applicable to American priests throughout the country. I scrutinized each item to assure its pertinence and necessity. In essence, the model schedule I employed was taken from the national survey on "Health Practices and Health Consequences" of April 1979, the results of which were made available through the U.S. Department of Health and Human Services in June 1981. This research instrument was also the basis of a long and complex questionnaire developed for the California Adventist Health Study, which we analyzed carefully before completing our own precise and simplified version.

I sought four categories of information in this inquiry. The first was simply an account of the ailments or "conditions" of ill-health that the priests experienced. The second asked what they were doing to preserve their health or to offset ailments. The third probed their work assignment and its relation to their health. The fourth requested a subjective appraisal of their current state of health compared to that of their age peers. When we met in Chicago to finalize the content of the questionnaire, the members of the bishops' committee suggested other items that were eventually discarded. These involved questions about family background, celibacy, parish and parishioners, education, and various problems.

Negotiations about the process and method of the study began early in 1982. The exchange of correspondence was mainly between Monsignor MacDonald and myself, but the content of questionnaire items was of interest also to others. Dennis Dease, who directed the earlier study of clergy stress, thought the purpose of the second study should be to test whether there were connections between psychological stress and physical health. Bishop Michael Murphy reported that the subcommittee met in June in Chicago to discuss in detail the content of the questionnaire I had submitted and indicated they were "interested in a wholistic context in the instrument of inquiry."

As is often the case in general discussion about prospective research projects, the members of the subcommittee wanted to gather much more information surrounding the lives of priests. This would have made the survey unmanageable and introduce many more questions than we could handle. I took into serious consideration all of the items mentioned by Bishop Murphy and sent him what I considered a workable instrument in July. All problems of content were ironed out by the beginning of September. At that point the Washington, D.C., office reproduced the final copy and was ready for distribution. By the end of October 1982, the questionnaires had been delivered to all twenty-one dioceses. By mid-December they reported that the responses were "winding down," with the cutoff date of New Year's Day approaching. When I received them at Loyola University they were neatly packaged, separately by diocese, with each envelope slit open. We had not yet installed a computer, but I continued to get excellent cooperation from Daniel Kileen and Norma Piacun, who processed the data for us at the Tulane University Computer Center.

The computer work proceeded quickly and efficiently, and by the end of January 1983, I was able to compose a four-page "overview" of the rough data for the benefit of clergy respondents who had asked for it. I soon learned that this quick and brief review of the findings could not be distributed until approved by the proper committee. The subcommittee met in Chicago at the end of February 1983, when its new chairman, Bishop Kenneth Angell, approved the overview of findings and allowed it to be distributed to interested respondents.

Meanwhile, Monsignor MacDonald had contacted all twenty-one chancery offices for information regarding certain health and welfare regulations, which had been requested by the committee members. We saw no sense in asking the individual respondents questions about age at retirement for priests, diocesan vacation policy, tenure of diocesan appointments, policy for medical checkups, the presence of a health committee, or the operation of pension funds. All of these matters could be answered from the chancery office and were pertinent to the diocesan environment in which the priests were reporting their health habits.

By the middle of May 1983, I had finished the analysis of the data and sent the complete typescript to Monsignor MacDonald, who had copies made for the members of the subcommittee, which was slated to meet in Chicago from June 8–9. At this time, they were to choose one of their members to write the book's preface. I still do not know who wrote that inappropriate introduction since I was not present at the meeting. I did subsequently receive some comments and suggestions concerning my interpretation of the research findings.

In a letter of September 14, 1983, the monsignor said the committee would be ready to meet with me for a final review of the report. "The subcommittee will ask you to overview the study, explain the process, give your own evaluation, and suggest some things the committee should do about it," he wrote. On the afternoon of October 5, I met with the Bishops' Committee on Priestly Life and Ministry and on the following morning with the Subcommittee on Priestly Affirmation and Support at the Ramada-O'Hare Inn. This was, in a sense, a careful double review of the final draft, which was, at that point, labeled "not for publication in whole or in part."

The hierarchical process always runs slowly, and, in this case, evidence is provided by Monsignor Daniel F. Hoye, general secretary, NCCB/USCC, in a statement of November 2, 1984, as a kind of *imprimatur* to the book:

> In its 1982 planning document, as approved by the general membership of the National Conference of Catholic Bishops in November, 1981, the Bishops' Committee on Priestly Life and Ministry, through its Secretariat, was authorized to address the question of the health of the American Catholic priests. A draft was reviewed by the Administrative Committee in September, 1984: "The following text has been approved by Bishop Michael J.

Murphy, Chairman of the Committee, and was authorized for publication by the undersigned."

There is no happy explanation for the delay of eleven months, between the October 1983, approval by the subcommittee and the November 2, 1984, approval by the general secretary. The study of clerical physical health, the first of its kind in the United States, seemed to be "hot" news crying out for reportage. The four-page overview had been distributed in January 1983 to several hundred priest respondents to the study with the caution that it was "not for publication." On May 31, 1984, I suggested that Washington "break" the story by releasing to the news media the "Afterword," which contained summaries and generalizations. This was not done.[2]

On October 17, 1984, the monsignor informed me that he was ready to go to the printers, who had set a deadline for the end of October. There was still further delay, as he wrote to me on February 7, 1985, and said, "there is a lot of slow molasses in our publication department." Finally on March 28, 1985, the book came off the press. It contained a gracious acknowledgment: "this study is significant in that it is the first scientific inquiry into the health of Catholic priests in the United States."

One may suggest that this national survey of the health of the Catholic clergy deserves special mention as a "breakthrough" of accurate information to replace hazy and erroneous earlier reports. A large majority (84 percent) of the priests reported that they are in "excellent" or "good" health. Almost nine out of ten (87 percent) had not been hospitalized during the previous year. Over half (56 percent) had not even been sick enough to take to their beds. The average number of days lost due to illness was only 1.7. These statistics compare favorably with the total population, where injuries and illness result in an average of 9.5 days of restricted activity and nearly 4 days of lost work during the year. [3]

The principal ailments reported in the survey affected a minority of the respondents, such as rheumatism (22 percent); sinus trouble (24 percent); back pain (20 percent); high blood pressure (18 percent); and hay fever (16 percent). In listing the number of priests who suffer these "principal ailments," we found no "cause for alarm" in either the overall state of health or in any specific area of ill-health. Compared to American adult males in other occupations and professions, the clergy appear to have lower rates of morbidity, both generally and specifically. We then safely concluded that the physical health of priests cannot be considered "one of the most crucial issues facing the Church today."[4]

The survey also provided accurate information about the "self-induced" disabilities that come from smoking, drinking, and overwork. Only 2 percent reported that they suffered from emphysema and more than three-quarters (76 percent) of all respondents do not smoke cigarettes. Widespread warning about the health hazards of nicotine have been heeded by almost half (48 percent) of the senior priests who quit smoking and by almost six out of ten (58 percent) of others who never took up the habit.

Another illness that also seems to have ameliorated through personal effort is alcoholism. More than one-third (37 percent) do not drink at all, and one out of five take two or three drinks daily. While statistics in the field of alcoholism are generally questionable, the research data on clergy alcoholism are fairly reliable, demonstrating that about one in twenty American priests is an alcoholic, active or recovering. The data from the priest health survey confirmed this national statistic (5.6 percent), which did not vary greatly from diocese to diocese among our respondents.[5]

The third example of a self-induced health threat is now called *burnout*, which is simply a popular term for an old-fashioned malady that everybody used to recognize as a nervous breakdown. Most speculation about the extent of clergy burnout seems to lack a reliable database. Even the bishops' published study, *The Priest and Stress*, presented only loose statistics on clergy stress. Not everyone who is overworked is a candidate for burnout, nor is everyone who feels a great deal of anxiety and stress. By our best calculation, only a minority (6.2 percent) of those priests have the combination of characteristics that make them probable candidates for a nervous breakdown.[6]

These clergy statistics call into question the exaggerated and unnecessary concern about stress and burnout. I was certain that much of the discussion about clergy burnout could be dismissed for lack of evidence or for conceptual confusion, but it is an issue that has to be confronted. Bishops and religious superiors tended to believe the worrisome rumors. The solid data I collected suggested that it was time to demystify the subject. I took the time to write an article about "the myth of clergy burnout" for the *National Catholic Reporter*.

The bishops tended to be sympathetic toward those concerns. They remarked that "the demands on a priest's time are burgeoning. Many over-zealous priests run great risks of suffering 'burnout,' or emotional, or physical illness." They talked about the "growing awareness of the problems of stress among American priests" and how it affected their priestly ministry. A quick overview of the research findings indicates that the great majority of the priests considered themselves quite healthy and not likely candidates for burnout. Only one out of ten said that their health was worse now than what it was two years previously. A much smaller minority (3.2 percent) remarked that ill-health "greatly affects the amount and quality of their ministry."[7]

The potential "victims" we uncovered in this study do not find themselves "depleted, run out of energy, unable to reanimate themselves." On the contrary, these priests are "on the go" all the time. They are not the victims of a rapid pace of change and transition, which is said to leave some Church personnel bewildered and frustrated. It seems erroneous or at least misleading to suggest that stress and burnout inevitably accompany the adaptations required in a developing ministry and modernizing Church. The dynamic, dedicated, modern priest thrives in this kind of situation. We are reminded by the experts that the person who works long hours and leads a busy life may be far less frustrated than the person trapped in a limited position with no sense of relief or accomplishment.

In summary, I think that our research data have placed the problem of clergy burnout in proper perspective and have allayed the fears of bishops and religious superiors about the extent of the problem. We all know that some priests are likely to have a nervous breakdown, and they deserve our deepest sympathy. On the basis of the data, we have concluded that the priest most likely to fall into this category is a diocesan parish priest in his mid-forties, who has more psychological problems than physical ailments. He fits the definition accepted by the bishops: overburdened, working longer hours, and experiencing a great deal of emotional strain.

The majority of priests, however, are not in such dire straits. Like other adult Americans, they are subject to the cultural and economic pressures of a narcissistic, consumerist society. The notion that clergy are suffering the fearful consequences of stressful overwork persists in the face of clear evidence that most Americans have long since abandoned the so-called Protestant work ethic. We have outlived our traditional reputation as a nation of industrious production workers and have moved toward an ethic of consumerism. Nevertheless, the normal and necessary work of the ministry goes on.

This survey focused on the physical health or illness of American priests, but one of the most clearly demonstrated generalizations from the data is that physical fitness is closely associated with mental health. The priests who suffer "often" from depression or who say that a great deal of emotional stress is attached to their life and work also tend to have various physical ailments in higher proportion than do emotionally balanced priests. The physically fit clergy were also the least tense and nervous, the least worried about things in general. The healthiest were much less likely (28 percent) than the sickest (54 percent) to say that they have had emotional, mental, or behavioral problems during the past year.

In the long run, the physical fitness of the Catholic clergy may well depend on their own efforts. One often hears that "they just don't take care of themselves." A physician who deals often with priests complains that "they won't do what you tell them." The fact is that clergy live longer than men in other professions, and this proverbial longevity has regularly been a feature of demographic research. The high proportion of physically healthy priests tends to support the assumption that longevity correlates with good health. The clergy can then be considered a population at "low risk" for illness.

The data revealed very clearly that physical exercise is an important factor in the maintenance of physical fitness. When we investigated separately the category of 419 of the "sickest" priests, we found that half of them are overweight, and the same proportion seldom, or never, exercise. Almost as many

(47 percent) do not take advantage of their weekly day off, while three out of ten take less than two weeks annual vacation. Such statistical comparisons always lead to the question of cause and effect. Do they not exercise because they are sick, or are they sick because they do not exercise enough to keep in shape?

In the world of conventional occupations, people supposedly reach the retirement age at sixty-five, and this ordinarily means that they stop working for salary or wages. The supposition is that such people no longer enjoy the physical stamina and intellectual capacity to perform their duties responsibly. Our clergy respondents do not fit this pattern. Among the 866 priests who have reached retirement age, six out of ten (61 percent) have not retired and are working an average week of 53 hours, while the others are retirees but are working 25.4 hours per week. A majority of the retirees (58 percent) say that they are in good or excellent health, while an even greater proportion (70 percent) of the nonretired make the same claim.

While waiting for the book to be published I wrote an article, "Cranky Old Priests," in the fall of 1986, where I presented evidence that "priests become more gracious and pleasant as they grow older." The popular literature on aging among nonclergy reveals that loneliness and depression are ordinarily associated with the life of senior citizens. The research data in this study, however, suggested that elderly priests are the exception. About half (48 percent) of the older priests reported that they *never* felt depressed during the past year, and the same proportion said that they *never* felt lonely. On the other hand, only one-seventh (14 percent) of the younger priests claimed that they felt no depression, and a slightly smaller percentage (12 percent) said that they never felt lonely.

There are psychological reasons why the aging process normally brings out mental and behavioral problems in the elderly. The normal expectation among laypeople, however, is not normal among older clergy. When we asked the priests whether they experienced any severe personal and emotional problems during the previous twelve months, a significantly larger proportion of the older priests (75 percent) than of the younger (56 percent) answered no. Indeed, and perhaps surprisingly, some of the younger men (14 percent) had problems severe enough to require professional help. These statistical comparisons suggest that the senior priests are more relaxed and, perhaps, more at peace with themselves.

People are less likely to be moody and irascible if they feel good. The fact that most priests move into their seventies while they are still physically fit, as the research data demonstrated, is probably one of the main reasons why they can face the aging process with greater tranquility. Admittedly, progressive physiological changes take place in human cells and bodily organs over the years. Most of the priests, however, escape the kind of disease and injury that increase the rate of biological aging, which helps to explain why clergy live longer than people in other professions.

One may say that the secret of a serene seniority for the clergy lies in the wisdom and experience they have achieved by the time they reach Erikson's "eighth stage" of human life. During this final stage people are forced to become aware of the finitude of life and the proximity of death. The crucial task of everyone is to answer the central questions: "What is it all about? Can I now say that my life has been meaningful and purposeful?" The elderly person who has no answer may tend to despair—may feel that life has been wasted—and develop a real fear of death.

The senior priest has been through all these experiences many times during his long life. What becomes an emergency for others is mundane for him. Aiding the sick and dying has been part of his regular routine. He has helped many people to understand the meaning and purpose of life and the inevitability of death. The religious life-style of the clergy, the tasks of their churchly vocation, and the spiritual mentality in which they perform their duties all contribute to their physical and psychological health in later years. For the most part, the elderly priests have "got it all together"; the grumpy, grouchy old priest is the exception.[8]

During the course of this survey, I took every opportunity to interview priests throughout the country about their attitudes and experiences on clerical retirement. The Second Vatican Council had recommended that bishops and priests retire because of the increasing burden of age or for some other serious reason. Yet even after the council, only sick priests and bishops were expected to relinquish their official appointments. Until the introduction of the clergy pension, the notion of retirement from active ministry due to age was an alien concept in the Catholic clergy. The vocation to the priesthood implied not only full service, "always on call," but also a lifelong ministry interrupted only by incapacity or death. It was a shock for priests to learn that retirement was now mandatory.

Yet a paradox of "necessary" resignation that still encourages continuing employment exists. The priest resigns from his ecclesiastical status, even while he continues to function in his priestly role. He is no longer a pastor, or an agency administrator, or diocesan official, but he is still engaged in the priestly ministry. Formal diocesan regulations tend to be flexible. In the diocese of Covington, Kentucky, for example, priests "may retire at the age of sixty-five, but *must* retire at the age of seventy, from positions of major administration. It is the bishop's hope that able-bodied priests will continue in other positions, such as associate pastor, chaplain, or priest, in residence at a rectory."[9]

Retirement practices differ from diocese to diocese. In the larger diocese, it is said that about half of the retired diocesan priests remain in a rectory, usually that of a priest friend. About one-fourth live in a nonchurch residence, such as the home of relatives and friends. The remaining minority look for a retirement community, perhaps in Arizona, California, Florida, or other warm-weather climates. I found that in several Florida dioceses the retired priests ("outsiders") actually outnumbered the native priests. The St. Louis archdiocese offers a retirement home, called Regina Coeli, which consists of a converted apartment building where each priest has his own apartment but also the benefit of a common dining room.

The statistics of the present survey point to a late age of retirement, whether mandatory or voluntary. Among the 476 priests who are seventy or older, two-thirds list themselves as retired. As diocesan and congregational regulations become more specific and effective, the proportion of retirees will increase, but the priests will continue to work. Their reluctance to relinquish active ministry simply reflects the traditional practice of older persons who work until they can no longer hold a job. Professionals generally take a negative view of retirement, and this is especially true of the clergy.[10]

When the fathers of the Second Vatican Council recommended resignation for bishops and priests they were motivated by the welfare of both the Church and its personnel.
They had no premonition that their recommendation would
prove to be too late and once put into effect would make the
situation worse. Who could have foreseen the drastic decline
in seminarians or the vast exodus of young clergy from the
Catholic priesthood? The growing proportions of priestly
retirees are now "making room at the top" for priests who are
no longer there to succeed them.

Regulations governing the retirement of religious order
clergy do not include questions of pensions or salaries, except
insofar as the priest may have been engaged for a fixed number of years under the jurisdiction of a bishop in parochial or
other diocesan employment. Even then, the regular clergy are
bound by a vow of poverty, transmit any income to the religious congregation, and tend to spend their declining years in
the particular community, or house, where they had conducted their ministry.

Unless the religious order priest works at an educational
institution that has its own retirement policy, he is likely to
continue working longer in active ministry than his diocesan
counterpart. While most diocesan priests spend their entire
career in parish work, the priest member of a religious community may be occupied in any number of ministries. He is
likely to have shifted from one kind of work to another on
several occasions so that the move to a "second career" is not
a traumatic experience for him. Most of the religious communities arrange to bring their aged members to a central infirmary only when they are in need of regular nursing care.

It was never the intention of any retirement program,
whether for diocesan or religious clergy, to prevent the level
of priestly work that the individual's age and capacity may
allow. The occupational ambiguity in the status of retired
diocesan priests is that they are expected to seek out their
own locus and type of ministry, whereas previously they had
been told specifically what they were to do and where they
were to serve. With the increasing shortage of priests, it
should be easy for the retiree to "find work," but a lifetime of
obedience seems to have adversely affected such an important and independent decision. One diocesan priest, age sixty-

eight, reflects such ambiguity and indecision: "I'm retired, and it's fun. I now do the things I'm interested in. We old guys should be asked what we would like to do. You would be surprised at the varieties of interests, and it helps our health. We cannot just sit."

4

Hospitals and Health Care

✚✚✚✚✚✚✚✚✚✚✚✚✚✚✚✚✚✚✚✚✚✚✚✚✚✚✚✚✚✚✚✚✚✚✚✚✚✚✚

In the fall of 1979 I enjoyed a sabbatical, scholar-in-residence status at the University of Notre Dame, where I was associated with both the Department of Sociology and the Catholic Committee of Urban Ministry, under the direction of Monsignor Jack Egan. I had hardly settled in my office there when I received a telephone call from Father Paul Besanceny, offering me a job as project director for the Center of Applied Research in the Apostolate (CARA) in Washington, D.C. We arranged to talk a few days later in Boston at the meeting of the American Sociological Association. On August 27, Father Besanceny described the research project for which the U.S. Department of Health, Education and Welfare was about to grant a contract to CARA.

When CARA was established in 1965, with a trained anthropologist, Father Louis Luzbatek, as its first director, I was a member of its Research Review Committee, which met infrequently. Unlike the scholarly and prestigious research institutes at universities such as Chicago, Columbia, Cornell, and Michigan, CARA was encouraged by the American bishops (with a heavy financial subsidy from Cardinal Cushing) to do practical and useful research for the Church. It was most fitting, therefore, that CARA should apply for a government grant to study the "Role of the Catholic Health Care System in Implementing National Health Priorities." The contract was awarded a month later, on September 26, 1979, with the termination date set for January 26, 1981.

I was not a stranger to the study of health care and was even then negotiating for the publication of my research report on the *Rehabilitation of Clergy Alcoholics.*[1] In *Religion and Pain* I had focused specifically on the health professionals who were concerned about the spiritual dimensions of ministering to sick people.[2] I have not hesitated to use some of the interviews I did for the CARA study in my subsequent book, *Healing Ministries.*[3] This research paid careful attention to the sick people themselves and to the professionals who took care of them. In the proposed CARA study, my job was to analyze the systems and the locations where health care was provided.

The first preparatory meeting for the research project was held at CARA's Washington, D.C., headquarters from October 9 to 10, when its director, Dr. Edward Sullivan, explained the details of the research grant and proposed the general methodology for our procedures. Paul Besanceny was our contact person at CARA. The assistant project director, Suzanne Ahern, MPH, was at hand too for this discussion. Her main responsibility was to conduct the extensive library research on the Catholic health-care system. A second part of the project was a statistical analysis of all existing data which was to be handled by Dr. Florence Rosenberg.

Meanwhile, CARA enlisted a number of experienced hospital professionals, both Catholic and non-Catholic, to function as a steering committee. They met with us at CARA headquarters on November 13 and discussed in detail the criteria to be used for the four hospitals selected as the subject of site visits the following summer. The contract required that "four exploratory case studies be conducted: one in a hospital representing each of the following kinds of sponsorship: 1) local government; 2) Catholic sponsored; 3) other religion-sponsored, and 4) other non-government, not-for-profit sponsorship."

The members of the steering committee were experienced and knowledgeable in the field of health care. We expected them to be consultants throughout the project, whenever we were in need of guidance. We asked them to comment on the hospitals that they knew and to provide the names of two or three additional hospitals in each of the four categories. With their list, we spent considerable time in comparative appraisals and did not settle on the final four choices until our meeting in Washington, D.C., in April.

The contract signed with HEW declared that the research project will "determine the extent current activities or operational characteristics of the Catholic health care system contribute to certain national health priorities." We were to identify certain particulars, such as how the system (a) maintains and improves services to inner-city and rural populations; (b) improves efficiency in the financing and provisions for health services, including interinstitutional arrangements; (c) develops HMO and other alternative delivery systems; and (d) strengthens ambulatory care or other community health services.

These were the core priorities contained in Section 1502 of the National Health Planning and Resource Development Act of 1974. CARA's attention initially pointed to the Catholic health system, for which the literature search was directed, and the statistical analysis was provided. What was the Church's role, and how was it being carried out? As a preliminary preparation for the study, I took every opportunity to interview Catholic health-care professionals while I was still on the Notre Dame campus.

I tape-recorded exploratory interviews of about two hours in length with one physician, three chaplains, and seven religious sisters from Catholic hospitals in Cleveland, Ohio; Detroit, Michigan; Dubuque, Iowa; Helena, Montana; Milwaukee, Wisconsin; South Bend, Indiana; and Yakima, Washington. In the three months, from October to December, I was able also to interview nine professionals from non-Catholic hospitals: one social worker, two physicians, two chaplains, and four hospital administrators. I made site visits to the Priests' Retirement Home on the Notre Dame campus and with the chaplains and nurses at St. Joseph's Hospital and Holy Cross Hospital in South Bend. On January 2, I flew to Detroit for consultation with the sisters at the Mercy Health Care System. Everywhere I repeated the same question: How do they deliver primary health care to poor people efficiently and inexpensively?

I was looking for precise definitions, and I searched for knowledgeable people who could explain the difference between Catholic and non-Catholic hospitals. A long-time hospital chaplain said that the quick answer of the man-on-the-street was: "It's a place where they don't do abortions." Another said that the sisters who run the Catholic hospitals strongly oppose the unionization of their lower-echelon employees. There was, of course, the notion of the "caring community," the total therapeutic community in which all workers, professionals and staff, cooperate for the benefit of the sick and dying. Some of the information I picked up in these exploratory interviews—even with honest and dedicated clergy and sisters within the system—was not entirely favorable toward the hospital administrators.[4]

In January I returned to Loyola University in New Orleans to teach in the Spring semester but spent considerable time studying the transcribed tapes of my numerous interviews. This was preparatory work on the project, and I made out "time sheets" for the CARA office. My work included telephone interviews with health professionals, such as Dr. John Rice of Chicago's Augustana Hospital and Dr. Jorge Prieto of Cook County Hospital as well as personal interviews in New Orleans with Jack Cooley of Baptist Hospital, Terry Buckingham of Touro Infirmary, and Dr. John Mary of St. Charles Hospital.

On April 17, 1980, the members of the steering committee met with us at CARA headquarters for an in-depth discussion of the activities and characteristics of certain hospitals, under the four different types of sponsorship. Each member was then asked to list, in order, a first and second choice of hospitals for study in each classification. The final consensus consisted of the following:

1) Santa Rosa Medical Center of San Antonio
   (Catholic-sponsored);

2) Presbyterian Hospital System of Albuquerque
   (other-religious sponsored);

3) Greenville, South Carolina, Hospital System
   (local government);

4) Mid-Maine Medical Center, Waterville
   (not-for-profit, nongovernmental)

The choices were put into effect within the week. Thereafter, back at Loyola, I began making negotiations with the chief executive officer at each of these health facilities. On Monday, April 21, I called vice-president Jeffrey Lefko, at Greenville; on Tuesday, executive director Sister Angela Clare, of Santa Rosa Medical Center; on Wednesday, vice-president Joyce Godwin, of Presbyterian Hospital in Albuquerque; and on Thursday, president Eugene Beaupre, of Mid-Maine Medical Center in Waterville. These people, of course, requested additional information. I sent them an outline of our proposed inquiry, including some of the most general areas we wanted to examine in their operations. In subsequent weeks, I talked with each of them several times and firmed up our visitation dates.

All arrangements were agreed upon before the first of June. I arrived in San Antonio on Friday, June 6, and was met at the airport by Sister Angela Clare and Sister Ann, who had booked me into the relatively expensive Hilton Palacio del Rio. We agreed to begin the interviews on Monday morning, and I meanwhile contacted two Jesuit Fathers, Joe Fengler and John Welsh, at the parish of Our Lady of Guadalupe, for Saturday night dinner at the Tower of the Americas, and later, the Folklorica and Arnesan *Fiesta Noche del Rio*. On Sunday I checked out of the Hilton, went with Sister John Sapp, O.S.B., to meet Suzanne Ahern at the airport, and spent the afternoon visiting four of the old Franciscan missions. I then registered at the Holiday Inn, within walking distance of the hospital, and found a worried telephone message from Sister Angela Clare, who said she had been "looking all over" for me.

On Monday morning, Suzanne and I met with Sister Angela and her contingent of five key staff people for a general introduction. As a matter of fact, they were prepared for us and were ready to schedule interviews with individuals and small groups. The center is under the auspices of the Sisters of Charity of the Incarnate Word, who established the facility in 1869. The original institution has now branched out to the Children's Hospital and the Villa Rosa Rehabilitation Center. Santa Rosa is a link in the network of seven "sister hospitals," which are operated by this congregation of religious women.[5] For five days we tape-recorded conversations with representatives from all parts of the center.

Although each of the San Antonio facilities has its own director, a common philosophy exists. Transfer and promotion of employees is fully operative among the three units. Employees may also transfer among the seven sister hospitals. Seniority earned in one hospital is recognized in others, with the attendant benefits and pension advantages. Santa Rosa is also able to help other hospitals with cost-cutting and the sharing of expensive and sophisticated equipment. Further, Santa Rosa belongs to the American Hospital Association, maintains membership in the Texas Hospital Association, and is affiliated with the American Catholic Hospital Association. It was a participant in a pilot project to establish a series of evaluative criteria for Catholic health facilities.

One of the local projects of urban development that it encouraged was the restoration of El Mercado, a renovated mall of shops, restaurants, and merchandise stalls that attracts tourists. It serves as the locale for the annual Gran Noche de Santa Rosa, a charitable fund-raiser. Santa Rosa is recognized as an integral part of the San Antonio community. As a voluntary, not-for-profit medical center, Santa Rosa can return to the continued health care of the community any surplus it engenders or added funds it can gather. In other words, the medical center carries a very heavy charity load of patients. The great majority of them are Hispanics of relatively slender financial means. The slogan of the administration is that "no one is turned away who cannot pay." The original mission of this nursing order of religious women was to serve the health needs of the indigent sick, of those who could not obtain adequate medical attention in any other way. Like other hospitals that received Hill-Burton funds, Santa Rosa was conscious of its obligation to provide a designated amount of health care for the poor, and it consistently exceeded this requirement. The cost of these services, which amounted to more than $8 million per year, could be listed as "bad debts," uncollectibles, or simply charity.

The Children's Hospital is a central feature of the Santa Rosa Medical Center, providing health services unobtainable elsewhere in southern Texas. In 1956, San Antonio's first fully licensed and approved heliport was inaugurated atop the eleventh floor of the Children's Hospital. The great majority of airborne patients are premature or high-risk infants. The hospital boasts a regional concentration of specialists in pediatrics: neurosurgeons, cardiologists, orthopedists, and others. The Children's Hospital presented a constant financial drain on the resources of the center. The birth rate tends to be higher in poorer families, and thus more of the maternity cases became free service. The sophistication and competence of the Children's Hospital spilled over into outpatient clinics, where 90 percent of the patients were children.

Much of the success of the Santa Rosa Medical Center must be attributed to the philosophy and practice of management. Its mission statement says that it meets "the needs of the sick irrespective of race, creed, color, religion, national origin, or social status." Santa Rosa was the first hospital in San Antonio to introduce the peer review process for accrediting doctors. Removing incompetent doctors is the "right thing" to do, according to the hospital's governing philosophy. Paying a just wage to all workers and hiring people regardless of race, sex, or religion is also the right thing to do as are refusing to allow abortions and sterilization operations, emphasizing the sacred value of life in the prenatal and neonatal stages, expending extraordinary efforts for handicapped and disabled children, and giving assistance to the indigent, the lonely, and the elderly.

The Pastoral Care Department, under the direction of Sister Sara Carter, has nine members, each of whom serves a hospital section as a "parish."[6] The department is accredited for clinical pastoral training. Two priests contribute sacramental visitation, and the program is benignly blessed by Monsignor Bernard Popp, pastor of the San Fernando Cathedral. The genuine Christian love of this department explains the remarkable morale exhibited by its staff. The employees recognize the loving and cheerful spirit of the center and often say that they feel a "real difference" at Santa Rosa compared to other hospitals where they had worked. We asked them whether this same spirit would continue if the fourteen religious sisters were no longer present. The general consensus was that the sisters would be missed, but their influence would carry on among the many dedicated individuals who think of their hospital work as a lay ministry.

On the afternoon of Friday, June 13, we had a final wrap-up session with Sister Angela Clare and her key administrators.

We were pleased not only with their splendid cooperation but also with the preliminary assessment we were able to make of our findings. We made an appointment to have dinner that night with Sister Angela and Sister Ann and to drive out to the campus of the Incarnate Word College, the motherhouse of the religious congregation. The next day I flew back to New Orleans to my own campus at Loyola University.

For several days I worked over my notes and the transcripts of research memoranda, but on Thursday flew to San Francisco for a conference at nearby Berkeley. I delivered a paper entitled "Youth in Search of the Sacred" at the Unification Conference on New Social Movements.[7] When the conference ended on Sunday, June 22, I flew to Albuquerque to begin the investigation of Presbyterian Hospital. Reservations had been made for me at the Crossroads Motel, across the street from the hospital. Father Frank Lynette met me at the airport and took me to the rectory of the Immaculate Conception Church, where I had a preliminary talk with Jesuit Brother Tom Sherman, one of the pastoral ministers of the hospital.

My previous telephone conversations and correspondence had been with Joyce Godwin, vice-president for management services. She met us on Monday morning and continued to facilitate all our appointments. During the next five days we interviewed more than thirty persons—trustees, administrators, department directors, surgeons, nurses, social workers, and office staff—and learned about the origins of this church-related hospital. In 1907 the New Mexico Synod of the Presbyterian Church authorized the establishment in Albuquerque of a "Presbyterian Sanitarium for indigent lungers." While the influence of the church and its ministers was significant in the early decades and while there was always a chapel, or meditation room, it was not until 1954 that the first official chaplain was appointed. The current chaplain, Reverend Dennis Saylor,[8] who had just published a book about hospital ministry entitled *And You Visited Me,* received the services of a Methodist chaplain at the Anna Kaseman Hospital and the assistance of a Jesuit brother in pastoral ministry.

The Synod of the Southwest continues to nominate three clergy board members. The expansion of the hospital system into the rural areas of New Mexico is said to be "an extension of the Church's call to mission." Aside from its relatively loose supervisory function, the Presbyterian Church appears to have little direct influence and no authority over the organization and administration of the contemporary center. Employees are not required to pass religious or confessional tests, and many of them come from the large Hispanic Catholic population of Albuquerque. The medical staff, like the rest of the professional personnel, represents a variety of religious affiliations.

Pastoral care and religious ministry are available to employees and staff as well as to patients and their families, but it appears that chaplains are utilized only in crisis situations. One does not sense a religious "atmosphere" in the midst of the daily hospital activities, where the concentration of effort and attention is on medicine, surgery, and nursing. The highly trained members of the counseling department, under the direction of Joan Gunzelman, were available on a "secular" basis to both employees and patients. The earlier spiritual emphasis seems to have yielded to a kindly humanistic interest that motivates people who are genuinely concerned about the sick and the suffering.

St. Joseph's Catholic Hospital, four blocks down the street from Presbyterian, had also originated as a sanitarium for tubercular victims who came from far and wide to enjoy the dry climate of Albuquerque. The two hospitals share a working arrangement at several levels. The medical staffs of both hospitals have a common affiliation and tend to send their patients to either or both hospitals. They cooperatively launched an ambulance service that employs trained paramedics and modern equipment. The ambulance team is on call mainly in Albuquerque and its suburbs but also often brings in critically ill patients from the rural areas. It operates at a deficit that is prorated according to the amount of usage by each of the hospitals.

A second cooperative venture that has since gone independent was the establishment of medical clinics in five rural areas, a joint response to the absence of doctors and nurses in the neighboring counties where there was a general lack of primary health care. A third significant cooperative project was the formation of Mastercare, a health maintenance organization, for which each hospital invested $50,000 in "seed money" to augment the supportive federal grant. Enrollment, which reached 18,000 people, was open to employees of local industries, companies, and institutions. Still another joint program was the establishment of home health care, or hospice, for patients who are under the care of a physician but are not needful of the constant attention given to hospital patients. Referrals for home care came from medical doctors, supervising the nurses and paraprofessionals who, in turn, would visit the patients in their home.

A conscious decision was made early on at Presbyterian to make sparing use of interns and residents so as to avoid becoming known as a "teaching hospital." The staff wanted to focus all available resources on the patients. The training of graduate medical students is expensive, time-consuming, and complicated. The reluctance to affiliate with the University of New Mexico Medical School in a formal program still allowed room for the existence of a full-time director of medical education within the Presbyterian system. Medical knowledge and health information were made available through seminars and pamphlets to all employees of the hospital as well as to large numbers of patients and their families. Unlike nearby St. Joseph's, which closed its nursing school, Presbyterian never offered a nursing program. On the other hand, a school of practical nursing was started in 1956 and expanded many times until 1965, when Presbyterian purchased the former temple of the Mormon Church for this purpose. This eventually evolved into a Department of Health Occupations, with five training programs for paraprofessionals in health care.

Some of the more outspoken physicians on the medical staff complain that Albuquerque is "over-run with medical specialists," especially in surgery. This bespeaks a great need for general practitioners, or family doctors. Over six thousand babies were delivered at Presbyterian in 1979, the numbers increased after St. Joseph's phased out its own obstetrics department. In general, more emphasis was placed on primary health care, on the human and personal needs of patients. The outlying affiliate hospitals had less need for medical specialists than for doctors trained in family medicine. This basic principle of personal concern extends to all hospital personnel.

At all levels of the occupational structure at Presbyterian Hospital Center our interviewees told us that they like their co-workers: friendly, cooperative, cheerful, and competent are some of the words used to describe colleagues. A top administrator told us, "If you force me to say which I like best, the work I'm doing, or the people I'm doing it with, I'm not sure I could answer that question." The majority of the nonprofessional staff said they would turn down a job offer elsewhere. Work satisfaction by the personnel was matched by general satisfaction expressed by the patients. More than nine out of ten respondents to a recent survey of patients said they would return to Presbyterian if ever a patient again.

After an interview with social worker Judith Walden and lunch with Sister Monica Ann, C.P.E., at St. Joseph's Hospital, on Friday, June 27, vice-president Joyce Godwin gathered her key group of administrators for a "wrapup" session. They were ready to examine several particulars of our findings and helped to clarify a few items for us. The following morning Frank Lynette picked me up at the Crossroads Motel for the trip to the airport. I arrived back in New Orleans before noon.

I had the entire month of July to do content analysis of the interviews from the two hospitals in San Antonio and Albuquerque and to make preparations for the next site visit in Greenville, South Carolina. Beginning on Independence Day, I attended the twenty-fifth anniversary conference of Alcoholics Anonymous at the New Orleans Superdome. I had almost completed research for my book *Rehabilitation of Clergy Alcoholics*, but in the meantime I had several additional interviews with recovering clergy to conduct at the conference.

From July 19 to 27, I participated in an ecumenical conference sponsored by the Unification Church in Acapulco, Mexico, held at the Hyatt Regency Hotel. My role was that of small-group moderator. By this time, I had sufficient experience and knowledge of the Unification Church that I could cooperate intelligently in their programs. I was still gathering data for my book about the Unification world movement.[9] Most of the American leaders of the church delivered lectures on the Unification ideology, including Mose Durst, Jonathan Wells, Pauline Pilote, William Bergman, Joseph Tully, Hugh Spurgin, and Lloyd Eby.

During the week before I left for Greenville, I completed the first rough drafts of the site visits in San Antonio and Albuquerque. I made telephone contact several times with Jeffrey Lefko, vice-president of the Greenville Hospital, who had sent me packets of preliminary materials. He had made reservations at the Howard Johnson Motel, where I checked in on Sunday, August 3. I immediately took a taxi to St. Francis Hospital for a lengthy interview with the director, Sister Bernardine.

On Monday morning, Lefko was ready with a small group of management people to review some of the background information that I had already learned in the brochures and pamphlets previously mailed to me. As the only "competitive" voluntary, not-for-profit hospital in the city, Greenville Hospital was established in 1932 by the Franciscan Sisters of the Poor in the depth of the economic depression. The Catholic population in Greenville is a small minority, and the two hospitals—Greenville and the Catholic-sponsored St. Francis—complement each other along ecumenical lines. Local doctors tend to affiliate at both hospitals. In 1976 the St. Francis Obstetrics Department closed, but the hospital continued its services in pediatrics. One surgeon who had no qualms about abortion left the hospital but opened an office in the same neighborhood where he continued to perform them.

The genesis of the Greenville Hospital System was begun by a group of doctors in the early part of the century. Then it became a city-owned enterprise until 1947—its thirtieth year—when it was the beneficiary of a unique piece of legislation passed by the South Carolina General Assembly. Approved by a county referendum, Act 432 vested ownership and control of the Greenville General Hospital in an independent, self-perpetuating board of seven trustees. In 1952 the hospital anticipated the national health priority that later encouraged multi-institutional arrangements. The link with the local hospital in the nearby town of Greer was the original example for the subsequent national trend toward the multihospital system. In 1963 Hillcrest Hospital in Simpsonville was affiliated, followed in 1974 with Greenville Hospital in the town of Travelers Rest.

In subsequent years the large "campus" evolved into a medical complex that consisted of the Marshall Pickens Psychiatric Unit, the Memorial Hospital for acute care, and the Roger Peace Institute of Rehabilitation Medicine. These were followed by the Center for Family Medicine and the Cancer Treatment Center. This expanding multiunit complex assured health services for both the inner city and the outlying areas. It also provided the kind of secondary and tertiary care that brought in critically ill patients from other parts of the country.

This network of eight health-care units within the Greenville Health Care System demonstrated an increased efficiency in health services and avoided the duplication of high technology. By calculating the health needs of the entire county population, the administrators agreed that there was no need for more than one cancer treatment center, one emergency trauma room, an intensive care nursery, an obstetrics unit, a cardiac catherization laboratory, and a cardiovascular surgery unit.

The hospital has also developed an improved system for ambulatory health care. Most people who seek medical aid are treated on an outpatient basis. There are approximately five times more visits to the emergency departments and the clinics than there are people admitted as inpatients. Each of the seven major clinics is subdivided into specialties, which are subsumed under clinics for eye, internal medicine, obstetrics/ gynecology, orthopedic, pediatrics, and surgery.

There was an overriding need to deliver primary health care to people of inadequate economic means, and the Greenville Hospital System answered this need by providing a cadre of general practitioners. For example, the faculty of the Center for Family Medicine is affiliated with the Medical University of South Carolina in Charleston. The program of medical education at the Greenville Hospital System attempts a corrective to the maldistribution (toward big cities and away from small towns) of physicians and to the disproportionate ratio of primary-care physicians to medical and surgical specialists.

Another innovation was the hospice program, which grew out of the Cancer Treatment Center. This program benefits outpatients who, in the words of one patient, "don't want to die in the hospital among strangers and hooked up to machines." The function of the physician is primarily pain control, but social workers play a central role in the program too. A chaplain is assigned half time and receives active assistance from family members and from many volunteers. Hospice is a primary example of home health care extending therapy beyond the walls of the hospital.

The Howard Johnson Motel where I stayed in Greenville was more than walking distance to the hospital, and I had to rely on hospital personnel for transportation since the town had not built a system of buses or trolleys. On Wednesday night, hospital president Jack Skarupa and his wife, Barbara, took us to dinner at the Country Club and for a tour of the city streets. He remarked that there were three Catholic parishes in town, St. Mary's, St. Anthony's, and Our Lady of the Rosary. The latter later came under the ministry of the Southern Jesuits.

Provisions are made for spiritual ministrations to the patients in all units of the system. The director of the pastoral care department has his office in the Memorial Hospital and has half-time clergy at several units. Fixed appointments for accredited chaplains became necessary after some of the fundamentalist seminarians from nearby Bob Jones University caused a disturbance among the patients. The Greenville Hospital System had previously maintained a curriculum for the training of clergy in clinical pastoral education, but this program was phased out as a means of containing costs. Fortunately, some of the local churches have well-trained volunteers who regularly visit their sick coreligionists.

On my final day at Greenville, David Bryant drove me to North Greenville Hospital, which reserves some rooms for the treatment of alcoholics. In the early afternoon, Jeff Lefko and three top management personnel conducted a final discussion of our generalizations. I stayed at the motel most of Saturday, August 9, to review the tape recordings of the week's events.

My first contact with the Mid-Maine Hospital in Waterville, Maine, had been on April 24, when I telephoned Dr. Eugene Beaupre, the executive director. I called again on May 21, suggesting that I might make a quick preliminary visit on the 27th, after celebrating the silver anniversary of my cousin's ordination in New York. The event was canceled, however, when my cousin suffered a stroke. Meanwhile, I had received all the usual brochures and other literature that gave an adequate description of the medical center. During the week after my return from Greenville, I analyzed the transcripts of the tapes I had made and also made preparations for the trip to Maine. On Wednesday, August 13, I had a long telephone conversation with Joan Coleman, second in command at Waterville, who said a room reservation was made for me at the Americana Motor Inn.

Waterville is a small city with a small airport. An Eastern flight brought me directly to Boston in the late afternoon of August 17. A twenty-seater Northeast Airlines prop plane made a stop at Augusta before arriving at Waterville. The medical center provided a car for our use during the week and, in general, offered warm hospitality. Dr. Beaupre and Joan Coleman took us to dinner at the Village Inn in suburban Belgrade Lakes. In a sense, this was a business dinner, at which we heard the fascinating story of the origin and development of the Mid-Maine Medical Center.

Systematic health care was first provided by the Daughters of Charity of St. Vincent de Paul, who established the Sisters' Hospital in 1913. Five dissatisfied members of the medical staff broke away in 1931 to organize the proprietary Thayer Hospital. In 1964, the sisters moved and renamed their new hospital after St. Elizabeth Ann Seton. For about forty years the "doctors'" hospital tried to keep up with the "sisters'" hospital, and there continued to be more competition than cooperation between Seton and Thayer. Through a series of fortuitous events the two hospitals consolidated in 1975 under the name of the Mid-Maine Medical Center. This is the smallest and the least urban of the four hospitals we visited.[10]

The concept of the multiunit institution was exemplified at Waterville in the process of consolidation. The long rivalry between Seton and Thayer was strongest in the medical staffs, even though most of the doctors had affiliation at both hospitals. Some held the vivid memory that Thayer was founded by doctors dissatisfied with the Sisters' Hospital. Deep loyalties had been nurtured over the years and were difficult to dislodge. Other doctors who favored the Seton Hospital spoke disdainfully of the Thayer unit as the "country club." Similarly, some whose allegiance was with Thayer spoke of the Seton unit as the "motherhouse." Even after five years of successful consolidation, a few still petulantly declared that they will "never set foot" in the other unit.

When the sisters withdrew from Waterville, Bishop Peter Gerety of the Portland diocese helped to bring about a friendly cooperation in the medical center. About half the population of Waterville is Catholic. There are three parishes. Chaplains, both Protestant and Catholic, provided pastoral care in Thayer as well as in Seton. When the merger came, the office of the Pastoral Care Department was located in the Seton unit, where the Catholic chapel continued in use for daily Mass. I had lunch and a long conversation with both chaplains. Father Ned Hogan, a Jesuit, is associate to the chief Protestant chaplain, Reverend William Brewster, who was accredited as supervisor of training for students in Clinical Pastoral Education.

A positive influence for mutual understanding among employees and a loving concern for patients carried over from the pastoral ministry that was previously active in both hospitals. The reorganized Department of Pastoral Care employed two full-time salaried clergy and incorporated the part-time services of local ministers and priests as well as lay volunteers from the churches. The concept of a caring community is a live option of the chaplains, who remain sensitive to the spiritual and emotional needs of suffering patients. They promote the ideal of a therapeutic community in which all members exhibit love and compassion.

The task force for the development of a therapeutic community consisted of five people from the management team. It eventually expanded to include department heads, physicians, nurses, volunteers, and rank-and-file workers. Physical changes were introduced, procedures were improved, and specific problems were investigated, discussed, and resolved. One of the administrators told us that "the caring environment at Mid-Maine is ongoing, pervasive, continually discussed, and reinforced. We see it as a major element of our responsibility as a health-care provider. We talk about the quality of care and about the efficiency of our operation, but the caring environment goes absolutely hand in hand with virtually every decision we make."

While the chief focus of the medical center is the health care of its patients, a high priority was placed on the transmission of health knowledge and techniques. A medical education consortium reaches out to the doctors and nurses in the smaller hospitals throughout the state. Mid-Maine supplied most of the instructors from its own medical staff, but it also invited professors to come from as far away as Tufts Medical School in Boston. Other instructors participated from the larger hospitals in Maine, such as Franklin Memorial at Farmington, Haddington-Fairview at Skowhegan, and the Kennebec Valley Medical Center.

The long-term trend in hospital care is to get patients out of bed and ambulatory as quickly as possible. The start of this trend in Waterville originated with the Mansfield Clinic, named for a fallen World War II hero. Doctors volunteered their time and talent for almost every medical specialty: surgery, pediatrics, ears, nose, and throat, and leukemia. Another clinic was the F. T. Hill Center for Communication Disorders, which specializes in speech pathology and hearing loss. There is also a free dental clinic open on Saturday mornings for children of poor families. A dental clinic for children was established at Jackman in northeastern Maine and another in Bingham in central Maine for both youth and adults.

Mid-Maine Medical Center provides primary health care for many underprivileged people who are too poor to pay for it. Underemployment is a chronic condition in rural central Maine, where the level of wages tends to be below the national average. Poor people come to the emergency department of the Thayer unit with minor ailments that are ordinarily treated in a doctor's office. Others who can pay for medical services prefer the emergency room rather than adapting their own schedule to the doctor's regular office hours. This is why one of the administrators calls the emergency room the "department of convenient medicine."

There is no public transportation system in Waterville, and poor people call the free ambulance service rather than use expensive taxis. Consequently, the emergency room functions as the main channel of admission of patients to a hospital bed. This was the case at Mid-Maine, but the numbers of ambulatory outpatients far outnumber the proportion who were assigned by their doctor to a hospital room. Another aspect of "convenient" medical attention was the increasing practice of day surgery. Adult patients were able to receive this treatment at the Thayer unit, youngsters at the Seton unit.

One of the perennial problems of rural areas is recruiting general practitioners. Fortunately, the Mid-Maine Medical Center is sufficiently complex and sophisticated to attract doctors in the chief medical and surgical specialties. The development of an extensive referral system channeled in a steady stream of patients requiring their services. On the other hand, the policy of supporting small hospitals and clinics in rural areas brings health care to the patients where they live and where they are commonly underserved. The medical center supports an ongoing program of training for medical residents in family practice. Further, the director of the emergency room is board-certified in family practice and imparts his enthusiasm for small town and rural medicine to the young interns in the program.

Continued outreach to the smaller hospitals of central Maine profited greatly from the extensive background of the medical center's administrators and staff. To avoid the charge of authoritativeness, the center's board of directors adopted the attitude that "we will help you whenever you come and ask for help." Then, a more assertive approach was projected by the "sales pitch" or potential "marketing" of the managerial and clinical expertise that is readily available through the vice-president for external affairs. Giving assistance to the autonomous small hospital is a deliberate effort to halt the centralization of medical resources. Mid-Maine Medical Center is dedicated to the proposition that health care be provided as closely as possible to the community where the patients reside.

The personnel of the medical center were enthusiastically cooperative in describing their experiences and aspirations. President Eugene Beaupre, although extremely busy, gave us what time he could, but central guidance came from vice-president Joan Coleman. We interviewed three board members on Thursday and had dinner with another physician, Dr. Charles Pratt of Mount St. Joseph. On Friday afternoon the vice-president gathered all the available informants for a final overview of our own conclusions. On Saturday morning I drove to the airport for the 11 a.m. flight to Boston.

Instead of going directly home to New Orleans, I flew to New York to attend two meetings: the annual convention of the Association for the Sociology of Religion from August 25 to 27 and the American Sociological Association from August 28 to 31. Both seminars were held at the New York Hilton Hotel. I flew back to Loyola University in New Orleans on Labor Day.

In the months following these site visits and before the end of my contract with CARA, I wrote a book-size report of the study. It has never been published. The site visits to these hospital centers were simply and deliberately exploratory, and the report of the findings was intentionally descriptive. The research proposal did not suggest a series of hypotheses to be tested against the findings nor the utilization of control categories for comparative purposes. The hospitals selected for study were not seen as typical, or representative, or the "best" in their classification. We studied them as imitable examples of constructive change and as models of hospitals that are striving to set a standard of national health care.

Aside from the fact that they are all commendable for their health-care delivery, these four institutions share some common characteristics. They are autonomous, voluntary, not-for-profit institutions, and, for this reason, are quite different from those owned by private proprietary corporations or those that are under the direct public ownership and auspices of state or federal governments. All have received, in small or large amounts, Hill-Burton funds, and voluntarily carry a greater load of charity patients than obligated. A considerable proportion of their patients are admitted and treated under Medicaid and Medicare. "Reaching the underserved," "taking care of the poor," and "turning no one away" are common slogans found in these hospitals.

Another uniform factor is the managerial competence exhibited by both top administration and middle management. It seems safe to say that the ability to plan, to organize and reorganize, and to maintain the hospital as a going concern are the central reasons for the overall success of each institution. This means the proper utilization of resources—physical, material, and financial—but also the employment of talented human beings at all levels of the system. Each of the hospitals has a dependable core of loyal and permanent employees although all of them share, to some degree, the general problem of labor turnover, which is more prevalent in the lower echelons of semiskilled and poorly paid workers. The shortage of registered nurses—and efforts to recruit them—were reported at all sites. The maldistribution of medical doctors, especially the shortage of general practitioners, or family doctors, is also a common theme in small towns and rural areas.

All four health-care systems subscribe to a holistic approach in medical and hospital service that includes the spiritual dimension of patient care. The Pastoral Care Department in each hospital is written into the budget, pays the salary of clinically trained ministers, encourages ecumenical sharing in spiritual ministrations, and involves lay volunteers in the visitation of patients.

Despite these commonalities, each hospital displays at least one special characteristic for which it is notable. The outstanding feature of the Santa Rosa Medical Center is its Children's Hospital, which emphasizes the sacred value of both ill-born and well-born infants. The Presbyterian Hospital Center appears most noteworthy for the manner in which it has been able to establish, or restore, health services to remote areas of New Mexico. The Greenville Hospital System received its original impetus for expansion from the unique provisions of Act 432, passed by the South Carolina General Assembly in 1947, which allowed it to pioneer the national trend toward multi-institutional hospital systems. What seems most unusual about the Mid-Maine Medical Center is its efficient consolidation of two formerly independent, rivalrous, and successful hospitals.

The story I tell here—about the "good works" done in these four hospitals—relies heavily on the professional contribution of Suzanne Ahern, whose research went far beyond the site visits. In compliance with the contract between CARA and the Department of Health and Human Services (formerly HEW), she composed the final and official report, "Analysis of the Role of the Catholic Health Care System in Implementing National Health Priorities." The summary included a statistical analysis of all U.S. Catholic hospitals, a review of contemporary literature dealing with Catholic health care, and the workshop "papers" delivered by expert hospital administrators at the completion of the research project.

All of these were interim reports that had to be explained in a personal presentation before the federal project officer, Lyman van Nostrand, and his agency staff. We appeared at the Human Resources Building in Hyattsville, Maryland, on January 14, 1981. CARA director, Ed Sullivan, gave the history of the project and explained the statistical analysis, Suzanne Ahern described the literature review and the workshop discussions, and I gave a briefing on the case studies. The final report was officially accepted on January 30, and the contract closed.

5

The Charismatic Renewal

❈❈

After an absence of fifteen years I attended, in 1987, a charismatic prayer meeting and liturgy at St. Benilde's Church in New Orleans. I had just read Mary Jo Nietz's book *Charisma and Community*[1] and was scheduled to lead a discussion about the Catholic pentecostal movement at the October meeting of the Association for the Sociology of Religion. The 1987 prayer meeting was essentially the same as the first charismatic gatherings I attended in 1972 at Loyola University of New Orleans. There was still the same enthusiasm and the same charismatic traits: speaking in tongues, praising the Lord, and especially witnessing people who received the Baptism of the Holy Spirit and special benefits from their prayers.

The Catholic pentecostal movement, as it was then called, was brought to the Loyola campus in November 1968, when Father Harold Cohen was baptized in the Spirit and called the first prayer meeting. Other Jesuits involved were Donald Gelpi, Henry Montecino, and Louis Poché. An article in *NCR* by Mary Papa, "People Having a Good Time Praying" in May of 1967, first—and fleetingly—brought the movement to my attention. By 1972 the Loyola campus was bustling with charismatics. The Jesuits, who had been "touched" by the Spirit, willingly instructed me to prepare for my first prayer meeting on Friday, August 18, 1972. The meetings were conducted twice a week on campus. Mondays were for the "core community" of about two hundred members who had already participated in two advanced seminars, "Life-in-the-Spirit" and "Growth-in-the-Spirit." On Friday nights the Eucharistic prayer meetings were open to the general public. Loyola students were always in attendance, but they were far outnumbered by parishioners attracted from the surrounding Catholic churches. On Thursday nights, the "overflow" crowd gathered for Mass and a healing service at the Church of St. Edward the Confessor in Metairie. An occasional born-again evangelical made noises that interrupted the meeting and was gently escorted to the door.

The pentecostal renewal, as a church organization, was relatively new in the Jesuit experience. The groups we promoted among the Catholic laity, such as the Apostleship of Prayer and the League of the Sacred Heart, were now declining in popularity. The once flourishing Sodality of the Blessed Mother that existed in Jesuit schools and parishes had been renamed Christian Life Community or otherwise vanished completely. Church services, liturgies, and devotions, conducted by Jesuits, were in the quiet and relatively somber Roman tradition. Except for the occasional public recitation of the Rosary and the litanies, Jesuits were not given to exuberance and excitement in the worship of God. The laity as well as the clergy were expected to behave quietly and routinely in church.

The joyful shouting at the charismatic meetings was something new in my religious experience. I was especially intrigued with the speaking in tongues, and I regularly carried my tape recorder to catch the patterns of glossolalia. These gentle nontranslatable sounds were murmured by individuals and occasionally rose in a kind of communal singsong. I was informed that the "gift of tongues" is enjoyed only by those who have experienced the Baptism of the Holy Spirit and thus are said to be "born again," a term not favored by the leaders. Such initiation to the charismatic renewal usually occurs with the laying on of hands by several members in a small prayer circle, which occurs at the same time that the newcomer takes the Life-in-the-Spirit seminar.

I had both curiosity and admiration for those charismatic Catholics, some of whom were old friends of mine. More than once I asked them, "Why doesn't this happen to me?" I was assured that the "Spirit bloweth where it will." It was also suggested that one has to be spiritually prepared for such conversion. It was not easy to keep separate the role of sociological researcher, which I tried to maintain throughout the study, and the role of Catholic believer, which was part of my everyday life. This was the prime case of participant-observer, which is sociologically appropriate in any study of community life.

Time and again I have been assured that the Pentecostal experience is a conversion experience, a change of heart, a spiritual *metanoia*. The hypothesis that the charismatic renewal has a personal effect on people is an obvious one, since the entire movement is geared toward changing the lives of participants. Something "happens" to people, so that they become committed almost in spite of themselves. There is a similarity in the "conversion" experience of recovered alcoholics.[2] Yet there are others who attend "Life-in-the-Spirit" seminars and receive prayer in the laying on of hands but walk away unchanged. In other words, it does not "work" for everyone. One of my Jesuit colleagues assured me, "it is the sort of movement my training and instincts have tended to keep me far from. I am involved because I believe that God has touched me and that I have responsibilities as a result of that touch and call."

It is not the task of the social scientist to attempt to rationalize this mystical metanoia, nor do I mean to suggest that it is an exclusively Catholic experience. In my interviews with Catholics who converted to the Unification Church they regularly reported such personal experiences. In the book I later edited about these former Catholics, I said that "every one of our authors reports at least one spiritual experience, a vision, a dream, a warm glow of feeling, in the presence of transcendence."[3]

Another similarity I later recognized among the Unificationists was their personal feeling for community. One of the factors that attract people to membership in the charismatic renewal is the close and friendly relationship that exists within the local prayer group. If human love is exhibited by warm embraces, joyful smiles, friendly greetings, and mutual encouragement, the casual observer at a Pentecostal prayer meeting might well exclaim: "These charismatics! See how they love one another!" When the Eucharist is celebrated at the meetings, the members join hands during the recitation of the

Lord's Prayer, and they exchange the Kiss of Peace in a manner that bespeaks their spiritual solidarity. For contrast, one need only observe the relatively aloof manner in which this ritual is performed at Sunday Mass in many parish churches.

The kind of fellowship exhibited in primary face-to-face relations among the Unificationists is also in evidence among Catholic charismatics. At the prayer meetings the members are on a first-name basis—a familiarity that extends to priests and religious sisters and brothers—and they often wear a first-name tag that invites this intimacy even from strangers. The concept of sharing is very popular among them, and they frequently express their willingness to "share" an experience, an idea, a prayer or teaching, or a prophecy. They are clearly searching for Christian community.

It is in the nature of group relations that when communities expand and multiply they face the need for administration and organization. Some enthusiastic charismatics wished to keep the religious experience at a grass-roots level of individuals in personal contact with God, supporting one another but without the benefit of an organization or structure. Early in the research project I had conversations with an active charismatic promoter, Father Philip Kelly, who liked to argue about terminology. He said there can be no human leaders among the charismatics. "The Spirit does the leading; not man. When man takes over, the Spirit takes his exit." He said further that "it is nonsense to insist that speaking in tongues is the infallible sign that the Spirit is present in my life."

Another word that bothered Father Kelly was *movement.* He vehemently insisted that the charismatic renewal is a "new life in the Spirit of Jesus, not a 'movement,' not an 'ism.' " This attitude is similar to the leading spokespeople who do not like to call it an association, an organization, a federation, or even a movement. They resist structures and institutions and insist that the work of the Holy Spirit must not be routinized in the lives of the people. In fact, however, all this was happening even before we finished the study, and the charismatic community has since then grown into an enormous bureaucracy. One charismatic group in Amarillo, Texas, the Disciples of the Lord Jesus Christ, for example, was formally inaugurated as a new religious congregation with forty sisters and nine postulants. In February 1991, Bishop Leroy Matthiesen accepted them as a "covenant commitment of fellowship in the Spirit."

Like most religious sects and cults at their inception, the original charismatic groups wanted to be free and spontaneous. There was no thought of structures, program planning, elective or appointive officers, leadership, or authority. As the membership increased and the groups multiplied around the country, the original concept changed, as it had to. Within two years of the famous retreat weekend in February 1967 at Duquesne University,[4] there was a cultic organization with programs to plan and with people "in charge." There had sprung up a representative group of mature leaders from around the country. The official bureaucracy began with the formation of a service committee consisting of two priests and five laymen, people who had been accepted as national leaders in the charismatic renewal.

Even when I conducted the research study in 1972–73, there was still an odd, almost unreal, reluctance to admit that the spontaneous spiritual communities had become a structured organization. The claim was made that because this was a spiritual renewal—an unorganized movement—there need be no authority structure within it. The only authority can be the authority that comes from services well performed. It is true, of course, that one of the principal functions of the authority figure in any type of organization is to be of service to all its constituents.

In the course of this research study it soon became clear to me that the Pentecostal renewal was a social movement, containing all the elements necessary for its survival: leadership, a program, an ideology, a communication system, and a favorable public image. At the national level, one had only to read the movement's periodical *New Covenant* to recognize the presence of all these sociological characteristics of organization. These born-again Catholics were organized in identifiable groups throughout the country, and they were open to sociological study as both a local community and as a well-structured national movement.

On the Loyola campus I was fortunate to have the guidance of two significant and nationally involved charismatics. One was Father Harold Cohen, a prominent lecturer and member of the National Service Committee. Working in the campus

chaplain's office was Patti Gallagher, who had been a participant in the original prayer weekend at Duquesne University
in February 1967. She gave me a copy of the 1972 national
directory, which listed names and addresses of prayer groups
along with the contact person, telephone number, time and
place of meetings, and the percentage of Catholic members.
One is reminded of the A.A. directory, which lists A.A. meetings held almost everywhere in the country.

In the fall of 1972 I was conducting a "Sociology of the
Parish" seminar at the diocesan Notre Dame Seminary as well
as a course in the "Sociology of Religion" to Loyola undergraduates. The topic of charismatic lay Catholics was of prime
interest to both seminarians and college undergraduates. The
decision to do a study of the renewal movement was reached
in consultation with the local Jesuit charismatics. I compiled a
tentative questionnaire with the experienced assistance of
Patti Gallagher and Patrick Bourgeois, a philosophy professor
who had been faculty advisor to the Chi Rho Scripture study
group at the Duquesne University. Meanwhile, I attended
prayer meetings and interviewed lay leaders and other participants. I pretested the items on the questionnaire with a number of local members, checked them against the clergy
experts, and was ready for the mail-out in early December.

Clearly influenced by Vatican II, many of the prayer groups
in the 1972 directory invited the participation of non-Catholics
in an effort to be ecumenical. I wanted to limit my investigation to Catholics, however, so I selected the survey sample
from the groups that reported more than 50 percent Catholic
membership, of which there were 464. From these I chose
every third group and with some difficulty verified their name
and address from the nearest Catholic parish listed in the official Catholic directory. I sent a preliminary request to the leaders of 155 lay groups, asking their willingness to distribute
questionnaires to three women and three men in the group.

The process of tracking down the group leaders became
complicated. At intervals of three weeks, until the middle of
March 1973, I followed up, or replaced, the group leaders
who did not respond to the postcard or who did not fit the
conditions of the sample. It turned out that only 60 of the
group leaders were laypersons; among the others were 57
priests, 27 sisters, and 11 brothers. In the 155 groups to whom
we sent 930 questionnaires we received 744 responses, for a

return rate of 80 percent. There were 375 men and 369 women, even though more women than men belonged to the groups and more women attended the prayer meetings.

I anticipated one other aspect of this inquiry that prevented it from being a representative sample of all adult lay charismatics. I expected that the contact persons, or group leaders, would probably select the more faithful and more knowledgeable members to answer the questionnaire. Given the accuracy of this assumption, the final report could not really represent the rank-and-file membership. Nevertheless, they were all laypeople, and they spoke for the faithful laity of the Catholic Church.

Although Catholic clergy and seminarians, religious sisters and brothers were attracted in large numbers to the charismatic renewal, the organizers and managers of the movement as well as the majority of members were laypeople. The Charismatic Communication Center at the University of Notre Dame was operated by laypeople; the movement's periodical *New Covenant* was managed and edited by lay leaders. The so-called National Service Committee, established in 1970, was composed of five laymen and two priests. In 1974, it expanded to nine members: five laymen, of whom two were deacons, and four clerics, of whom one was Bishop Joseph McKinney.

The American beginnings of the Catholic pentecostal movement can be traced to the laypeople who conducted the first discussions and prayer meetings without benefit of Catholic clergy. In the early 1970s they began to call themselves the Catholic charismatic renewal. One of their clergy advisors, Father Killian McDonnell, O.S.B., insisted that "the movement is dominantly lay in character. The theology and rhetoric are essentially lay." He added that "it would be a sad day if the movement were to become clericalized and lose its lay character."[5] Even the episcopal moderator of the renewal, Bishop Joseph McKinney, of Grand Rapids, told me in March 1973 that he advises the laypeople not to "pass the mantle of leadership" over to the institutional Church. "Because this has so authentically risen from the grassroots, I point to them as the New People of God, those who believe in Christ and are reborn."[6]

The questionnaires were mailed in packets of six to the group leaders over the months of January, February, and March. I allowed ninety days before the cutoff date. As the

replies arrived we coded them for the use of the Tulane
University computer. This process was very rapid, so that by
the end of March 1983, I was able to distribute a confidential
overview of the raw data to the group leaders who had distributed the questionnaires. The generalizations I discuss here
are fixed in time, place, and people and reflect lay charismatic
Catholics during the winter of 1972–73. It is now at best a
source for comparison, if the survey were replicated twenty
years later.

All of the respondents said they had experienced repentance and Baptism in the Spirit: "I know how it feels to repent
and to experience the forgiveness of sins." A large majority
(85 percent) received the gift of speaking in tongues. Catholics generally do not ask the evangelist question, "Are you
saved?" Yet more than half (55 percent) of these lay Catholics
agreed that "accepting Jesus as my personal Savior means that
I am already saved." They were not sure that religion is more
emotional than intellectual, but half agreed that the Holy Spirit
speaks to the heart—not the mind. Seven out of ten leaned
toward millennialism, that is, they believed that the Second
Coming was imminent.

They clearly indicated that experience in the charismatic
renewal strengthened their spiritual and religious habits.
Everyone claimed to read the Scriptures more often. The
majority (77 percent) said that they attend Mass and receive
Holy Communion more frequently. They visited the Blessed
Sacrament more (63 percent). Smaller proportions (37 percent) said that they go to confession and recite the Rosary (30
percent) more frequently.

We listed a series of personal benefits, or "graces," that are
said to come to charismatics. We asked them to list these benefits in order of importance and found that the three principal
benefits were:

1) a feeling of God's presence in their life;

2) appreciation of God's special goodness;

3) a genuine conviction of their personal salvation.

Catholics are expected to be loyal to their local parish. Some pastors were apprehensive that the renewal groups were drawing people away from the parish, but this was not generally the case. While the majority (68 percent) said they met regularly in prayer groups outside their own parish, nine out of ten (89 percent) also attend Sunday Mass in their parish church. Six out of ten said that their home parish is a genuine Christian community. However, a minority of one-fourth say that they are not, or never have been, active in parish groups and societies. All of them continued to contribute money to their parish, and some of them (52 percent) gave only since becoming involved in the charismatic renewal.

A number of conservative clergy felt that the charismatic renewal could get out of hand, in the sense that theirs was a direct and personal way to God. Yet most of the respondents showed a certain reverence for and trust in the hierarchy of the Catholic Church. Eight out of ten (78 percent), for example, firmly believed that the pope (who was then Paul VI) was the infallible Vicar of Christ. More than half (55 percent) said they would obey their bishop if he were to prohibit charismatic renewal meetings in the diocese. Only about one-third (35 percent) favored the popular election of bishops.

These people wanted changes in the Church, but they were not rebels against the system or the clergy. Indeed, they appeared to have good relations and generally positive attitudes toward the Catholic clergy. They depend on the priests. Three-quarters of them said that charismatic renewal could not get along without the assistance of priests. More than half (55 percent) reported that they had their parish priest as a guest in their home during the previous year. About half (52 percent) said they approved optional marriage for priests (21 percent disapproved). They also supported a clergy committed to social action—almost six out of ten (57 percent) agreed that priests have a proper place on picket lines (27 percent disagreed).

Catholic pentecostalism was clearly compatible with "progressive" social attitudes, especially in the matter of interracial justice. The great majority (86 percent) favored racially integrated schools. About three-quarters (77 percent) expressed support for the civil rights movement, and almost as many (74 percent) favored the enactment of legislation for open housing.

Nine out of ten (89 percent) favored the Medicare program, and a large majority (77 percent) approved an increase in the hourly minimum wage.

A difference existed, however, between social attitudes and social activism. Very small numbers of charismatics took part in social movements and activist programs. Only one in five of the respondents had been a participant in the Catholic interracial movement. Only one out of six gave support to the grape or lettuce boycott promoted by Cesar Chavez. About one of ten had been involved in peace demonstrations or had worked at voter registration for minorities. This was not a youth movement—the average age was 40.2 years. Eight out of ten respondents (79 percent) were married; 14 percent were converts to the Catholic Church. Hardly any (2 percent) Black Catholics were among them.[7]

In other words, the population of Catholic charismatics belonged to the comfortable white middle class. It is noteworthy that two-thirds of them either attended (27 percent) or finished (39 percent) college. This relatively high level of education was reflected, of course, in the kinds of occupations they held. Only three out of ten reported that they were blue-collar workers. As may be expected from their status of education and occupation, only a small proportion (11 percent) said their income level was below average.

At the beginning of our survey I was told that several well-known charismatic priest-leaders had left the movement and the priesthood. Of the original list of contact persons taken from the 1972 directory, we had to replace the names of five priests to whom I had sent postcards of inquiry. One responded quite frankly, "I am no longer a member of the Roman Church." Three were on "leave of absence" from their religious order and eventually departed the priesthood altogether. Another was a prominent national leader who administered the only officially established charismatic parish in the United States and who felt that he was not giving up the ministry when he threw in his lot with Protestants. This particular priest had been praised by his bishop as having "the proper theological background to give proper direction to the large number of people who are becoming involved in the Charismatic movement in this diocese."

Despite such defections, the large majority of charismatics saw the clerical role as essential to the movement. One woman from California wrote: "We don't really have pastoral guidance of the Charismatic Renewal in our area. I wish there was a team of charismatic priests and laypeople traveling about the country to speak in the Catholic churches and visit our individual prayer meetings. We have had some Catholics getting rebaptized in other churches, and some have left the Church."

Collectively aware of the increasing influence of the charismatic renewal on many Catholics, the Catholic bishops released a statement in November 1974. The Bishops' Committee on Pastoral Research and Practices warned against the "possibility of self-deception when dealing with the manifestations of the Holy Spirit." They further advised against the "elitism" of a closed circle of the saved and against a biblical fundamentalism that ignores "the intellectual and doctrinal content of faith and reduces it to a felt religious experience." The bishops "strongly urged" priests to take an interest in the movement and in the formation of lay leaders who are "well grounded in the teaching of the Church and in understanding of Scripture."

This relation between clergy and laity in the movement called for further investigation, and I pursued it with the lay leaders after the report was finished. I sent a one-page set of questions to 171 lay leaders to ask about priests who subsequently left the priesthood. Several told me that just the opposite occurred. They knew priests who came to the prayer meetings as a "last resort" when they were in the midst of a "vocational crisis" and getting ready to leave the priesthood; instead they found a new life. The charismatic renewal strengthened their vocation and, in two circumstances, they became "fervent leaders" in the diocese. As in the case of so many born-again laypersons, some priests found in the movement an impulse for conversion.[8]

Despite such glowing reports, there is contrary evidence to suggest that the experience of Pentecostal fundamentalism attracted some away from Catholicism. One of the lay respondents reported that "a priest-leader in the diocese concluded that reliance on the Bible and on direct personal relationship with God dispensed with devotion to Mary and the saints. He got himself rebaptized by immersion with the Assembly of God. Since then, he has become obsessed with demon-hunting." In one mid-America diocese, three members of a religious order left the priesthood at the same time and are now preaching and healing with the Protestant Pentecostals. Their frustration with the institutional Church required "delivery" from celibacy, and they are, without exception, married men. Two celebrated charismatic clergy who subsequently left the priesthood were Francis MacNutt in the healing ministry and Carey Landry, a leader in the music ministry.

While in the process of digesting the survey data and analyzing its meaning, I continued attendance at the Friday night prayer meetings and became friendly with the local leaders and thus began to receive invitations to discuss the survey results. I was invited to participate in the International Charismatic Conference at the University of Notre Dame from June 1–3, 1973. This was like "coming home" to the campus where I had taught sociology in the academic year, 1955–56, and had conducted the research for my book *Parochial School*. I stayed with Monsignor Egan at the Moreau Seminary and was surprised at the presence of thousands of charismatics who attended the conference.

On the first day I discussed priest-laity relations among the charismatics with Jesuit priests from around the country, who were also chaplains of prayer groups. I pointed out that they themselves were learning from lay members and were practicing a kind of meditative spirituality they found new but still could be squared with Ignatian meditation. In the afternoon I attended a panel discussion of charismatics in the urban ministry. On Saturday a panel entitled "Reform and Renewal" was co-chaired by William Storey and Vinson Synon.

While the charismatic renewal is always advertised as a predominantly lay movement, there were hundreds of priests in attendance at the Notre Dame conference. In a lively discussion with a score of these priests we were able to reach some general conclusions: The shortage of spirit-filled priests results in some laypeople moving to evangelical churches; the priest-led groups tend to emphasize traditional prayers and practices; all the priest leaders have experienced the born-again metanoia, but a few have decamped to fundamentalism; charismatic priests are hindered in their renewal ministry where bishops discourage, and even forbid, the movement; the Pentecostal movement was growing so fast that the supply of properly trained priests could not keep up with it.

On Saturday afternoon a panel discussion on reform and renewal was chaired by William Storey, a Notre Dame professor of religion and an early enthusiast of the movement. In later years Storey would leave both the movement and the Church. Nevertheless, charismatic enthusiasm continued to be high as the day wore on. The charismatic Mass at the campus crypt was concelebrated by twenty-eight priests. The spirit of repentance spread, and there were too few priests to hear confessions. I was invited to take over a confessional, but declined to do so. I remembered the remarks of the woman who said, "you can always tell if the priest hearing confessions is a charismatic." Since I had not joined the movement, I felt that penitents might expect more of me than I could give.

All the charismatic leaders from Louisiana were at the conference at Notre Dame and must have been satisfied with my performance since in August I received an invitation from Father Richard Chachere to be a guest speaker at the forthcoming Second Annual Charismatic Renewal Conference, on the campus of Southwestern University in Lafayette. Actually I was scheduled to conduct three seminars the weekend of November 23–25 there. I was listed on the program as an "outsider to the movement" who will give a "sociological interpretation" to the survey findings. I responded to the request for a photo and resume to be used "for publicity release as soon as possible." The photo, sent from the university's public relations department, depicted me in a collar and tie. The diocesan newspaper altered the picture by "painting in" the turn-around clerical collar.

The first discussion I led attempted to answer the question: "Does schism lurk in the charismatic renewal?" Some of the members felt that they had been "set apart" from ordinary Catholics by their Baptism in the Spirit. Participating in a special cult within a large church has been part of Catholic experience through the centuries. But this need did not have to be sectarian. A few charismatics, however, exhibited "breakaway" tendencies. A minority (25 percent) said that the movement did not need the guidance of priests. Almost as many (22 percent) were not sure about papal infallibility. Perhaps more unexpected was the number (45 percent) who said they would refuse to obey the bishop's prohibition of prayer groups in the diocese.

The questionnaire contained several items that we would normally expect Catholics to reject. I called these beliefs heterodox rather than heretical, because they are open to orthodox theological interpretation. Practicing Catholics do not ordinarily talk in fundamentalist terms; yet a majority (71 percent) were willing to say that "the Second Coming of Christ is imminent." More than half (55 percent) affirmed that "accepting Jesus as my personal savior means that I am already saved." Half (51 percent) were willing to say that "the Spirit speaks to the heart—not the mind." It is easy to see the influence of Pentecostal fundamentalism in such expressions. Another important factor was Catholic education. When I compared the 215 persons who accepted all three of these doctrines with the 100 who rejected them, I found the most important factor opposing heterodoxy was the amount and kind of schooling they had attained.

A second seminar I conducted at Lafayette dealt with the role and status of women in the renewal movement. At the prayer meetings I observed that females far outnumber males, yet they seemed to have no position of authority and management in the group. They were being taught by the theoreticians of the movement to be submissive to male authority. The traditional doctrines of the patriarchal Church are fully endorsed in the charismatic renewal; the wife must be submissive to the husband. When a woman submits to her husband and acknowledges his authority, she is submitting to the will of God. In the light of this ideology, it was not surprising that only three out of ten (29 percent) of the respondents agreed that the Catholic Church should support the women's liberation movement, and only one-third of them favored women's ordination to the priesthood.[9]

In spite of such patriarchal doctrines, women do play a "principal" role in 45 percent of the 155 groups from which I collected research data. I observed at the actual prayer meetings that women expressed themselves more often in witness, in prophecy, in spontaneous quotation from Scripture, and in other paraliturgical ways. From an organizational perspective, many "ministries of service" were performed primarily by women. Women take care of altar linens, provide refreshments, befriend newcomers, pray with individuals for special intentions, visit sick members, and babysit on days of renewal. The women in the audience for this seminar made no protestations for equality, and several who did speak said I had "no right to find fault" with the scriptural and divinely approved system of gender relations.

The third topic I discussed at the Lafayette conference was the contrast between social justice and personal religion, a subject that political activist, Susan Anthony, had addressed at the Notre Dame conference. She complained that when you suggest social action to charismatics you are greeted with "silence and withdrawal." On more than one occasion, Father Louis Poché had challenged me: "The focus of the group is on prayer, not on social work." Catholic pentecostals were probably as aware as other people of the suffering and injustice in modern society. They were not satisfied with the world as it was. Their basic conviction seemed to be that reform starts at home, in one's heart, and somehow spills over into other homes and other hearts, until all of society is reformed.

The data of our study indicated that the charismatic person is ready to give personal assistance to anyone in need but prefers not to join reform movements. One sister remarked that any discussion of social problems would cause the death of the prayer group. Although they pray together, their social attitudes differ greatly. I was able to discern the difference between the "liberals" and the "conservatives" among the respondents. A minority of 21 percent agreed with all three "test" items:

1) Priests have a place on picket lines;

2) The Church should lead in social protest movements;

3) The Church should support women's liberation.

On the other hand, three out of ten (29 percent) disagreed with all three statements. Whether liberal or conservative, all were engaged in the corporal works of mercy, but they agreed with the famous Pentecostal preacher, Reverend David Wilkerson: "Our calling is not first to addicts, widows, the weak and poor. Our ministry is first and foremost of Christ! We are called first to His praise and glory. To meet His need before we feed the multitudes."[10]

Although there is great emphasis on individualistic piety, which manifests itself in a joyful relationship with the Holy Spirit, there was also much talk about "sharing" and much writing about "community" among the members. Local prayer groups have primary, face-to-face relations, but the members do not commit themselves to a full-time vocation within the movement. The question of how charismatics are to relate to parish and diocese occasioned some tension among charismatic members of the New Orleans archdiocese. One segment, with its mainly Jesuit leadership, proposed that the prayer groups remain close to their parishes. The other segment emphasized formation of "covenant" communities that are nonparochial.

One of the chief charismatic spokesmen, Stephen Clark, explained the need of covenant communities as a means to "build a new society within the shell of the old." This implies a separation from the sordid sinful world, even though it also has a tendency to distinguish charismatic groups from the rest of the Catholic Church. The dispute among the charismatics themselves centered on the exercise of authority within the community. How great was the obedience of the member to the leader, usually a layperson? In some instances, this relationship was said to resemble that between a penitent and a confessor, between the religious novice and the superior. The most outspoken opponent to this type of covenant community in the early stages of the renewal was J. Massingberd Ford, who was actually excluded from the conference because of her "disruptive and divisive behavior."[11]

Another and more serious kind of split came after my book, *The Catholic Cult of the Paraclete*, was published. This emerged from a prophecy uttered in Rome in 1975 at the international conference. The prophecy, given from the high altar of St. Peter's, warned people to prepare for the calamities of the end-time, for the Age of Darkness descending on the earth. The Word of God community in Ann Arbor, Michigan, and its satellites promoted this eschatological type of preparedness. The People of Praise community, based in South Bend, Indiana, were not quite so enthusiastic about the "gloom and doom" ideology. The ideological split between the two groups became more apparent as time passed. At the same time a so-called third force that had been latent began to seek more autonomy within the renewal. They felt that the covenant communities, whether tied to Ann Arbor or to South Bend, had too much power and control over the movement. Although unorganized and nameless, this "third force" could be identified all over the country from Los Angeles to New York.

Without continuing the kind of detailed research I had done for the book (which was published in 1975), I tried to keep up with the activities of the charismatic renewal. The prayerful solidarity of the movement was disrupted further in 1981. The divorce that took place between South Bend's People of Praise and Ann Arbor's Word of God seemed at first to be an ideological rift between incarnationalists and eschatologists. Each center had developed a number of covenant communities that identified with it. At this point it looked as though two separate renewal movements were in competition: the organization of covenant communities versus the broad charismatic renewal. The leaders on both sides exercised a dominant influence on their satellite groups, and after 1981 these two groups did not speak to each other. Variant ideologies simply provided a rationale to cover a power struggle within the charismatic covenant communities.

The National Service Committee tried to represent both factions but found it difficult to function in the midst of such rivalry. The members agreed to withdraw from the committee, allowing one representative from each side. Steve Clark from Ann Arbor and Ralph Martin from South Bend retained control of the *New Covenant* publication in Ann Arbor, while Kevin Ranaghan and Paul DeCelles at South Bend provided headquarters for the National Service Committee and organized the annual international conference at the University of Notre Dame. Meanwhile, the Word of God group in Ann Arbor expanded into the Sword of the Spirit, which decided to have its own set of conferences. The first one, which was held in New Jersey and drew thirteen thousand people, occurred under the acronym FIRE (Faith, Intercession, Repentance, Evangelization).

FIRE and the Sword of the Spirit had large ambitions and ample financial subsidy from Tom Monaghan, owner of Domino's Pizza. There also appeared to be an ultraconservative link with the Central Intelligence Agency and the contras through a Nicaraguan editor, Umberto Belli, who joined the faculty of Franciscan University in Ohio. The leaders of the Sword of the Spirit seemed intent on multiplying covenant communities under their own direction. They wanted to be recognized as a kind of Catholic fellowship with a special relationship to the Vatican and were said to have deep admiration for the manner in which Opus Dei was organized.

At the same time, the People of Praise were developing their own satellite covenant communities and had their own newsletter, *New Heavens—New Earth*. The South Bend group always had control, even possession, of the annual national conference and objected strenuously that the twenty-fourth anniversary conference was to be held in Providence, Rhode Island. They insisted that the 1991 conference take place in Notre Dame—they even copyrighted the title, "1991 National Conference of the Charismatic Renewal in the Catholic Church"—and planned to hold it one week before the Providence conference. Both groups advertised in the *New Covenant*.

Many of the Catholic charismatics have lately been drawn in the direction of Medjugorje and have embraced membership in the MIR organization, which consists of a loose network of devotees of Medjugorje (*mir* roughly translates as the Yugoslavian word for "peace"). In December 1990, a MIR-sponsored conference attracted as many as seven thousand people to the Rivergate Auditorium in New Orleans. In general, attendance at the annual charismatic conferences has been declining, while the supporters of Medjugorje have been multiplying. One of the strongest and most devout promoters of the Medjugorje movement in the United States has been Father Michael Scanlan, president of the Franciscan University of Steubenville, Ohio.

Father Scanlan experienced Baptism in the Spirit and was an active charismatic, having been involved in the renewal with Father Jim Ferry since 1968. He was rector of the Franciscan seminary at Loretto, Pennsylvania, when the board of trustees at Steubenville—and his provincial—asked him to take over the presidency. The school had been on the verge of closing when it was revitalized by Father Scanlan in 1974. His effort to revivify the campus with the thorough Christian message of the renewal was not a quick and easy struggle. He was an active leader of a covenant community, Servants of Christ the King, toward which students and faculty were gradually drawn. He said that "at some point in the late 1970s the charismatic, faith-filled life of the center became the dominant culture on campus."

As the student body grew and the college prospered, Father Scanlan rose in national prominence. He was elected chairman of the National Service Committee, and the campus, after a conference of charismatic priests converged on the facilities in 1976, became an international Catholic conference center. Prior to Steubenville there had been no recognized intellectual center for the renewal movement. Now, for the first time, an educational institution was able to put itself at the service of the charismatic renewal. Steubenville also became the rallying point for American pilgrims to Medjugorje.

In May 1981, charismatic leaders from around the world held a Prayer and Healing Conference in Rome. A Yugoslavian Franciscan priest, Father Tomislav Vlasic, attended as a representative of his country. A prophetic vision was allegedly vouchsafed with a message to the charismatic leadership, "I am sending my mother to you." The next month, in June 1981, the apparitions of the Blessed Mother began at Medjugorje. While this charismatic relationship is attested by the members themselves, no mention of it has been made in Medjugorje. Yet, the first Americans to spread the news about Medjugorje were, in fact, charismatics.

When Father Scanlan went to Medjugorje for the first time, he was privileged to kneel with the visionaries during an apparition. He felt a very powerful urge to defend these children and to try to pastor their spiritual development. Thus, Steubenville has become the center of American enthusiasm for Medjugorje and has promoted a record number of pilgrimage tours. Steubenville is identified with Sword of the Spirit and houses the editorial board of *New Covenant*, even though the editor remains in Ann Arbor. They do tend, however, to separate themselves from the People of Praise community. They too feel a sense of urgency with the millennialists who see Mary's Medjugorje message as one of conversion, repentance, prayer, and fasting.

The lack of technical research competence on the Steubenville campus led me to volunteer to process the data of their student survey through our Loyola computer facilities. The comparative data revealed the Steubenville students to have a high level of moral and social values, but because of the haphazard manner in which the data were collected I could not judge it a scientific study, nor could I lend my name to their press release of the findings.

Catholic charismatics are a modern phenomenon existing in a church that traditionally has not shown itself favorable to shouting fundamentalists. Despite their spiritual enthusiasm, they tend to be sociologically and politically conservative. The manifestation of the Holy Spirit is proclaimed by a segment of the Catholic population that preaches penance and anticipates the return of the Messiah in the "final time."

6

Holy Family Sisters

✸❂✸

In August 1951, the trustees of Loyola University took the first timid step toward the racial desegregation of the student body by authorizing a number of tuition-free scholarships to the Sisters of the Holy Family. President Father Thomas Shields asked me to visit the Mother Provincial and arrange for two of her sisters to take up the offer. Mother Philip was appreciative of this generous gesture but hesitant to accept it because, as she said, "the assignments of the sisters have all been made for the coming semester." Nevertheless, on registration day, Sister Laetitia Senegal and Sister Catherine Waiters, two religious women of color, signed up to take academic courses in the Saturday classes. They told me later that it was a "normal" experience, much like registering at Xavier University, where they had been taking undergraduate courses.

About a decade later I talked again with Sister Laetitia, who said she had continued as a part-time student at Loyola, taking courses on Saturdays, at night school, and during the summer sessions. She finally received her bachelor's degree in 1960 and said, "I was the first Sister of the Holy Family to graduate from Loyola." Sister Catherine had to drop out of Loyola because of ill-health, and she died in 1958. Meanwhile, two other minority women, Sister Clare and Sister Yvonne, attended as full-time students and graduated in due time. In the fall of 1952, two Xavier graduates—also black—Norman

Francis and Benjamin Johnson, were admitted to the Loyola Law School.

In subsequent conversations with Sisters of the Holy Family I heard vague accounts of an earlier experiment—nicknamed "Loyola #2"—with the Jesuit educators that dated back to the 1920s. I made sporadic inquiries about this "rumor," and learned from the late Father John Hynes that he had approved the interracial arrangement. I talked also with the late Father Harold Gaudin, who denied that "colored" sisters had ever received academic credits from Loyola University. I did not make a serious effort to unravel this contradictory story until years later, in 1985, when I was elected to the advisory board of the St. John Berchmans Manor, a high-rise residence for the elderly poor conducted by the Sisters of the Holy Family.

This religious congregation of women is native to New Orleans, having been started in 1842 by Henriette Delille, a "free person" of color. Their ministry was at first to needy, sick, and elderly black people, but soon expanded into schooling for young children. They lived and worked through the last decades of slavery and into the Reconstruction era of "separate but equal" accommodations. They were not publicly involved in any civil rights movement, but some of them regularly attended the annual Catholic Interracial Sunday, beginning in 1948 and sponsored by the intercollegiate students' group, the Interracial Committee.

The official records and archives of Loyola University provide no information that the Sisters of the Holy Family had received academic credits as early as 1921 through a special version of the Loyola Extension Program. In 1985 I interviewed the Holy Family archivist at the motherhouse, but she also bemoaned the lack of historical records. Much of what the sisters told me was admittedly hearsay, but I had a lengthy interview with the self-styled "last survivor," Sister Ann Simpson, who entered the convent in 1919. She said the other sisters "don't really know what went on back in those days."

The ingenious manner in which the Jesuits and the sisters circumvented the prevalent patterns of racial segregation had to be pieced together from other sources. What had triggered this decision was the establishment in 1921 of a new state board of education, which was authorized to "prescribe the qualifications, and provide for the certification of teachers."

The sisters wanted their high school diplomas accredited and their normal school diplomas approved. The new state regulations, scheduled to go into effect in 1924, pointed to the futility of operating a private summer school unless it were affiliated with a college recognized by the state.

The religious sisters were forbidden to attend secular or "Protestant" colleges. The only Catholic campus at that time in Louisiana that could grant college credits for prospective teachers was the Jesuit-run Loyola University.[1] Given the circumstances of racial segregation, even in church facilities like parishes, hospitals, and schools, it was not likely that the Loyola administration would seriously entertain the notion of admitting black nuns to their classrooms. The Jesuits looked for a strategy to allow their "lily-white" campus to provide teacher training for black sisters that would enable them to qualify for teacher certification. It is part of the folklore among the Holy Family sisters that the scheme to sidestep educational segregation originated with Archbishop John Shaw, who arrived in New Orleans in June 1918.

The archbishop appointed as a superintendent of the archdiocesan school system a Loyola faculty member, Father Francis X. Twellmeyer, who was also director of the extension program and the summer school at Loyola. Since the sisters were not admitted to the Loyola campus they could not take the required courses from approved college instructors on the Jesuit faculty. Both the archbishop and his superintendent realized they would have to look elsewhere for college teachers who could fill this need. They soon found willing cooperation from the Sisters of Charity of Greensburg, Pennsylvania. These sisters ran Seton Hill College for Women, one of the first Catholic colleges to encourage the attendance of young black women students.

In my search for verifying documents I visited the archives of the Seton Hill sisters in Greensburg, where I found copy of a letter, written in August 1937, from Sister Anne Elizabeth Regan of the Sisters of Charity to the registrar of Loyola University. The letter stated:

> In 1921, at the entreaty of Father Twellmeyer, Director of the Summer School of Loyola University, through the Catholic Board for Mission Work Among the Colored

People, the Sisters of Charity of Seton Hill College, Greensburg, Pennsylvania, opened and established a Normal School for the Sisters of the Holy Family, at 717 Orleans Street [in New Orleans], to work in conjunction with the Jesuit Fathers of Loyola University. In other words, the Catholic Board for Mission Work Among the Colored People supplied the finances; the Sisters of Charity supplied the teachers, and the Jesuit Fathers supplied the source of credit for the credits earned.

This letter had to be written in 1937 because there were apparently nervous administrators at Loyola who at that time were afraid of getting in "trouble" over the segregation laws. Blacks and whites were not permitted to cohabit. Thus, the Greensburg sisters were not permitted to live in the residence of the Holy Family sisters. Instead they stayed at the uptown Rosary Academy Convent of the Religious of the Sacred Heart. The house journal of June 21, 1921, states that the Sisters of Charity "have come at Father Twellmeyer's invitation to give courses to the Sisters of the Holy Family. As they cannot stay with those Sisters, they are glad to have hospitality here for six weeks."

It appears, however, that state authorities at this time were relatively benign and cooperative. At the end of July 1924, the state board teachers' examinations were conducted for the Sisters of the Holy Family at their motherhouse under the supervision of Father Twellmeyer and Sister Bertha Shea, director of Sisters of Charity Normal School summer courses. Ten of the black sisters passed the examination. In September, the Louisiana State Board of Education sent the teacher certificates for these sisters to Father Twellmeyer, who then personally presented them to the newly elected provincial of the Holy Family sisters, Mother Eusebia. At that time, state officials apparently saw no violation of the segregation statutes in this unusual educational program.

Changes in the personnel of Loyola administrators did not affect this complicated program. Father Twellmeyer became president of Loyola in 1924, but died within a year. He was succeeded by Father Florence Sullivan, who appointed Father Joseph Kearns director of the extension programs. He was also appointed superintendent of archdiocesan schools. On behalf of Archbishop Shaw, Father Kearns asked the Sisters of Charity to continue with the Loyola #2 summer school and invited the mission board to continue its financial support. When Father Kearns retired in 1928 because of ill-health his position with the Loyola #2 project was taken over by Father John Hynes, then dean of Arts and Sciences. President Sullivan wrote to the Seton Hill sisters: "I assure you that it will be more than a pleasure to Father Hynes and myself to cooperate with the good Sisters of Seton Hill in any way to help make their work in the Holy Family School the same success it has always been."

Sister Boniface Adams, who was appointed archivist of the Holy Family sisters in January 1987, found a document that proved beyond any doubt of this Jesuit educational involvement. The document, a summer school certificate, attested that Sister Francis Borgia Hart, a black student, "has been in regular attendance during six weeks at the Loyola University Summer School No. 2, from June 24, 1924 to August 4, 1924, and that she has received the following averages for the term." It was signed by the director, Sister M. Bertha, and countersigned by F. X. Twellmeyer, S.J.

Father Hynes continued the perennial struggle of obtaining the official teacher certificates for the Holy Family sisters. The chief purpose of Loyola's involvement was to assure that the academic credits be recognized by the state board of education. The official in charge of certification, however, had problems interpreting its validity because the requirements were changed every year or two, and these requirements were different for black teachers. A temporary certificate had to be renewed every three years, at which time the "papers" were sent for verification to the Loyola registrar. This was not always handled promptly, so that teaching sisters worried when they did not receive notice. Father Hynes assured them in May 1929, "I apprehend no difficulty in this regard. If necessary, Father Sullivan and I will make a trip to Baton Rouge to see the state officials." One of these state officials, A. C. Lewis, visited the Holy Family motherhouse in September of that year to discuss the certification of the sisters and to inquire about the affiliation with Loyola University.

The applications for teacher certification, especially for their renewals, were generally processed through the Sisters of

Charity, who acted as director of the summer school. These applications were then routinely sent to the state official in charge of teacher certification in Baton Rouge. This official, E. J. Lombard, in the spring of 1937, returned these applications to the registrar of Loyola University, who turned them over to Father Percy Roy, then dean of the College of Arts and Sciences. He consulted with the president, Father Harold Gaudin. All three of them—registrar, dean, and president— were newcomers to Loyola and disclaimed any knowledge of Holy Family nuns who had taken courses in Loyola's summer extension program.

Father Gaudin became president in December 1936. Although four of his predecessors (Cummins, Twellmeyer, Sullivan, and Hynes) had endorsed the enrollment of the black sisters in the Loyola extension program, Father Gaudin apparently felt otherwise. When I asked him about this, thirty-five years later in January 1973, he wrote to say that the question of academic credits to the Holy Family sisters "was brought to my attention by Loyola's Dean, Father Percy Roy. He was excited and frightened that credits, about which we had no record, had been issued as from Loyola. At that time we had been accepted for membership in the Southern Association of Colleges and Secondary Schools. We were due for an inspection. Our membership would be jeopardized if we accepted as from Loyola credits from a school over which we had no jurisdiction. Yet, to repudiate the credits would have worked untold harm to the nuns."

Meanwhile, the Sisters of Charity of Seton Hill were routinely preparing for the summer session of 1937. That year's summer school director, Sister Anne Elizabeth, writing for the first time to President Gaudin, suggested tentatively that "you have in all probability been told of the summer school we carry on in the name of Loyola, at 717 Orleans Street, for the Sisters of the Holy Family. We shall again be in New Orleans for this purpose this summer, opening the school Tuesday, June 22, and continuing for six weeks. During our stay we live with the Religious of the Sacred Heart, on St. Charles Avenue, and sometime during the summer we hope to meet with you on the work."

On June 17, 1937, President Gaudin replied that he was glad the sisters were returning to New Orleans for their "fine work" with the black sisters, but he expressed surprise that

Loyola University was said to be connected with their work. "You say that you carry on this work in the name of Loyola. I do not understand exactly what this means. I am sure we do not give credits towards a college degree on this work. I do not understand how we could." There is no question that President Gaudin recognized the potential embarrassment of the interracial connection and had no intention of promoting racial desegregation. "Inasmuch as the laws of Louisiana and the regulations of the Southern Association forbade integration in schools, segregation had some bearing on the case," he wrote.

Gaudin telephoned the dean of Xavier University and suggested that she accept the credits in question as coming from Xavier. The "problem" was not that easily resolved, however. In fact, the academic credits could not be granted from Xavier University because the sisters from Seton Hill were teaching the summer normal school under the accreditation program of Loyola, not Xavier. Later that summer, President Gaudin remonstrated with Sister Anne Elizabeth for using stationery marked "Loyola Summer Extension" for her correspondence with Mr. Lombard of the Louisiana State Department of Education. He insisted again that Loyola University had no record of academic credits by the Holy Family sisters. He requested that "you do not give Loyola's name in the summer school, over which we have no supervision and for which accordingly we can give no credit."

The president also contacted Father Edward Kramer in New York, then director of the mission board that was financing the program. "In no letter, nor in any data that I have in my files, was there ever question of recognizing the work by the Sisters as work done by Loyola University," he wrote. Father Kramer insisted that the academic courses taken by the student sisters "must have a source of credit." He told President Gaudin in March 1938 that "this source can be no other than Loyola Summer School Extension, organized, urged, and directed by your predecessors, as appears from letters of which you and I have copies. Many of our Colored Sisters have during the years obtained certificates from the State through Loyola University, by the instrumentality of Loyola's Presidents. To renew, or validate these certificates, as is required, and as frequently as is required by the State, the credits must stand under the name of Loyola University."

Nevertheless, the administration stubbornly insisted that documentation of these courses was not on file at Loyola University. One of the unfortunate consequences was that some of the black sisters who had received Loyola credits were later denied renewal of their teaching certificates. Registrar Margaret Carey simply refused to admit that any black sister had ever received college credit from Loyola University. Thus, a number of sisters had to repeat at Xavier University courses essential for periodic renewal of their teacher certificates. When I visited Seton Hill College, I found that the archives of the Sisters of Charity contained complete records from 1921 that gave names and class grades of sister students, names of faculty, and course offerings of the summer normal school. Until 1937 inclusive, the course load of the individual student was entered on 5 x 8-inch record cards. At the top was printed: "Loyola Summer School Extension, 717 Orleans Street, New Orleans, LA." It was apparently the fear that such "incriminating" documents would reach the hands of the state department of education, that first frightened Dean Percy Roy, then registrar Margaret Carey, and later, President Harold Gaudin.

When the Loyola summer extension courses were closed down by President Gaudin in 1937 the sisters from Seton Hill switched to the faculty of Xavier University. In spite of the "severance" from Loyola University, Mother Elizabeth of the Holy Family sisters believed, "it will be imperative for us to maintain a normal school at the Motherhouse in order to keep renewal of certificates." She saw also a real need for the continuing services of the Sisters of Charity from Pennsylvania. These sisters continued to teach summer school in New Orleans until 1957. By mutual agreement of the major superiors of the Sisters of the Holy Family and the Sisters of Charity, their long-standing (1921–57) cooperative educational program came to an end.

By this time, and in spite of white citizen councils and a white racist state legislature in Louisiana, educational opportunities were becoming more available for black students. Loyola University was one of the first private white institutions of higher learning to open its doors to blacks. When I began to investigate the history of Loyola summer extension #2, there were already black teachers and students as well as black administrators.

Over the years I continued my sporadic contacts with the Sisters of the Holy Family but took a deeper and specific interest in the early 1980s, when they began planning to extend their ministries to housing for the elderly poor. The Sisters of the Holy Family undertook their venture at the inspiration of Archbishop Philip Hannon, who was alerted to the shortage of housing from his first days in New Orleans. On his arrival in 1965, he was greeted with the devastation of Hurricane Betsy, which was especially hard on the homes of the poor.[2] He was met by Josephite Father Eugene McManus, a trained sociologist with experience in the local black parishes, who urged applications for federal loans under Section 202 of the 1959 Housing Act.

Meanwhile, the Sisters of the Holy Family negotiated for a government loan for the construction of the Lafon Nursing Home, across the road from the motherhouse. When the center opened in 1972, Mother Provincial Rose Hazeur spoke with Archbishop Hannon about the archdiocesan housing program for the poor. He then mentioned the 1971 White House Conference on Aging, which had recommended the construction of 120,000 units of housing for the elderly annually. He had already instituted the Horizon Project, with long-term loans and rental subsidies from the Department of Housing and Urban Development (HUD). The Horizon Project consisted of ten archdiocesan housing projects that provided 1,835 apartments for the elderly poor and handicapped in the New Orleans area. The archdiocese could ultimately boast one of the largest privately sponsored housing programs in the United States.[3]

In my sociological course on social problems I regularly focused on the widespread American problem of substandard housing, suffered by millions of American urban families. I had involved my students in surveys of the public housing projects and invited managers of these projects to address my classes. When I interviewed the Sisters of the Holy Family about their work among the poor they told me about a proposal they voted for in their 1978 annual chapter. They had been informed by the archdiocesan lawyer, Mr. Denechaud, that they were eligible as a religious community to apply for a HUD 202–8 project.

The apostolic ministry of the Holy Family sisters had always focused primarily on poor blacks. For almost one hundred years they operated two orphanages, Lafon Home for boys and St. John Berchmans for girls, both of which have since become day-care centers for young children.[4] For many decades they ran the Lafon Nursing Home, which gradually became overcrowded and its facilities inadequate. They built the new home in two stages, completing the first phase in 1973. With a substantial contribution from the Lafon Trust, another from the archbishop's Horizon program, a grant under the Hill-Burton Act, and considerable assistance from the Holy Family Alumni Association, the sisters were able to complete the second stage of construction in 1978. At this point the archbishop asked if they were willing to undertake a HUD project for housing the elderly poor. They agreed. Considering their extensive experience among the poor, it was appropriate that the sisters should expand their apostolate into the modern concept of congregate housing for needy and disabled senior citizens.

Tentatively the sisters discussed the feasibility of constructing a fifty-unit complex immediately adjacent to the new nursing home, with the logical expectation that it would be a convenient residence from which some of the elderly citizens might "graduate." This was to be named Delille Inn, after the venerable founder of the congregation. Plans were eventually postponed and shifted to the prospect of a large complex of 150 units at a location next to one of the day-care centers. The proposal for the construction of the St. John Berchmans Manor came to a vote at the 1978 chapter meeting when the Holy Family sisters decided to make application as a religious community for a HUD loan that involved full responsibility for the complete undertaking.

Despite the considerable competition around the country for federal funds, it seemed a propitious time for the Sisters of the Holy Family. They had a friend in Moon Landrieu, former mayor of New Orleans, who was then in Washington, D.C., serving as secretary of HUD. Another New Orleanean in Washington was veteran Representative Lindy Boggs, ready to lend any needed political support to the sisters. Although the application was approved, there were the usual delays. The Manor was not ready for occupancy until December 1982.

The sisters are not custodians; the Manor is not an institution. Sister Rose likes to think of the Manor as a kind of informal community, even a "big family," in which all the residents are encouraged to participate. The resident council meets once a month with the administrator. The loneliness of old age is assuaged in this type of congregate housing, as the smaller groups plan their own parties, bingo games, song fests, and Bible discussions. Each resident is a "guardian angel" for the person across the hall, and vice versa. Tenants who do not come out of their room during the day are reported to the floor representative, who immediately checks the apartment.

One need only walk through the hallways with Sister Rose to recognize the loving confidence in which she is held by all the residents. She finds it easy to "build rapport," as she says, and to keep communication open. Aside from such informal friendliness, she has evolved a kind of representative participatory community in which everyone relates to everyone. Sister Rose makes an annual inspection, a friendly visit, to each apartment, chatting with the residents about their welfare and needs. "When I visit them, they'll say over and over again how much they appreciate living here with us," she remarked. "There is a real good relationship between the staff and the tenants."

My contacts with the sisters and the elderly residents at St. John Berchmans gave me a knowledge and experience with the elderly poor not available in textbooks. With some of my sociology students I attended "special events" at the Manor, such as occasional bingo games, an annual fair, and Cajun chicken dinners. I also helped to provide transportation for the residents. Sister Rose even asked if I were interested in joining the advisory board of the Manor, made up of business and professional persons of both races. I agreed and was elected to the board in November 1985, and attended my first meeting on January 17, 1986.

On the basis of participant observation and many interviews, I was able at this time to publish an article, "Shelter for the Elderly," in *America* in early 1986. In March, work began on the Delille Inn, the smaller 51-unit housing project that had been planned by the Holy Family sisters prior to the opening of St. John Berchmans Manor in 1982. The Inn lies adjacent to the Lafon Nursing Home and shares the spiritual ministry of Chaplain Timothy Pieris. Besides three sisters of the Holy

Family, it is staffed by dedicated and competent laywomen. The residents are older than those of Berchmans Manor and leave reluctantly to move next door to the nursing home. Blacks outnumber whites; there are more women than men. They share with the home such benefits as concerts, fiesta, bingo games, and other entertainment.

Another exciting area of spiritual activity in which the Holy Family sisters are involved is the canonization of the Mother founder, Henriette Delille. In his April 13, 1988, dedication of Delille Inn, Archbishop Philip Hannon said that "most religious congregations are devoted to one particular program of charity. Mother Henriette Delille was dedicated to all of them: the aged, the uneducated, the homeless, the lonely, the hungry, the outcast—in their homes, on the streets, in her institutions. Through these she reached to their spiritual well-being as well." Archbishop Hannon knew that the sisters had already applied to Rome for permission to initiate Mother Delille's canonization. He continued to support the sisters even after he retired on February 14, 1989. He was succeeded by the Most Reverend Francis B. Schulte.[5]

Meanwhile, Mother General and her council reached a decision on a matter that had long been discussed among the sisters. This was the prayerful expectation that Mother Henriette Delille might one day be recognized as a saint of the Church. She had long been revered, not only by the members of the congregation but also by large numbers of the faithful who knew her reputation for holiness. An appeal was made to the Vatican that she be considered for sainthood. The petition was accepted and approved by Angelo Cardinal Felici, Prefect of the Congregation for the Causes of Saints. The Cardinal wrote to Mother Rose on March 17, 1989, informing her that a historical commission must be established by the archbishop to investigate her life, writing, works, and sanctity. Accordingly, on September 17, Archbishop Schulte appointed Monsignor Clinton Doskey as postulator for the cause of canonization and appointed me to membership on the commission.

Three professional historians had been appointed to the same commission, but none were able to contribute to its work. Father Charles O'Neill lived in Rome as director of the Jesuit House of Writers, which prevented his participation in

New Orleans. Dr. Charles Nolan, archdiocesan archivist who chaired the commission, and Father David Ker Texada, were employed full time and thus could act only in an advisory capacity. Instead, Sister Boniface Adams, provincial archivist for the congregation who had previously supplied all available data about the sisters' earlier experience with Loyola extension #2, became the driving force of the group.

The initial meeting of the historical commission was held on Tuesday, January 9, 1990, at the Holy Family motherhouse, but in the absence of Chairman Nolan. Monsignor Doskey presided with an explanation of the commission's mandate from Rome, its responsibilities and tentative budget. It was obvious that a research biographer had to be employed for the task, and a highly qualified historian was contracted, Father Cyprian Davis.[6] Sister Boniface had gathered all available evidence. There were no "relics" of Mother Henriette besides her personal prayer book and the annotation of some cash transactions she had made. She did not keep a diary, nor is there any correspondence to her or from her. The public testimony of her virtues was made after her death on November 13, 1862, in the archdiocesan newspaper *Propogateur Catholique*.

There was no diarist or biographer among the early companions of Mother Henriette, and within a few years after her death there were only five sisters remaining in the congregation. The oral history of her life was published in 1976 in a booklet *Henriette Delille, Free Woman of Color* by Sister Audrey Detiege. The task of writing the history of the Holy Family sisters had been assigned to Sister Francis Borgia Hart in the spring of 1916. She tells of the many interruptions and alternative work assignments while trying to gather historical data. She was one of the sisters who earned college credits from Loyola Extension in 1924 and finally presented her history as a senior thesis in 1931 for the Bachelor of Arts degree at Xavier University. Much of her data came from the "reminiscence" of twenty-eight sisters, whom she named in her book *Violets in the King's Garden*.

Monsignor Doskey asked that I prepare a description of the sociocultural environment of New Orleans during the lifetime of Henriette from 1812 to 1862. I studied the most recent research publications about the "free people of color" in New Orleans during the last century. It appears that the quadroon

balls, at which Henriette's mother and older sister were supposed to have contracted *placage*[7] with their consorts, were
fictionalized and glamorized by novelists. These biracial
descendants of French Creole fathers and African-Caucasian
mothers were baptized Catholics and registered as parishioners at the St. Louis Cathedral, where the free blacks shared
religious services with white Catholics.

Henriette and her companions were born into a social class
clearly distinct from the slave society and the white Creoles.[8]
Free people of color had as much right to a church wedding
as did white Catholics, but the placage contract was not sacra-
mentalized by the Church. Even so, local custom apparently
"normalized" family life under this arrangement. Although
there was no school in the cathedral parish, the Ursuline sisters conducted a school for black children, taught by
Carmelite nuns. The more fortunate received a French classical education that allowed some males an education in
France. Although free persons of color came from a wide
occupational range, more belonged to the working class than
to the professional class.

Free people of color did not have the legal right to vote or
to hold public office, elected or appointed. The Louisiana
State Supreme Court, however, declared there is "all the difference between a free man of color and a slave, that there is
between a White man and a slave. The free man of color is
capable of contracting. He can acquire by inheritance and
transmit property by will." In their recreational or social activities, they participated in theater and other public amusements,
but usually seated in a separate gallery. Strict segregation was
not always enforced in taverns and gambling places, however.
It appears from police blotters of the time that whites had
higher rates of crime and imprisonment than the free people
of color.[9]

In presenting a brief twenty-one-page sketch to the second
meeting of the historical commission on Tuesday, February 5,
I concluded with the observation made by sociologist Franklin
Frazier: "Economic competency, culture and achievement
gave these families a special status and became the source of
a tradition which has been transmitted to succeeding genera-
tions. These families have been the chief bearers of the first
economic and cultural gains of the race, and have constituted

a leavening element in the Negro population wherever they have been found."[10]

Present at this second meeting of the historical commission was Father James Fitzpatrick, O.M.I., Roman postulator for the cause of Mother Henriette, who had compiled a handbook on the process of canonization. He explained that we had to have a "historical" commission because the contemporary eyewitnesses were dead, and testimony was available only from written sources. He pointed out that canonization is the Church's public recognition of a person's sanctity and intercession. There must be proof that Mother Henriette in her lifetime had a reputation for holiness (*fama sanctitatis*) and that this reputation endures to the present day. A second requirement is *fama signorum*, that is, the proof that special graces, or even miracles, have been received from God through Mother Henriette since her death.

I was unable to attend the third meeting of the commission on Tuesday, March 5, at which Dr. Nolan and Father Texada said they were each employed full time and "could not be counted on for any of the work needed." They thought that Dr. Rudolf Detiege, now employed officially for the project, needed help from other scholars in the area. They suggested that professors of history and social science at Loyola, Xavier, Southern, and the University of New Orleans ask their students to help with the research. Sister Boniface, who had already gathered archival materials, continued her search and turned out to be the chief representative of the Holy Family sisters.

The historical commission did not meet in April, but I kept in fairly regular telephone contact with Sister Boniface. On Friday morning, April 27, she called to say that we ought to look into a reported miracle due to the intercession of Mother Henriette. The incident was described by Mary Pons, a wealthy woman in the community, who prayed regularly to her. In the middle of the night, on Saturday, April 7, Pons was awakened by a call from her housemaid, Yvonne Ashley, who asked to receive prayers for her seriously injured husband. "At the time she called, her husband was in the operating room of Charity Hospital where the doctors were trying to save his life," Sister Boniface recalled Ms. Pons as saying. "I have been praying to Mother Henriette for other hopeless cases. So, I started praying to her right then, plus the Blessed Mother, and all the saints and angels in Heaven."

In simple terms, the sisters believe that the prayers for Mother Henriette's intercession with God, and the unexpected recovery of the injured man, could be submitted under *fama signorum*. I spoke with the surgeon, Dr. Bruce Shanavant, who performed the operation and asked whether the event was an unusual happening that medical science could not explain. He said, "I think the miracle in all this is not what we did for him, but the fact that at least a yard of [a] broomstick went through his entire right lung and between the vessels in his heart and through his left lung. It didn't damage a single structure. That's the part that amazes everyone. It's very unusual because normally people like this will die. There is just no way that a structure could go through all these vital organs and the guy lives and walks."

The patient was discharged from the hospital on Good Friday, April 13, but was invited to return the following week at a "demonstration class" for medical interns at Charity Hospital, Mercy Hospital, and the Ochsner Foundation. The sisters heard about the accident and recovery from Ms. Pons, who provided an enthusiastic report of his miraculous convalescence. On Sunday, April 29, I drove with Sister Boniface and two companions to the Ashley residence, where I tape-recorded a first-hand account from him and his wife. They are practicing Baptists with a strong faith in the Providence of God and have no doubt that Mother Henriette intervened on their behalf.

In an article entitled "A Saintly Person of Color" that ran in the February 29, 1992, issue of *America*, I wrote that "I am personally, if noncanonically, convinced that Henriette Delille, the New Orleans foundress of the Sisters of the Holy Family, is now with God, a conviction held by all members of her community." At the time the article appeared I was on sabbatical, which I spent at Emory University during the fall and at the University of Notre Dame in the spring. This absence from New Orleans meant that I was unable to attend meetings of either the historical commission or the board of John Berchmans Manor.

One of the little-known facts about the Sisters of the Holy Family is their part in the establishment of a new congregation of religious women in Nigeria. In 1974, Bishop Patrick E. Ekpu, of the diocese of Benin City, Nigeria, decided that white missionary sisters were "Europeanizing" his Catholic people. He appealed for assistance to the Sisters of the Holy Family in New Orleans, who sent Sister Sylvia Thibodeaux, S.S.F., to his diocese. With the bishop, she is the cofounder of the Sisters of the Sacred Heart, and became the mistress of novices when the first candidates were admitted on Easter Monday 1975.[11]

Sister Sylvia has remained in Nigeria, and the Sisters of the Holy Family continue their outreach and support of the African congregation that now has more than fifty members. In September 1992, I interviewed Sister Benedicta Ulokoaga, S.S.H., and Sister Justina Emiawaguan, S.S.H., who were undergraduate students at Xavier University while living at the Holy Family motherhouse. Many of their members are from first-generation Catholic families, and they are enthusiastic about the growth of the Church in Nigeria. Applicants for the novitiate must have finished high school with academic credits in English and mathematics. The mode of religious life and their type of apostolic ministry have evolved under the influence of the Sisters of the Holy Family.

7

The Unification Church

The growth of the Holy Spirit Association for the Unification of World Christianity during the 1970s aroused an intensity of religious bigotry similar to the anti-Catholicism of the Know Nothing Party in the last century. Among the loudest critics were Catholic clergymen, Father W. Kent Burtner in San Francisco and Father James LeBar in New York, both of whom dabbled in exorcism and crusaded against "cults" in which Satan was reportedly at work. The American press, secular and religious, carried an almost systematic program of defamation against the "new" religious movements, such as Children of God, the Forever Family, Hare Krishnas, the Unification Church, and The Way.[1]

Like everyone else who watched or heard the news, I learned that members of these religious groups were sometimes kidnapped, held in restraints, and deprogrammed of their religious beliefs. Ted Patrick, who urged parents to save their children from the clutches of the "cults," received the most publicity. Several Unificationists, whom I later interviewed, said that their parents had hired a deprogramming agency called Citizens Engaged in Reuniting Families (CERF). One of the most prominent deprogrammers was Rabbi Maurice Davis.

On several occasions deprogrammers, such as Ted Patrick and Galen Kelly, were found guilty of criminal kidnapping of adults, and their deliberate effort to force religious reconversion was declared unconstitutional. The most frightening charge made by the anticultists was the insistence that religious conversion was a new kind of mental illness. According to them, the religious dissident is said to have suffered a mental sickness called *snapping*, a sudden personality change.

A new hysteria about the growing cult movement emerged with the mass suicidal deaths of members of the People's Temple in November 1978, in Jonestown, Guyana. Although there was never an even remote connection established between the Jonestown believers and the Unification Church, the catastrophe in Guyana was constantly cited as a warning of what was sure to happen in the growth of Reverend Moon's organization. Such rumors persisted despite the testimony of theologians, sociologists, anthropologists, and other scholars who repudiated these charges.

Sociologists have been in the forefront of the analysts—and opponents—of racism and sexism. Major research studies had delved into the routine prejudice and discrimination exhibited in anti-Semitism, for example. Thus, it was clear that the religious bigotry aimed at the so-called Moonies demanded attention from both social scientists and church people. Indeed, my first knowledge of the Unificationists came from a study made by sociologist John Lofland in 1965 of a small group of pious people called the "doomsday cult."[2] A more comprehensive study, *Sun Myung Moon and the Unification Church*, was conducted by Frederick Sontag in 1977.

My first personal contact with some of the Moonies was at the seventh annual International Conference on the Unity of Science (ICUS) held in San Francisco in November 1977. Academicians of national repute attended, including philosopher Robert Caponigri of the University of Notre Dame, sociologist John Doby of Emory University, and theologian Jude Dougherty of the Catholic University of America. On the sidewalk outside the Fairmont Hotel, people paraded, carrying placards of protest against Reverend Moon and his dangerous "cult." This demonstration of religious bigotry contrasted with the quiet ecumenical civility and scientific objectivity of the participants inside the conference halls.

The ushers and escorts for this large gathering were well-groomed and conservatively attired male members of the

Unification Church. As I talked with them during the several days, I asked each one what religion he had practiced before joining the church. The majority of them (seven out of eleven) said they had belonged to the Roman Catholic Church. This gave me another important reason for undertaking a research study of their group: Why had they switched religions? What attracted them away from Catholicism and toward Unificationism? These young men assured me that they had no complaint about their earlier experiences in the Catholic Church. They said also that "you have to talk with Dean Theresa Stewart, who used to be a religious sister."

My conversation with Dean Stewart, on Sunday, November 25, was the first of countless taped interviews, invariably courteous and informative, I had with members of the Unification Church. What she told me was quite similar to the conversion stories I had heard from many others. Her spirituality as a Catholic nun involved a deeply personal devotion to Jesus, interrupted sometimes by the distractions of work and people. While taking summer courses in New York, she met Betsy Jones, a social worker and former Catholic, who introduced her to a group of fellow Moonies. She was immediately impressed by the warm friendly embrace of the members, who showed genuine affection for the newcomer. "This was the real Christian community, at a level I did not experience in religious life," she remarked.

Of course, I replied that "this is nothing new. The idea of Christian community is as old as St. Paul's Mystical Body of Christ." I tried to argue that unity, collegiality, and brotherhood are essentials in the lives of Catholics. She gave a quiet response that I have never forgotten: "Yes, Father, but these people actually do it." In other words, the close-knit community, the expression of family love, is a basic fact of life in the Unification Church. My subsequent and frequent attendance at seminars and conferences gave me further knowledge of the doctrines and practices of the church.

The manner in which young people became converts to the Unification Church was of particular interest to me not only because it is a religious conversion but also because of the widespread calumny that converts were entrapped, deceived, and "brainwashed." During the next few years I talked with large numbers of young Moonies and in many instances asked them about their recruitment, or conversion, to the church. I later published the personal account of eighteen of these interviewees.[3] Each had their own specific backgrounds and individual experiences, but four factors were common to them all.

Perhaps the most significant pattern was the initial friendliness of the church members. This was a universal experience, emphasized by the scriptural notion "how they love one another." The importance of family and community was demonstrated from the beginning. Another pattern was a kind of spiritual experience, different for each individual, such as a sudden insight during a lecture, an experience of God, or a revelation through reading or in conversation. It need not be as dramatic as Paul's incident on the road to Damascus, but it was real for each one.

A third factor of conversion was the study and understanding of the *Divine Principle*, the catechism and the Bible of the movement that provides the theological basis of the church's belief system. The acceptance of this teaching—even if not fully understood—was a condition of conversion. Finally, there was the almost mystical presence of the true parent, Sun Myung Moon, hovering over the membership. One had to believe in the spiritual power of the leader. In the final analysis, this meant that they believed in and prayed to God, the Divine Father and Creator. None of them, however, really accepted the notion of Reverend Moon as the divine messiah.

The practice of community is, of course, a central concern of the sociologist and calls for study and research. My first published writing about the Unification Church was an article in the Jesuit magazine, *America*, entitled "Marriage, Family and Sun Myung Moon" that ran on October 27, 1979. This aroused the usual amount of criticism from people who were sure I knew nothing about this "dangerous cult." There were several inquiries from Germany, after the German version had appeared in *Neue Hoffnung*. It was also published in France and brought a scolding from the Jesuit editor of *Etude* in Paris, whose protégé, a young Jesuit seminarian, had left the order to join the Unification Church. At the same time, two former diocesan seminarians also became active in the French Unification Church. A complaint was lodged against me with the Jesuit Curia in Rome concerning the French version of my article.

The unusual custom of "arranged marriages" attracted widespread criticism, both in Europe and America. Reverend Moon matched couples at large engagement blessings and officiated at simultaneous "mass" weddings of hundreds of people. This was a "foreign custom," completely out of touch with the modern American world. I was severely criticized by two French Catholic laymen, one whose daughter had joined the church eight years previously and who was then in the United States. He was sure her marriage was involuntary and begged me to use my influence with the Unification leaders to "release her from captivity." As a matter of fact, I asked Dr. Mose Durst, then president of the church in America, to arrange a meeting for me with the daughter, Christiane Viala. I met with her in New York in December 1982, and found her a charming young lady with deep religious convictions, who was busily engaged in church activities in New Jersey. I wrote a cheerful letter to her father, assuring him of his daughter's love and of her good health.

The ICUS meetings had begun in New York in 1972, with only twenty people. The next year it was held in Tokyo, with sixty participating. In 1974, attendance at the London conference doubled to 128 and doubled again in New York and Washington, D.C., in 1975 and 1976, respectively. I attended my first ICUS conference in San Francisco in 1977, followed by conferences in Boston, Los Angeles, and Miami Beach. The largest gathering—808 participants—was in Seoul, South Korea, in 1981. I attended two somewhat smaller affairs in Philadelphia in 1982, and Chicago in 1983. Invitations to subsequent ICUS gatherings were extended mainly to non-Americans and involved smaller numbers.

These international meetings were the subject of much criticism, often by professors who were not invited or who spurned them because they gave "validity" to a disreputable cult. There may have also been some envy in the criticism of "all expense-paid junkets" for so-called gullible college teachers. A criticism, directed personally at me, came from a New England professor, Robert Lenz, who had accepted full hospitality from the Moonies—including round-trip fare and three days' lodging and meals—for the ninth ICUS at the Fontainbleau Hotel in Miami Beach. He later wrote to all academic participants, warning them against the evils of Mr. Moon, and admitting that he had himself surreptitiously accepted this benefice in order to seek out his son Douglas, whom he later kidnapped and deprogrammed.[4]

Although the founder, Reverend Moon, always gave the opening address and spoke of absolute values and the power of God, there was never, to my knowledge, any church proselytizing. No one was "brainwashed" directly or indirectly. On several occasions, I gave the benediction at the closing banquet. The proceedings, including research papers and theoretical scientific proposals, were regularly published and distributed by the International Cultural Foundation.

Reverend Moon believes that "world problems can be solved in a harmonious global culture based on absolute values." He insists that these absolute values can be developed and expressed through promoting dialogue among responsible intellectuals essentially at annual meetings such as the International Conference on the Unity of Science. The concepts of absolute truth and immutable values tend to find questionable support in our relativistic culture. Yet Unification Church leaders continue to invite scientists and humanists, philosophers and theologians to dialogue and come together on the basis of absolute values.

The Unification Church organizes smaller conferences of scholars, usually on a university campus that focuses on the "new" religious movement. At Berkeley in June 1980, an English sociologist, David Martin, moderated a discussion entitled "Social Impact of New Religious Movements" with eight Unificationist graduate students and fifteen scholars from various university faculties. My own paper, "Youth in Search of the Sacred," addressed a topic I was then researching among converts to the church. This was one of the more successful academic gatherings of my professional experience. It was small, intensive, intellectually stimulating, and academically rewarding. In his welcoming address, David Kim, president of the Unification Theological Seminary in Barrytown, New York, admitted that professors sometimes "jeopardize their academic and scholarly status by associating with us." He offered his respect and admiration for our "courage in coming and participating in a conference such as this one."

Another small academic conference was held at Loyola University of Chicago in 1983, and brought together seven graduate students and twenty-two faculty members. From the papers contributed to this conference came a book which I edited, *Alternatives to American Mainline Churches* in 1983. Both the conference and the book tried to reach beyond the

Protestant-Catholic-Jewish "catch-all" and investigate alternative religious organizations that have often been called "fringe" groups.[5] Basic conceptualizations were attached to the church by one speaker, Rodney Stark, and to the cult by the moderator, David Martin. Papers on metaphysical alternatives discussed scientology, thelemic magick, and spiritual fellowship. Alternative religious groups included Krishna, electronic churches, Catholic traditionalists, and the Unification Home Church.

In addition to these academic and scientific gatherings, I participated in a series of instructional seminars designed to explain the teachings and practices of Unificationism. These were usually three-day meetings in which senior members of the church took turns lecturing on the *Divine Principle*, which was accepted as the sacred scripture of the church. The audience was then subdivided into four or five subgroups, each with its own discussion moderator. Over the years, I served as moderator in seminars held at various locations, including Barrytown seminary, the New York headquarters, and at hotels in San Juan, Acapulco, Tenerife, Quebec, San Diego, and Seoul.

What I learned from the instructors of these seminars, and from the literature they distributed, formed the basis of my book about the Unification Church, *The Holy Family of Father Moon* in 1985. In my analysis of Unificationism, I outlined the four essential elements of organized religion:

1) The belief system—that is, the creed—centers on God the Father, who is wounded by the sins of His children but embraces them in a universal salvific love;

2) The moral code is basically that of the Ten Commandments, with strong emphasis on chastity before and during marriage;

3) The liturgy emphasizes prayer and meditation and the celebration of special holy days in the year. There is one central "sacrament," that of the marriage blessing;

4) The organizational scheme of membership is from the newest devotee to the "true parent," that is, the Reverend Sun Myung Moon.

These four essential elements distinguish an organized church from a volatile sect or cult.[6]

To share knowledge of a non-Catholic church, and even to assist in explaining it, leads to the development of ecumenical relations. Commentators who insist on a strict interpretation of the Vatican II document on ecumenism, *Unitatis Redintegratio*, maintain that the ecumenical movement limits ecumenism to "those who invoke the Triune God and confess Jesus as Lord and Savior." (Art. 1) The Unification Church does not accept the doctrine of the Holy Trinity—only the Father is God—nor do they accept the Divinity of Christ. This presents a dilemma in dealing ecumenically with an association that is committed to the Unification of World Christianity, but it still leaves space for another council document dealing with non-Christian religions, *Nostra Aetate*, which declares that, "The Church is giving deeper study to her relationship with non-Christian religion." The Church gives "primary consideration to what human beings have in common and to what promotes fellowship among them." (Art. 1)

On the basis of these experiences I received a three-year appointment to the supervising board of the Ecumenical Research Association (the "New ERA"), which planned conferences for clergy and church leaders from the inner city. It was an attempt to provide opportunities for theological exchange among ministers of deep faith and experience but with relatively meager seminary training. Many of these church people had already been in contact with young Unificationists who worked among the urban poor. I attended all the board meetings and participated in two conferences, one in Nassau, Bahama Islands, the other in Seoul, South Korea.

The more contact I had with the Unificationists and the more I studied their teachings and practices, the more invitations I received to participate in their programs. As I moved into the status of *emeritus* (teaching every other semester) at Loyola University, I was able to accept their invitations. In the autumn of 1985 I taught "Sociology of Religion" for a half-semester at the Unification Theological Seminary at Barrytown. The thirty-four students who took the course were academically competent and generally had the mature experience of street "witnessing" for the church. David Kim was president of the seminary, and Theresa Stewart was academic dean. The seminary custom was to begin each class with a prayer. The seminary consisted of a community of brothers and sisters sharing the same faith, which contasted with the students I had taught at the Harvard Divinity School who came from a variety of church denominations.

The following spring I received an invitation from the chairman of the Professors World Peace Academy (PWPA) to participate in a lecture tour of Japan and Korea. This program involved fifty-one teams, each composed of a Westerner, a Korean professor, and a native guide-interpreter, who translated the Westerner's lecture. The schedule called for each team to speak in four locations. I was assigned to Ma San, an industrial city in the southern part of Korea, from where I went out to lecture in three smaller towns. I visited the local Catholic Church wherever I could find one and also paid my respects to the "rock shrine" in Pusan, dedicated to the memory of Reverend Moon's spiritual experiences.

We then moved to Japan, where the program was less extensive. There were twenty-three teams, each with three lecturers—a Westerner, a Korean, and a Japanese. The two Asiatics spoke their native language, but the guide translated the American lecture into Japanese. I was assigned to lecture in Osaka, Okayama, and Hiroshima.[7] On the feast of St. Ignatius Loyola, I attended Mass at the reconstructed Peace Church, formerly ministered by the Jesuits. I placed an American bouquet at the cenotaph in the Peace Memorial Park, the actual site of the A-bomb catastrophe of August 6, 1945. The audiences in both countries were adult, middle-class persons, more male than female, apparently of conservative educational and religious background.

Before returning home I visited Sophia University in Tokyo, where the Jesuit faculty showed little fondness for the Unificationists. They gave me a copy of the pastoral of the Japanese Catholic hierarchy, which was distributed on July 7, 1985. The bishops declared that the Unification Church had been a source of confusion among Christians, and even among priests. They said that "to consider the whole of humanity as one big family is praiseworthy enough, but the sect cannot be called Christian, and surely not Catholic. It is not a partner for ecumenical endeavor." The bishops listed the tenets that they considered heretical; namely, the denial of the

Divinity of Christ, the fullness of revelation in Him, and the salvific value of His Death and Resurrection.

The purpose of the lecture tours in Asia was to promote the manifestation of an international, East-West fellowship. World peace and interreligious friendliness were the general themes running through all the speeches. Interestingly, none of these lecturers was a member of the Unification Church, nor were any of them right-wing conservatives. They spoke of the universal values of justice, democracy, peace, truth, and love. My own lecture, which appears in the book *The Future of the World*, analyzed the religious bases of a peaceful world and described how the teachings of the church included the principles of morality, family, social solidarity, fraternity, and democracy.

The book contained the lectures of thirty participants from the Japan-Korea tour. It was translated and published in several languages, with the Italian version catching the attention of one of the Vatican prelates. This led to a letter of protest about me to the Jesuit General, Father Hans von Kolvenbach, who in turn relayed it to me through the Southern Jesuit Provincial, Father Edmundo Rodriguez. The complaint in its original Italian accused me of praising Reverend Moon, which I did, and of promoting his heretical teachings, which I did not. My short response to these allegations, quoting the appropriate documents from the Vatican Council, seemed to satisfy the Roman authorities, who did not push the matter further.

One of the more ambitious programs of the Unification Church is the Council for World Religions, which was founded by Reverend Moon in 1984. Its purpose is to "foster harmony and mutual respect among the religions and religious believers of the world." The grand plan is to operate at three levels:

1) To conduct an *intrareligious* discourse within a major religion, such as Christianity, Islam, Judaism, and Hinduism;

2) To bring together at a regional level *interreligious* meetings of the different religious bodies;

3) To bring together an assembly of all the world's religions.

These strictly ecumenical meetings among churches within Christianity began at San Diego, from December 4–6, 1986, under its own title, "The Way Forward in Christian Ecumenism." My own contribution to the discussion was a sociological analysis of the nontheological factors that tend to bring Americans together almost in spite of religious differences. I discussed such "social factors" among the mainline Christian churches as inclusiveness, voluntarism, internal pluralism, bureaucracy, democracy, and cultural accommodation.[8]

For the next three years the interreligious conferences on ecumenism were held outside the United States. The general theme of the July 1987 conference in Grainau-Eibsee, Bavaria, was "Christian Ministry in Ecumenical Perspective." I explored celibacy and marriage within Catholicism in my paper, "Married Priests, Women Priests and Ecumenism."[9] Being in Germany also provided me with the opportunity to interview Father Edgar Glöckner, a married Lutheran minister who had been ordained to the Catholic priesthood.

The next ecumenical conference was slated for Jerusalem in May 1988, but the domestic disorder in Israel made it necessary to choose another site. The title of the meeting, "Christianity and the Wider Ecumenism," was just as appropriate at the Hotel Etap Marmara in Istanbul. The topic I chose to discuss was "Christianity as a World Minority." There are fewer Christians in Turkey than in Israel. On this occasion we had an audience with the All Holiness Ecumenical Patriarch Demetrios of the Greek Uniate Church. We also visited the beautiful Blue Mosque, the dilapidated Sophia Basilica which attracts more tourists than the well-kept royal palace. We ended the final segment of the meeting in Bosphorus and then Bursa, from which we made a short visit to ancient Nicea.

In 1989 the Intra-Ecumenical Conference was held in Dubrovnik, Yugoslavia, where the theme of discussion was again the search for ecumenical unity and understanding among Christians. In this communist country the downtown churches were in operation; nuns wore their religious habits on the streets, tourists attended Mass. On Saturday morning, after the close of the conference, most of the participants were transported to the village of Medjugorje to visit the site of the Marian apparitions, but I did not accompany them.

The largest and widely inclusive interreligious program inaugurated by Reverend Moon is the Assembly of World's Religions. Other international religious groups, like the World Council of Churches or the ecumenically minded Vatican of Rome, were "scooped" by Reverend Moon's decision to pre-empt the centennial celebration of the World's Parliament of Religions in Chicago in 1993. An elaborate plan was worked in a celebration in "three steps": the First World Assembly was to be held in 1985, the second in 1989, and the third in the centennial year itself, 1993. The first assembly was indeed held in November 1985 at McAfee, New Jersey. According to news reports, more than six hundred men and women of different faiths from around the world gathered in the spirit of fellowship and goodwill.

My own contribution to the First World Assembly was a paper about the development of the religious sisterhoods in the Catholic Church, which fell under the general heading of "Recovering the Classical Heritage."[10] Our section was moderated by a young rabbi who seemed uncertain of the existence of God and allowed a garrulous old preacher to talk too long. The persons in this session were mainly women who kept God in some faraway place, out of contact with human beings. On the "free" day of the assembly, when most of the participants went to visit the churches of Harlem in New York, I took the opportunity to baptize my niece's newborn twin boys.

The Second World Assembly was scheduled to take place in Seoul in 1989, but the disturbed conditions of the Korean citizenry made it imperative to switch date and place. Thus, the Second Assembly of the World's Religions, which carried the slogan, "Transmitting Our Heritage to Youth and Society," was held at the Hyatt Regency Hotel, San Francisco, in August 1990. My group's general theme was "Transmission and Development of Doctrine," which was heavily populated with theologians and metaphysicians who tended to stay at the level of theory. I tried to bring them down to the practical world with a discussion of social justice in my paper "Option for the Poor in the Papal Encyclicals."

An ecumenical feature, introduced at the First World Assembly, was the daily opportunity for prayer and meditation—altogether a choice of services at six different locations. There were daily meetings for Christians, Buddhists, Hindus, and Moslems, and interim schedules for African traditionalists, Jains, Sikhs, Native Americans, and Zoroastrians. I attended a different service on each of the five mornings. Every evening at ten o'clock there was an interfaith meditation.

The dramatic awareness that bigotry and hatred still are directed at the Moonies became clear in the regrettable fact that Reverend Moon needed the protection of a bodyguard. He appeared at the opening of the assembly to give the annual founder's address and again at the grand banquet on the closing night. Everybody had to be frisked by passing the electronic security check before entering the auditorium and the banquet hall. I asked some of the guests from the African and Asiatic countries how they felt about this need to guard against the assassination of a religious leader. For the most part, they had not been aware that threats were being made on Reverend Moon's life. At any rate, there were no disturbances, nor were there were any protests by placard-carrying dissenters.

One of the obvious goals of the Unification Church is to make its teachings known to as many Christian groups as possible. The people they reach in the massive conferences of ICUS and the interdenominational assemblies of world religions tend to be the top leadership, especially scientists, academicians, and theologians. Meetings with representative people from other religions brought a respectful acceptance of the Unification leadership as authentic religionists. There was probably no expectation, nor was any attempt ever made, for evangelizing and converting these participants.

The New ERA conferences were closer to grassroots religion by addressing mainly local church people with the intention of "gaining friends" and winning ecumenical acceptance. One of the most important aspects of the Unification ideology is its inclusiveness. Members are not pressured to abandon their original church. Indeed some members have told me that they do not hesitate to accompany their family to Catholic, Methodist, and Presbyterian services when they are home on a visit. The frequent conferences of New ERA reached out to the ministers and people of Christian churches who were not members of the so-called mainline American denominations. They sought to inspire them to fellowship, Christian love, and unity.

A new approach was introduced in early 1988. The Advanced Interdenominational Conference for Clergy was specially designed to bring together active clergy from all denominations. Only pastors with at least a seminary-level education were invited. The conference, held in Japan and Korea, was different not only because it took place in the countries where Unificationism was "native" but also because the invitees were deeply involved in preaching and pastoring. The value of Unification teaching is expressed in their daily life and ministry. A special attempt too was made to bring the presence of the Holy Spirit into the meetings rather than conform to a strictly academic atmosphere.

The guests for this unusual conference were invited to spend several days in Japan (February 2–5) and several days in Korea (February 6–11). The Unification policy was stated quite clearly: "The Church is not sponsoring this Conference in order to convert anyone to the Unification faith, but to offer the Unification Principles for consideration. Participation by any individual does not represent his or her endorsement of either Unification doctrines or life-style." Ironically, after the initial presentation of Unification theology one ministerial couple, fundamentalists from Georgia, withdrew from the program and returned home.

My own assignment was to act as group moderator and panelist. The first day in Tokyo was mainly an explanation of the history and activities of the Unification Church, including an introduction to the East-West encounter between Buddhism and Christianity. The next day provided a serious introduction to Unification theology, focusing on God and the creation principle. In the afternoon we took a bus to the Shinto shrine of Meiji-Jingo. But we were delayed in heavy traffic and arrived too late to witness the annual Demon Exorcising Bean-Tossing Ceremony, a popular Japanese folk custom, at the temple. The bus ride was graced by the presence of Belgian Catholic missionary Father Andre Broekaert, who gave an excellent theological explanation of Buddhist and Shinto theology. In the early evening we attended a youth rally for new Japanese members of the Unification Church. The enthusiastic shouting was louder than a Notre Dame football rally.

When the conference moved to the Sheraton-Walker Hotel in Seoul, the agenda took on a more formal structure. The theology lectures followed the regular sequence: "Fall of Man"; "Principles of Restoration"; "Jesus, the Messiah"; "God's Work in History"; and "Eschatology." After each session, the small group of which I was moderator raised questions and commented about the talk. Following the discussions, a plenary "critique panel" assembled, and the group moderators, acting as panelists, fielded questions.

On the evening of February 10 we were bused to the Little Angels Academy and Performing Arts Center, where we enjoyed a formal banquet and a special performance of the Little Angels Dance Troupe. On the last day the church had arranged transportation to the demilitarized zone separating North Korea from South Korea. This all-day excursion promised to require much more exertion than I wanted to expend. The final banquet that night was capped with closing ceremonies. Reverend Moon did not appear at this Korean conference, and he could not attend in Japan either since convicted felons were excluded.

Reverend Moon was sentenced to a federal prison in Danbury, Connecticut, having been judged guilty of criminal tax evasion. Carleton Sherwood begins his book *Inquisition* with the words: "The Reverend Sun Myung Moon and Takeru Kamiyama were found guilty on the afternoon of May 18, 1982, on charges of tax evasion and conspiracy. After the defendants were convicted and the jury dismissed, defense counsel filed post-trial motions; they were argued and denied between July 5 and 14. Two days later, Moon and Kamiyama were sentenced and fined, although they remained free on bail pending appeal."[11] It appears that Moon had been found guilty of a practice that I believe is common to every Catholic bishop in the country: he held a discretionary fund of church money under his own control, spent it on church needs, and paid no taxes on it.

I cannot claim close friendship with Reverend Moon, although I met him personally and chatted with him and his wife at the ICUS meetings and at the three assemblies of world religions. I have made clear in my speeches and writings that I cannot accept his theology, nor his salvation history, which are the basis for church membership. Nevertheless, I have been deeply impressed by his generosity, charity, and concern for social justice. The enormous funds he has expended in promoting ecumenical meetings have not been matched by any other Christian church. From a sociological perspective he has been a positive force for youthful morality, respectable marriage, and steadfast family life.

It is a common conviction among large numbers of Americans that Reverend Moon was "railroaded" into prison. I was only one person among the many individuals and organizations who volunteered as witness on his behalf. I submitted *amicus curia* (friend of the court) briefs to the United States Supreme Court "in what to the untrained eye appeared to be a minor tax case involving an unpopular religious figure," wrote Carleton Sherwood, "whose Asian origins and unusual theological notions had earned him in this country a small following and little sympathy from established religions."[12]

Reverend Moon quietly endured his prison sentence. Revered for his spiritual counseling of other prisoners, he appeared to many to be a silent martyr to religious bigotry. His request for parole was extended for seven months and finally denied in April 1985. He was released early due to good behavior under the provision that he live out the rest of his term at a halfway house in Brooklyn. Forty-six days later, on August 20, 1985, he became a free man.

The publicity surrounding Moon's jury trial for tax evasion, and his subsequent incarceration, were instrumental in an attitudinal revision toward the religious leader. The anticult movement, with its program of kidnapping and forced reconversion of members, seemed to lose its virulence to the extent that one got the impression that the anti-Moonie propaganda had lessened to some degree. A public celebration in Washington, D.C., and a testimonial banquet in Moon's honor brought together representatives of the mainline religions for this occasion. People who had little interest in the beliefs and practices of the Unification Church manifested their personal approval of the man who had suffered the price of religious bigotry. They rallied to the public support of a remarkable man.

The leaders of the Unification Church in the United States always seem ready for more missions. One organization which I have never become involved in is CARP (Collegiate Association for the Research of Principles), which discusses religious principles on college campuses. The disturbances in the Middle East prodded the members to combine campus activities with serious discussions about the search for peace.

The first effort, sponsored by the Unification Campus Ministry Association, to initiate this peaceful pursuit took place on the campus of Boston University from October 12–13, 1990. The title of the conference was "The Quest for World Peace: The Challenge for Campus Ministry and Higher Education in the Post Cold War Era." There were forty participants, of whom twenty-four were not members of the Unification Church. Two introductory speakers, Marvin Bordelon and Joon Ho Seuk, struggled with the challenge of world peace, just at the time when a threatening military buildup was occurring in Saudi Arabia.

The two-day program consisted of four workshops:

  I. Moral Education and the Development of Character;

 II. The Role of American Higher Education in a New
     Global Context;

III. Responsibility, Sacrifice, and Love in Campus
     Ministry;

IV. Is World Peace a Realistic Possibility?

While the discussions that accompanied and followed these workshops embraced major problems of the world, the tentative solutions culled from the literature of the two-day event tended toward personal virtue, such as: "Issues of justice have a special appeal at this time, but underlying such issues are matters concerning the human spirit." Thus, the challenge of campus ministry is first a challenge to ourselves. We have to go beyond the selfish habits of the heart and, according to conference participants, "replace such habits with a heart of reconciliation, a heart of service, a heart of love."

The second campus ministry conferences were held on the Berkeley campus of the University of California, from February 8–10, 1991. In essence, it was a one-day conference preceded, as it was, on Friday night with an address by Durwood Foster, professor of theology at the Pacific School of Religion in Berkeley. The plenary session on Saturday morning was conducted by Mose Durst, former president of the Unification Church of America. The morning workshop, conducted by Dr. James Gaffney, discussed whether ethics is possible without religion. The afternoon workshop by Dr. Gerald Jones examined historical theology. The facilitators of each of the sessions then analyzed the theology of peace and justice. The closing banquet at the University Faculty Club featured an address by Dr. Joon Ho Seuk.

The Reverend John Morris, director of the Unification Church in Louisiana, invited me to act as facilitator at the next campus ministry conference, held in New Orleans, from October 4–6, 1991, at the Dominican Center. The opening banquet was addressed by Professor Richard Rubenstein, a nonmember, whose scholarship contributed to the organizational development of the church. On Saturday the opening plenary remarks were again made by Dr. Joon Ho Seuk. The theme of religious response to diversity was discussed by Dr. Edward Warner, who explored at length the concept of religious pluralism. Because of illness in his family, Dr. Raymond Carter was unable to attend, but I read his paper and led a discussion of its contents.

The papers presented at these campus ministry conferences were edited by Reverend Morris, published in bound volumes, and distributed to the participants. Two central theses were proclaimed: (a) that all knowledge and science in every field of study forms a basic unity and (b) that aside from the relative values of each field of knowledge, there is an overarching set of absolute values. This also describes the vision of Reverend Moon: "world problems can be solved in a harmonious global culture based on absolute values." He had faith that these absolute values could be recognized, expressed, and developed through promoting dialogue among responsible intellectuals.

The Unification Church attracted nonmembers at another level through the *Divine Principle*, the religious doctrine of the founder's sacred writing. These writings took the form of seminars, in which I sometimes acted as moderator: at the Caribe Hilton in San Juan, Puerto Rico, in June 1979; at the Hyatt Regency in Acapulco, Mexico, in 1980; and at the Hotel Ybarra Semiramis, in Tenerife, Canary Islands, in 1981. In October of that year, I attended a conference on marriage and family at Marburg University, in Germany. In 1984, I presented a paper at two conferences, in June at the Athens Chandris Hotel, and in August at Hotel Lotte in Seoul, South Korea.

Reverend Moon's dedication to the learning process and his subsidies of organized education have been demonstrated from the start of his evangelical career. He established the Unification Seminary at Barrytown and urged his followers to do street preaching. CARP was established to cooperate with campus ministry. The annual meetings of ICUS gave birth to an international association, the Professors' World Peace Academy (PWPA), which, in turn, inaugurated the most ambitious of his educational programs.

Reverend Moon had been searching for an opportunity to establish a worldwide university system. This project started modestly in Korea with a college in 1985, which was raised to university status in 1989 and named Sung Hwa University. PWPA served as the Unification's agency for establishing a university campus in the United States. The opportunity arrived with the announcement of threatened collapse of the University of Bridgeport in Connecticut. In its bankrupt condition, the university was slated to close at the end of the spring semester in 1992, but PWPA came to the rescue with funding.

According to the association's statement of objectives, "PWPA seeks to foster a first-class university in the United States where people of all races and nations will be educated as world citizens. This undertaking is one part of a large plan to establish a number of universities throughout the world in order to prepare young men and women to live as global citizens in the 21st Century. As presently conceived, this world academic system would establish at least one major university in each of the world's dominant cultural spheres, namely, the Far East, Middle East, Indian Subcontinent, Europe, and, of course, North America."

In the spring of 1992 I was on sabbatical at the University of Notre Dame when I received an invitation from Dr. Gordon Anderson to become a member of the board of trustees of the University of Bridgeport. In exchange for its vital fiscal support, PWPA agreed to exercise influence over the institution by electing sixteen of the board's thirty-one members. The association deliberately chose to nominate academicians and prominent citizens who were not members of the Unification Church but were favorably disposed to its cultural and intellectual objectives. A preliminary and introductory meeting was held at the Bridgeport Hilton on Friday, May 15, when the new "owners" were cordially received by the university representatives.

While the anticult bigotry against the Unification Church had largely subsided around the country, a small "coalition" of students, faculty, and local citizens protested the incipient takeover of the university and took their concern to the media. On October 30, 1991, the *Chronicle of Higher Education* reported that "last week about 300 students, professors, alumni, and others, showed up at a trustees' meeting to oppose the proposal." Two weeks later, on November 11, the *New Yorker*'s "Talk of the Town" column mentioned "the Unification Church's reputation for exerting a strong grip on the thinking of its members," and doubted that this particular body could be "trusted to uphold academic freedom." But on May 10, 1992, the *New York Times* editorialized favorably that "Mr. Moon has as much right to run a college as anyone, so long as he does not impose his will on its faculty or the 2,600 students."

A news reporter from Hartford asked me, "How does a Jesuit get mixed up with the Moonie take-over of the University of Bridgeport?"[13] She suggested that I was "being used" to lend respectability to the suspect and unpopular Unification cult. Nevertheless, her article, entitled "Jesuit Moonlighting," did include my comments about the high moral standards of thought and behavior that the new owners intended to introduce to the Bridgeport campus. The first full meeting of the newly constituted board of trustees was held on September 25, 1992.

The Coalition of Concerned Citizens was not in evidence as we arrived for the introductory board meeting. It had held protest meetings in the previous weeks and picketed the campus in the belief that the university's reputation "will be tarnished by its association with Moon, whose church has been accused of exploiting young people." The following spring, on April 30, 1993, the coalition filed suit against the university and asked that "the Court find the UB-PWPA agreement in violation of state trust law and the University's non-sectarian character."[14]

The University of Bridgeport declares itself "non-sectarian and non-denominational" but is committed to "assist students in the process of integrating and developing their intellectual, emotional, social, psychological, cultural, philosophical, and spiritual aspects of their personalities." There is no officially designated campus chaplain, but facilities are provided for the

Newman Club, the Hillel Foundation, and a Protestant chapel. Counselors are available, and there is a loose interfaith center. Significantly, the academic program does not include a department of religious or theological studies.

The "new" members of the board of trustees are representative of the PWPA, which, of course, is supported by the Unification Church. It is one of Reverend Moon's greatest commitments that Bridgeport "become one of the finest universities in the world." Reverend Moon is first and essentially a religious leader, deeply interested in the moral integrity of students and their religious and ethical behavior.

Despite continued and prejudicial opposition—seemingly less vehement than in the early years of the movement—the Unification Church has established local branches in most large cities of the country. *Unification News*, the monthly publication of the church, provides spiritual and theological encouragement to members, including information about international aspects of the movement. One of the more significant developments has been the "opening" to the Russians, among whom Mr. and Mrs. Moon have become celebrated visitors.

The third meeting of the Assembly of World Religions was held in Seoul, South Korea, in August 1992. This was also the occasion of a mass wedding of 20,825 couples at the Olympic Stadium, a phenomenon I witnessed firsthand. At a banquet on the previous evening Reverend Moon delivered the most important message of his life. He announced that in the Providence of God he is the Messiah; indeed, he and his wife are co-Messiahs. Many years ago I had asked Mr. Moon if he was the Messiah. When he proclaimed that "We are the Savior, the Lord of the Second Advent, the Messiah," he was not claiming divinity, however.

Unification theology worships God the Father, but not the Son and the Holy Spirit. Jesus was both the human prophet and the Messiah who failed, but he was not divine. In other words, Mr. and Mrs. Moon are special human messengers from God sent to bring peace, unity, and salvation to all humanity.

While I continue to cooperate in a friendly ecumenical manner with the Unification Church and its leaders, I stay far removed from its doctrinal system and theological interpretations. My interest from the beginning has been an effort to "explain" why so many people—especially Roman Catholics—

were attracted to the Unification Church. I still insist that to replace bigotry with tolerance and ignorance with information seems a worthy objective in a democratic society.

8

Values and Education

✝✝✝✝✝✝✝✝✝✝✝✝✝✝✝✝✝✝✝✝✝✝✝✝✝✝✝✝✝✝✝✝✝✝✝✝✝✝

Like many other Jesuit professors who have devoted their lives to the apostolate of education, I have often wondered about the moral results or "value outcomes" of our teaching. The network of Jesuit educational institutions was intended from the beginning to provide something more than academic training. In the old days there was no hesitancy to say that we want to "form moral character" of the students in accordance with "Christian ideals of education."[1] There are doubters now, even among Jesuits, who question whether this objective is measurable or even attainable. On the other hand, we regularly and confidently measure the academic product of our teaching as we rejoice when the student "makes" an A grade and console the student who fails to "make the grade."

On two occasions, one at the high school level and the other among college students, I gathered research data that attempted to answer the question, "Is there any way of estimating the real, factual extent of the influence which our schools exert on the moral and spiritual life of our students?" The research study of Jesuit high school boys was done twice. The responses taken from 7,307 students in April 1965 were reported in a book entitled *Send Us A Boy—Get Back A Man* in 1966. The follow-up survey of 7,588 boys was taken in April 1968, when the freshmen of the first survey had become seniors. The results were published in a privately circulated book, *Jesuit High Schools Revisited,* in 1969.

When I initiated the high school survey in 1964, I was still working in Chicago on the special report about *Graduates of Predominantly Negro Colleges* which was done under government contract at the National Opinion Research Center.[2] I finally completed this report after I had begun my term as Stillman Professor at Harvard University. In October 1964, I received a call from Father Bernard Dooley, executive secretary of the Jesuit Secondary Educational Association, who expressed the central intention of the proposed survey: "We want to know how successful we have been in forming these young men in accordance with Christian ideals of education." He explained that the planning committee for the workshop on the Christian education of high school students had requested a "survey of the attitudes of the young men who will graduate from Jesuit high schools in 1965, or at least of a few typical groups of these graduates."

The inspiration for this research project seems to have emerged from the often-quoted 1962 Loyola Workshop on the Role of Philosophy and Theology at the college and university level. The final report of that workshop included a description of the "profile of the Jesuit college graduate," but it also made the realistic recommendation that "a large-scale attempt should be made to evaluate scientifically the effectiveness of our efforts to form the attitudes of our students: This would involve construction, administration and analysis of appropriate testing devices." Finally, at the 1963 meeting of Jesuit high school delegates in St. Louis, the following question and statement were put forth: "To what extent are we achieving our ideal in moral and religious formation of our students? It was felt that our most critical need in this area is for more factual information about the value patterns of our students."[3]

I felt that it was up to Father Dooley and his staff to elicit the cooperation of the principals in the forty-four high schools under Jesuit direction. He demanded a promise of their participation in the study and asked them to submit a list of the five most important questions concerning the moral education of their students. This means that the substantive content of the questionnaire did not come from educational or sociological theorists but from the everyday collective experience of competent teachers.

The two main concerns of the high school principals were the moral and religious habits of their students. The most frequently asked questions involved dating, cheating, drinking, or laziness during study hours. The second main category concerned religious practices, such as attendance at Mass, reception of Holy Communion, frequency of prayer, confession, and other devotions. From these comments I put together a tentative questionnaire and with the cooperation of Father Donald Nastold I administered the first pretest to a junior class at St. Ignatius High School in Chicago, on February 26, 1964. On the basis of this trial run I revised the questionnaire and tested it on another class of juniors at the same school on March 11.

I suggested that the survey of the graduating seniors be expanded to include the freshmen of these same high schools. This would provide an internal comparison to test the general assumption that the seniors, having had a full Jesuit secondary schooling, would show up "better" than the freshmen. I wanted to gather the data toward the end of the school year, when freshmen had been there long enough to make valid judgments of their experience and when the seniors could give us the benefit of their full four years' tutelage under Jesuit educators. The principals agreed to this extension. The final version of the questionnaire was then printed under the supervision of Father Dooley in Baltimore, and distributed by him to all the high schools during the first week of April 1964. Packets of the completed questionnaires were sent directly to me in Chicago for editing and coded identification. The total number of responses—3,740 freshmen and 3,567 seniors—were then computerized by Father John Keller of Loyola University at New Orleans.

After receiving the raw data in the marginal tables from New Orleans I looked first at the comparative responses of freshmen and seniors. I then selected five significant items on which to make a rough judgment of the usual "trend" assumptions:

1) The longer the student remained in a Jesuit high school the greater would be his appreciation of the school and its faculty;

2) Seniors would be better Catholics, as shown by their beliefs and practices of Catholicism;

3) Seniors would adhere to higher ethical standards of conduct and demonstrate greater moral integrity than freshmen;

4) Seniors would show an increased appreciation of the intellectual, moral, and artistic influence that the school has to offer;

5) Seniors would demonstrate more progressive social attitudes and a keener awareness of modern social issues.

The only one among these hypotheses that "tested out" was a relatively indirect finding of the survey: that students at Jesuit high schools receive a good academic training and that the seniors recognize and appreciate this experience more than freshmen. It is a well-known fact that Jesuit secondary education competently prepares boys for academic success in college. Since at least 85 percent attend college, there was no need to gather further evidence. Rather the purpose of the survey lay in another direction: to measure the moral improvement and character formation of the students from freshman to senior year. In this regard, the freshmen were "better" than the seniors.[4]

One of the assurances I had at the beginning of the high school study in 1965 was that the findings would not be filed away and forgotten. I was invited to present the report at a two-week workshop on the Christian formation of high school students at Loyola University in Los Angeles. The workshop was partially supported by a grant from the Lilly Endowment. The application for the grant stated: "it is expected that this workshop will have a profound effect on Jesuit education in the United States and around the world." This may have been an overly enthusiastic expectation, but the delegates to the workshop had every intention of achieving a "profound effect" on their schools as a result of the conference.

The task force that commented on my research report said that "the real value of the study will necessarily lie in the studies and analyses of findings at the local level, preferably by entire faculties of each school, and then in the changes introduced at the local level in accord with local findings." There was disappointment in the negative results of the survey but also a renewed resolution that improvements could be introduced at the points of greatest needs in the individual school. Recommendations and resolutions for pragmatic improvement of moral and religious training of high school students were formulated at the Los Angeles workshop.

As I look back at my report of this survey I am most interested in the chapter "Building Christian Character." Perhaps it was to be expected that "the ideal objectives far outreach the practical results, a discrepancy that is a kind of universal condition of personal and social behavioral aspirations." The students, especially the seniors, did not find Jesuit training more spiritual than academic. On the positive side, the overwhelming majority of all students thought that their character had been strengthened in some degree during their stay at the Jesuit high school.

Of course, there were delegates to the workshop who had reservations about surveys and statistics, but since both the survey and the workshop were encouraged by the top superiors in the Jesuit order I felt no need to defend the study and its methods. There was a kind of minority hesitancy expressed by the suggestion that I was reporting on the "pooled ignorance" of the students; that these boys should consider themselves the beneficiaries, not the critics, of an educational system distilled from the wisdom and experience of the Jesuits; that the information they provided about family background was surely inaccurate; that they never take anonymous and nontest questionnaires seriously; that April was the worst time of the school year to make a survey of students; and that the inherent quality of the Jesuit schools could not be captured in quantitative and statistical tables.

Actually the great majority of the delegates to the Los Angeles workshop did not question my research techniques, and even those who disliked the findings did not challenge any of the research data. The general willingness to accept the results of the survey may at first seem remarkable because the findings were basically negative—indicating that the high schools were not really successful in "forming these young men in accordance with Christian ideals of education."

Perhaps the delegates were less surprised and disappointed with my report for two reasons: First, they knew the factual situation because of their day-to-day experience in the schools themselves, and second, because they had just spent a year in the honest group appraisal and self-evaluation of the objectives and attainments in each Jesuit high school.

Among the resolutions passed at the workshop, I strongly urged that the 1965 survey be replicated in the spring of 1968 with exactly the same survey instrument. This would look at the 1968 seniors who had been freshmen three years earlier and provide a comparison between the previous seniors and the new freshmen. I had no intention of volunteering to repeat the survey. I had hopes that some other Jesuit sociologist would take up that task. Even so, in early May 1967, Paul Siegfried, the new executive secretary of the Jesuit Secondary Education Association, asked if I would undertake the second study. I was at that point fully immersed in writing the analysis of research data from my survey of diocesan priests, *America's Forgotten Priests*, but I was willing to cooperate with any social researcher ready to replicate the high school study.

For a brief time it appeared that a researcher had been found in the Catholic Educational Research Center (CERC) on the campus of Boston College. The director of this center, John Walsh, conferred with Siegfried in Washington, D.C., and with Joseph Shea in Boston, and submitted a "tentative estimate" of $19,000 to conduct the second survey. This seemed a reasonable bid, especially since it included the cost of printing five hundred copies of the research report and of the marginal tables for each school. Further negotiations, however, led to the proposal being rejected.

The discussions with CERC clarified for me the difference between educational testing and sociological research. I looked upon every answered questionnaire as a sociological document that had to be separately scrutinized for completeness, consistency, and conformity, even before its precoded information could be entered into the computer. Educational Testing Service simply used Digitek "answer sheets," on which respondents made checks at the appropriate places. Furthermore, CERC revised the original questionnaire, introducing so many changes and new items as well as rewording old items that there would not be the maximum comparability that I considered essential between the 1965 survey and the proposed new survey.

Siegfried was growing impatient over the delay and asked me to prepare the questionnaire for the second survey and to supervise the collection of data from the high schools. The number of high schools had increased to forty-seven (while four other new schools hadn't been open long enough to have a senior class). On March 19, 1968, the questionnaires were sent in packets to each school from the Washington, D.C., office of the Jesuit Educational Association with instructions that they should be administered to freshmen and seniors during the second week after Easter.

The responses were sent to me in Cambridge where, by the end of June, I had edited them, appended identification codes to them, and sent them for processing to John Keller at the Computer Center of Loyola University of the South. As in the previous project, the data processing continued smoothly throughout the summer months but with the expectation that some sociological reporter other than myself would write up the findings.

The search for someone to analyze and report these findings had been going on since March. My failure to find a sociological reporter to take on this task was a frustrating experience. Some of the Jesuit commentators on the 1965 report felt that the analysis and interpretation of data could best be done by a Jesuit who was either in high school work or had "more recent experience" in high schools than I had. I was more than willing to cooperate with this suggestion, even if it meant training a young Jesuit graduate student in sociology to do the reporting. I regretted that the Jesuit-run Cambridge Center for Social Studies had not developed into a research organization where such training would be available for young scholars.

When it became apparent by December 1968 that no one could be found to do the interpretive analysis of the research data, I reluctantly agreed to do it myself. This time I looked for collaboration among Jesuits who were actually engaged in secondary education. I asked Paul Siegfried to review each chapter and to give copies to other Jesuits. He found three men who provided excellent critical commentaries: Joseph Duffy of Boston College High School, Leo Lackamp of St.

John's High School in Toledo, Ohio, and Robert McGuire of Regis High School in New York City.

In April 1969, I was ready to answer the question on everyone's mind: Have the schools shown any improvement since 1965 in their program of Christian formation and training as seen through the eyes of the students themselves? At the meeting of the Jesuit Commission on Secondary Schools, held in Detroit at Easter time, I presented a progress report to the group of ten high school presidents and eleven principals. Perhaps these commission members—on the basis of the interim statistics I had distributed—were braced for the "bad news." Whatever their expectations, they now learned that the results of the second survey were largely negative.

The findings from the first survey were repeated in the second study. The moral and religious character of the Jesuit high school student showed no improvement between freshman and senior years and was no better than it had been three years earlier. The trend had not been reversed, nor had there been a measurable "closing of the gap" that might indicate some improvement. The 1966 Workshop on the Christian Formation of Jesuit High School Students—with its enormous preparatory studies and its serious concluding resolutions— seemed to have no measurable effect over the three-year period. As Raymond Schroth wrote in *Commonweal* in the January 30, 1970, issue, "the workshop promised change, and there is no evidence in the survey that the schools followed up the workshop with substantial reforms." The answer out of the mouths of the students themselves was still negative.

One of the dismal findings of the 1968 survey was the ineffectiveness of the teaching of religion in Jesuit high schools. The religion course became less palatable the longer the student stayed in the school, and there was no demonstrable improvement during the three-year period between surveys. For the great majority of students, every other subject was more interesting than religion. Some of the teachers of religion, however, received comparatively high ratings from the students, but the topic itself, they felt, was essentially dull.

A second and unexpected finding was the inference that students felt a difference between "Christian formation" and "character training." I concluded that the Jesuit secondary system was more successful in strengthening the character of students than in making Christians out of them. What showed up clearly in the survey was that a student cannot be a good Christian unless he loves God. On the other hand, a student could have a strong character without being a good Christian. It would appear then that these Jesuit high schools were succeeding admirably in promoting a secular version of character training. As the students saw it, strong character is a personal development quite separable from the religious and spiritual foundation on which the Jesuit theory of education rests. I felt compelled to say in the survey report that "perhaps the time has come to demythologize the religious ideology of Jesuit education and to reassess the whole concept of the impact of religion on character training."[5]

The published reports of these two surveys were printed for private circulation. Throughout both studies I preserved the utmost confidentiality, and I was protective of the reputation of the schools in my published reports. As far as I know, there was no undue publicity in any journal article or news media during the months immediately after the distribution of *Jesuit High Schools Revisited*. Raymond Schroth agreed to do an article for *America* in the autumn of 1969, but it appears to have been unacceptable to his editors. He worked closely with some of the members of the Jesuit Secondary Commission, revised the article, and had it published in the special education issue of *Commonweal* at the end of January 1970. Thus, the survey report came to the attention of the public, even while it continued to circulate privately among the Jesuits.[6]

❋❋❋❋❋❋❋❋❋❋❋

It is a long jump in years—almost two decades—to the double survey of the moral and social values of the students of Loyola University in New Orleans. The first of these was undertaken in 1984 as a combined project of the Department of Sociology and the Department of Campus Ministry. It seemed an appropriate time to make a study of this kind. A task force on Jesuit identity had recently researched the entire university enterprise and produced the Loyola "Character and Commitment Statement," approved by the board of trustees in 1980. It made the forthright declaration that the "mission" of

Loyola's Jesuits is "essentially religious but specifically intellectual and educational in the broadest and deepest sense."

Reflections about the mission of Loyola, its Catholic and Jesuit character and the need to place greater emphasis on issues relating to moral, religious, and social values, were the practical inspiration for a research survey. Much of the discussion previous to this study was impressionistic on the part of the faculty, speculative on the part of the administration, and almost euphoric among the promoters and public relations personnel. Little, if any, empirical information had been available on how the Loyola students themselves thought or behaved regarding religious beliefs, ethical values, or the university's advertised moral reasons for its existence.[7]

As instructor of sociology since the fall of 1948, when I assumed the chair of the department that I occupied for fourteen years, my own contact with Loyola students was personal and long standing. I got to know the students intimately in my courses, which included "Anthropology and Social Psychology," "Introductory Sociology" (in which I used my own textbook), "Social Problems," "Theory and Research," "Race and Minorities," and "Sociology of Religion." I also moderated the intercollegiate interracial organization and enjoyed the services of student assistants in a series of smaller research projects. Thus, I had a fairly comprehensive knowledge of student life and behavior on the Loyola campus.

Over the years, on the basis of my religious commitment as a Jesuit and my humanist commitment to the values of social science, I appreciated the ideological persuasion that Loyola University had to be different from other universities that are secular and not church related. In 1983, Tom Madden, dean of campus ministry, and several other faculty members met with me to discuss the question: "How well do we succeed in the special educational mission for which Loyola was founded?" We needed more than the assertion of the goals statement, which proclaimed that both teachers and students are reaching for "truth and Christian wisdom" or the promise of the brochures that we are "motivated by the Christian vision of reality." There was nothing original in our decision to study the value outcomes of a college education, which had been done off and on in other universities over many years.[8] There was also little original in the list of items we included in the research questionnaire. Most of them had been asked at other Jesuit colleges, but we wanted to reword them for the specific audience of the Loyola campus. This preparatory process evolved in the course of six months, from August 1983 to January 1984, mainly in consultation with the chaplains of campus ministry and the faculties of theology and behavioral sciences. During this period four versions of the questionnaire were written, and the draft at successive stages was submitted to twenty-one faculty members, of whom sixteen responded with suggestions and ideas.

I thought it was impractical and unnecessary to question every undergraduate student on campus, but I could reach a representative sample by focusing on the common curriculum courses that every student had to take every semester. We drew a random probability sample from the 164 common curriculum courses offered in the spring semester of 1984 that involved 916 students. About one-fifth (22 percent) of the registered students had either dropped the course or were absent from class on the designated day. Thus, the full sample consisted of 681 usable questionnaires, representing 29 percent of the 2,348 undergraduate students registered in the common curriculum courses that semester.

The generalizations that emerged from the survey cannot be compared to results from similar studies made in either Catholic or secular colleges. We were able, however, to make two kinds of comparisons. Measured against the criteria proposed by Loyola University, students are supposed to devote as much attention to moral and religious values as to intellectual and academic achievement. From this perspective, the conclusions we drew from the research data may be summarized as follows:

a) Assessing the Loyola values most important to them, the students are much more appreciative of the academic quality of the university than they are of the ethical and social values that the Loyola goals and commitment statements proclaim;

b) Most Loyola students are religious believers who profess the existence and providence of God. The university helps them to maintain this religious commitment.

As expected at a church-related institution, they meet the criteria of a personal religious faith;

c) The practices of religion, however, are at a lower level than the beliefs of religion. Less than half of the students say they "often" perform the various religious rites listed in the questionnaire although Loyola makes available opportunities to do so;

d) While there are degrees of seriousness and culpability in every system of morality, Loyola students seem to lack a balanced code of moral conduct. They strongly oppose hard drugs and cheating but are permissive on other matters, such as drunkenness and premarital sex;

e) In the area of public social issues, Loyola students tend to reflect the conservative mood of the country rather than the forthright social teachings of the Church. On all issues, except the nuclear arms freeze, they do not muster a majority on either side; and

f) In their aspirations for the "ideal" future work situation, the students want a job that promises both security and the opportunity for human service. Most of them are not anxious to make a lot of money and seem willing to settle into routine jobs.

Unlike the surveys of Jesuit high schools, which focused only on freshmen and seniors, I included students in all four classes at the university. For purposes of internal comparison, however, I again selected the answers of only freshmen and seniors for closer scrutiny. Here again, we were able to test the hypothesis that as a result of the Jesuit educational experience the seniors would be "better" than the freshmen. Besides the length of stay on the Loyola campus, several variables must be recognized in the statistical differences of response. The first is obviously the age spread, with freshmen averaging 18 years and seniors 21.7 years. The freshmen were more than twice as likely as the seniors (45 percent v. 19 percent) to have a room in a campus residence. A higher proportion of freshmen (80 percent) than of seniors (69 percent) are Catholic. More of the freshmen (63 percent v. 53 percent) report that they graduated from a Catholic high school, but the gender proportions are about the same—52 percent were first-year females, 54 percent senior females.

On almost every available measurement, the freshmen consistently provided responses that were more compatible with the values espoused by Loyola University. A greater proportion of freshmen than seniors (47 percent v. 38 percent) said they would "definitely" recommend Loyola to their young friends and relatives. They were more appreciative of the value advantages that Loyola offered, both academic and social. The freshmen appeared to be closer to their church and in general to have a stronger religious faith than the seniors. For example, they believed that religion gives meaning to life (72 percent v. 58 percent); they believed in a future life (75 percent v. 65 percent); they believed that sin is an offense against God (76 percent v. 55 percent); and they believed that God forgives the penitent sinner (88 percent v. 75 percent).

In a list citing examples of moral behavior, we found that only one behavior pattern, cheating on exams or term papers, was condemned more by seniors (78 percent) than by freshmen (71 percent). The widest percentage spread concerned the regular use of marijuana, where a much smaller proportion of seniors (35 percent) than freshmen (55 percent) felt that this was "very wrong." The seniors also condemned in smaller percentages the peddling of hard drugs on campus (75 percent v. 87 percent), but the same minority in both classes (27 percent) said that drunkenness should be denounced. On the morality of sexual behavior, such as premarital sex or homosexual relations, the freshmen were generally more condemnatory than the seniors.

I had a personal interest in probing the social awareness of Loyola students in the expectation that the university's promotion of social justice and the Jesuit concern for the poor and underprivileged would gain ample recognition. Was there a way to discover whether this student body was conservative or liberal? The two social issues that received the highest approval were the proposal to freeze nuclear weapons and passage of the Equal Rights Amendment for women. In contrast, the least approval was given to two equally progressive proposals: the abolition of the death sentence and the unionization of migrant farm workers. Another liberal proposal, the guaranteed annual family income, was favored by less than four out of ten respondents. There are no striking differences between freshmen and seniors, but in combining the responses we found a smaller proportion of conservative freshmen (32 percent) than conservative seniors (37 percent).

At a convocation of the full faculty on April 18, 1984, I presented these research data and moderated a panel discussion on some of the more notable findings. There was a general consensus that Loyola students fell well below the moral objectives described in the university's commitment and goals statement. The most disturbing statistic was the "downward curve in moral attitudes and spiritual values" from the freshman to the senior year. I meant neither as an explanation nor an excuse when I said that Loyola reflects the common research finding that college life in America tends to be a secular experience, so much so that by the time students become seniors their religious values decline.

Wherever the Allport-Vernon-Lindzey Test of Values had been administered, the results demonstrated a decline in religious belief and practice. The only place where this downward curve in moral attitudes and spiritual values did not occur was in fundamentalist schools such as Oral Roberts University in Tulsa, Oklahoma, and Bob Jones University in Greenville, South Carolina. Loyola University is not a fundamentalist campus, of course, but I had hoped we would be an exception. While I was not satisfied with Loyola's minimal moral and spiritual influence on the students, I had not really expected the university to work miracles or to produce large numbers of saints.

This does not mean that I was discouraged about the prospects of renewal or reform of religion on the Loyola campus. Campus chaplain Tom Madden distributed bound copies of the ninety-page report to all departments and made it available in the university library. In a short preface, President Father James Carter said that the results of the study were both encouraging and discouraging, but he asked that they be used extensively in "developing courses and programs" and in counseling the students to form values. Unfortunately, I did not discover any plan or program to implement the research findings or to remedy and improve student values. Like the aftermath of the Jesuit high school surveys, the practical application of research generalizations was difficult to achieve.

❖❖❖❖❖❖❖❖❖❖

Nevertheless, I thought we should try again three years later. Father Madden had resigned the campus chaplaincy and moved to the Jesuit Spirituality Center in Grand Coteau, Louisiana. He was replaced by Father Neal McDermott, who had done survey research at the National Opinion Research Center in Chicago. He agreed to my suggestion that we seek the president's support and approval in replicating our earlier survey in the spring of 1987, when the college freshmen of 1984 had become seniors.

We again selected a random sample of the common curriculum courses listed for the spring semester and received the ready cooperation of instructors to distribute and collect the questionnaires in the week after Easter. We had usable responses from 712 undergraduates who closely matched the earlier survey by gender, religious affiliation, and academic year. They were probably representative also in their appreciation of Loyola. The majority said they would "definitely" (43 percent) or "probably" (39 percent) advise a close friend or relative to attend the university. As in the previous survey, the students put great value in the dedicated faculty that provided good career preparation but with relatively few (22 percent) expressing appreciation that Loyola is a Catholic university.

One of the "explanations" offered for the discrepancy between the opinions of the freshmen and seniors from the 1984 study was that more than a third of the seniors had transferred from other colleges and did not have the benefit of four full years of a Jesuit higher education. In the 1987 survey we took this into consideration and were able to compare the transfer seniors with the seniors who had spent four years at Loyola. On every item concerning religious belief and practice the transfer students scored lower on "religiosity." They attended religious services less frequently, and prayed and read the Scriptures less often. Their moral standards were lower when it came to "sinful" behavior. On two specific social issues—immigration laws and annual family income—they were significantly more conservative than their fellow seniors. Thus, they were more willing (46 percent v. 32 percent) to deport illegal aliens, and they were less likely (31 percent v. 50 percent) to favor a guaranteed annual family income. The transfer seniors were also less ready to assert that God forgives the penitent sinner; that there is life after death; that God reveals Himself in the Scriptures; and that the Devil really exists.

What about the 1984 freshmen when they became seniors in 1987? Both as freshmen and as seniors, these students were more likely to admit that they have a personal relationship with God and that religion gives meaning to life than they were to put these feelings into external practice, such as attending Mass or receiving communion. As freshmen, only one-third said grace at mealtime; by the time they reached senior year this proportion dropped to one-fifth. It is quite clear from these comparisons that the religious influence of Loyola University failed to maintain its hold over the students.

The purpose of the second student survey in 1987 was to compare the data of the previous study. It is a sad fact that we detected little or no "improvement in the moral and social values of Loyola students over this three-year period." The responses to the 1987 survey were so similar to those of the 1984 study that we had to ask whether any fresh ideas and approaches had been introduced, any extra effort had been expended by the faculty, or whether anything "new" had been attempted by the administration. It was as though Loyola's moral and religious values were held in moratorium for three years while the students came and went unchallenged through the halls of higher learning.

The results of this 1987 survey were not an occasion of joy for either the dean of campus ministry or myself. We provided a copy of the report to anyone interested on the campus and for placement on the reference shelves of the library. Neither did I ask for a faculty assembly in order to discuss the study and its findings. It apparently got scant notice among faculty and students, except for a short news summary in the student newspaper.

The conclusions we drew from the research data may be summarized as follows:

a) Most Loyola students are religious believers, but their practice of religion is at a lower level than their beliefs;

b) They are much more appreciative of the university's academic quality than of its proclaimed ethical and social values;

c) They seem to lack a balanced code of moral conduct. While they strongly oppose cheating and hard drugs on campus, they are permissive regarding other behavior, such as heavy drinking and premarital sex;

d) In the area of public social issues, they tend to reflect the conservative mood of the country rather than the forthright teachings of the Church; and

e) The freshmen, barely touched by Jesuit influence, consistently provided responses that were more compatible with the values espoused by the university.

What happens to the moral standards and ethical values of students who spend four years at a Jesuit institution of higher learning? The most disturbing statistic of both Loyola studies was the downward curve in moral behavior and spiritual values that occurred from freshman to senior years.

We had hardly adjusted ourselves to the "dead end" of this values research project when word went out from the task force of Jesuit Higher Education that a general assembly of representatives from all Jesuit colleges and universities was to convene at Georgetown University. In August 1988, I was invited—and urged—by Jesuit Provincial Edmundo Rodriguez to share our research findings with the assembly secretary, Jim Cone. Our "capsule" summary contained the following thoughts: "How well do we succeed in transmitting the moral, social, and religious values of Catholicism? Is there some way of testing the success of our promotion of religious faith and social justice? We say that these are the values that set us apart from secular universities. How can we get some assurance about this?"

For the actual crowded session on the morning of June 7, 1989, at Georgetown University, I was able to gather an all-professional team: the moderator was Ray Noll of the University of San Francisco; the speakers were Joe Fitzpatrick of Fordham University and Ross Scherer of Loyola-Chicago. Loretta Morris of Loyola-Marymount had administered my questionnaire to her students and found remarkable similarity with the data I presented from the Loyola campus in New Orleans. David Moberg discussed the results of three student surveys he had conducted at Marquette University in Milwaukee and concluded that "objective evaluation of the outcomes of Jesuit education is possible only if there is a consensus about its ideals and an identification of specific attitudes and behavior that those ideals imply."

Two months later, in August 1989, I attended the annual meeting of the Association for the Sociology of Religion in Cincinnati and participated in a session entitled "Measuring the Effects of Religion in the University." Research reports by Dean J. Patrick Murphy of DePaul University and psychologist William Holmes of LeMoyne College were also included. In addition, Loretta Morris presented further analysis of her student values research while Jesuit Daniel Ross, sociologist from the Catholic Fu Jen University of Taipei, Taiwan, formulated plans for a congress to discuss student values in his part of the world.

During the ensuing two years Father Ross, a missionary from the California province who had earned a doctorate in sociology from the University of Notre Dame, conducted values research at his own Chinese university but also inspired similar research at other Catholic universities in the area.[9] He obtained a generous grant from a European Catholic philanthropist and scheduled a symposium entitled "Value Development and the University Classroom," from October 20 to 24, 1991, at the Taipei campus. The opening ceremonies included a welcoming address by Archbishop Lokuang, president of Fu Jen University (which contained about 200 Catholics among its 13,000 student body) and the keynote address by myself. I had studied all the research papers that had been prepared for this symposium and was able to present a rough composite of the findings.[10]

The symposium participants came from various Catholic universities of the Far East. Besides the Chinese of Fu Jen and the Koreans of Sogang, there were two Japanese universities, Sophia and Nanzan; two from the Philippines, De La Salle and Ateneo de Manila; and two from Indonesia, Sanata Dharma and Atma Jaya. For purposes of comparative analysis, Dan Ross had also invited some American sociologists to attend, including J. Patrick Murphy of DePaul University in Chicago, Donald Kirby of LeMoyne College in Syracuse, New York, and Kathleen Weigert of the University of Notre Dame in South Bend, Indiana.

The publication of the papers and the discussion topics from this international symposium prevents easy generalizations. These Jesuit educators are working in "mission" countries where many of their faculty colleagues, and most of their students, are not of the Catholic faith. (Of course, the exception is the Philippines, where most administrators, professors, and students are indeed Catholic). Everywhere we have observed a thrust toward secularism. Emphasis today is on business and the sciences, not theology and the humanities. Is it any surprise that there has been an almost universal upheaval in the Jesuit educational dedication to moral and social values?[11]

9

Liberal Catholic Journalism

❋❋

I had barely settled into the Stillman Chair at Harvard Divinity School when Donald Thorman invited me to join the board of directors of the *National Catholic Reporter*, a weekly newspaper published in Kansas City, Missouri. Its popular "Cry Pax" column was quoted in the faculty club by scholars who otherwise had little interest in Catholic journalism. The first task I was assigned was to survey the readership, which was growing spectacularly, and of whom two-thirds were Democrats and 45 percent clergy and nuns. It was a well-educated group: nine out of ten were college graduates who attended professional conferences and traveled abroad. The readers and subscribers were multiplying at an extraordinary pace.

The editorial competence of Robert Hoyt and the reporting skill of Robert Olmstead were the attraction that sparked the readers' interest. They gained the praise of *New York Times* correspondent Robert Blair Kaiser, who remarked that "the *National Catholic Reporter* was the most liberating force in U.S. Catholicism, in that it gave American Catholics information hitherto denied them by their own bishops and officials in Rome." Columnist Donald McDonald said, "The *National Catholic Reporter* is among the most important things that have happened in the American Catholic community in this century." The paper originally had its offices in the diocesan chancery, with the blessing of Bishop Charles Helmsing, but it was never under his control. Rather it was the product of dedicated Catholic laypeople who removed themselves from Church censorship. Ultimately they "made the bishops honest" by demonstrating that even diocesan papers could report news not always pleasing to the hierarchy.

The ownership of the paper was legally under the auspices of the board of directors, with Chicago publisher Dan Herr acting as president of the board. Charter members included fundraiser lawyers Frank Brennan and Jack Fallon and journalists Bob Burns and Joe Cunneen. In 1966, the two additional directors were Martin Marty and myself. An early concern was that the business office of *NCR* was, to quote one board member, "in a shambles. There was no bookkeeping. Everything was done out-of-pocket, like the old *Catholic Worker* days. They put the money in a pot, and those who needed it helped themselves. There was no accounting of income and expenditures. They had no idea what their costs were and whether subscriptions were paid. They got no bids from anyone; it was totally unbusinesslike." Everyone agreed that help was needed.

The lack of efficient cost-accounting practices was not the result of laziness or ineptitude. It was part of the ideology of an artistic and creative mentality. Attending to business was not Hoyt's style. He had a kind of aloof, intellectual attitude about the bottom line. The editorial department was disdainful of the grubby money concerns of the paper. There was something almost un-Christian about business transactions. The rigid demands of the budget were more disciplinary than Hoyt wanted. He did not wish to be held accountable to anyone but himself. He wanted to be creative and "do his thing" without supervision.

The journalistic brilliance of the paper was in utter contrast to the shoddy and amateur performance of its business office. Dan Herr, supported by the board members, was appalled that the business operations had gotten out of hand. He invited Donald Thorman to come in and "straighten out the mess." Thorman moved to Kansas City in December 1965, when the *NCR* enterprise was still located in the diocesan chancery office. The paper had passed its first anniversary and was expanding at an unprecedented rate of subscriptions when he took over as publisher in the beginning of 1966. Soon there was money in the bank. *NCR* then moved into a four-story building on Armor Avenue and expanded its work force. The editorials and news reporting were gaining nation-wide attention, but the organizational structure was still under repair. Thorman was an experienced newsman—he had been a successful editor of the Ave Maria Press in South Bend, Indiana. In the long run, he deserves credit for keeping *NCR* alive and successful. Without his dedicated and innovative professionalism the whole enterprise would have collapsed. Over the subsequent twenty years, most of the board meetings I attended were devoted mainly to the budget and to the means of staying financially alive.

In the world of newspaper publishing there is always a functional distinction between the publisher, who has to make sure that the enterprise is "fiscal," and the editor, who provides the "content" of the paper. The editorial staff of the *Reporter* came out of another tradition, a kind of community activity reminiscent of the youth movements of the 1960s. There was faith that money would always be available, as it was in the Friendship Houses. The first publisher, Michael Greene, wanted to restore order and to assert some authority over the editorial office. In the subsequent disagreements between him and Hoyt, Greene gave an ultimatum to the board: "One of us has to be in charge; him or me." The board sided with Hoyt, and the paper was without a publisher until Thorman arrived.

Under Thorman's guidance, an early attempt was made to clarify the relationship between himself and the editor and to understand the authority of the board of directors over both. Hoyt was asked, for the first time, to make a formal report to the board of directors meeting on September 13, 1966. He did so reluctantly, but he wanted assurance that this "concession" would not jeopardize his editorial freedom. His detailed report was an excellent description of a professional editor at work, but he wanted to keep the board at arm's length from his editor's desk. He felt that "it is not possible for a committee that meets four times a year to establish policies sufficiently nuanced to cover week-to-week decisions." This was a reasonable defense of the editorial "turf," but the implication was that the experienced professional men—there were no women—on the board had little to offer, except as guardians of the purse.

Meanwhile, earlier in the year, Hoyt and Thorman were approached by a group of diocesan priests from St. Louis, who requested *NCR* sponsorship and publicity for a research project to study the "problem" of clerical celibacy. This clergy group, which later organized as the National Association for Pastoral Renewal, gained some partial financial help from *NCR*, "with the understanding that the paper would be able to break the story on the initial results of the survey." The questionnaire I composed was mailed to 5,936 diocesan priests— every third name in the Kenedy directory of 1966—who were neither pastors nor monsignors but ordinary curates.[1] The survey dealt with the entire gamut of priestly life and work and devoted only seven out of more than seventy questions to the topic of priestly celibacy.

With the issue of December 14, 1966, the *National Catholic Reporter* made a coup that nettled the diocesan bishop-patron as well as the Apostolic Delegate, Egidio Vagnozzi. The *NCR* headline revealing that optional celibacy was favored by 62 percent of the priests was considered a "breakthrough" of a "fearful" topic that Church officials said should not be discussed. This broke open too the whole public discussion surrounding the marriage of priests who were opting out of the active ministry in the aftermath of the Second Vatican Council. Local bishops challenged the finding that bishop-clergy communication was inadequate and that bishops took little personal interest in their priests.[2]

What irritated the hierarchy more and aroused national attention in the survey report was the "sensationalism" of optional clerical celibacy. The news story headlined the fact that 62 percent of the priest respondents favored freedom of choice for diocesan clergy to marry or to remain celibate. This "fearful" topic, which had been banned from the floor of debate at the Second Vatican Council, was now out in the open. Indeed, it had been an open question among the priests themselves; more than eight out of ten said they had discussed it with fellow diocesan priests during the previous years.[3]

Meanwhile, the organizational personnel of the newspaper began to run smoothly, as the subscriptions continued to increase, and the finances took reasonable shape. There were no unexpected or immediate crises in meeting the budget. The relationship between publisher Thorman and editor Hoyt appeared to be tolerable. Both the chairman of the board, Jack Fallon, and the treasurer, Frank Brennan, lived in Kansas City and were available for legal and fiscal counsel. The regular quarterly meetings of the board offered a kind of oversight role and were usually conducted in Chicago, where the president, Dan Herr, had both his business and his residence. Burns and Marty were also from Chicago. Cunneen came in from New York.

The paper continued to publish the available news during the winter of 1966–67 while anxiously awaiting a decision from the so-called birth control committee, then holding hearings in Rome. The pope's commission discussed contraception and the pill in the first half of 1967 and delivered their report to the pontiff on June 28: "The Commission's Episcopal members had agreed not to submit majority and minority reports, just one report for the Commission. But archconservatives Father John Ford and Cardinal Ottaviani felt they had a right and a duty to warn the Pope away from it." The fact is that the commission was guardedly in favor of the pill, or some other form of contraception, but they realized that papal acceptance of their findings would call for a revision of the traditional ban against birth control. In other words, the concept of "responsible parenthood" had to include the "regulation of conception."

The commission's report was a secret document intended only for the eyes of the Holy Father, yet it got into the hands of the editor of the *National Catholic Reporter.* The name of the Vatican insider who released the document is still not revealed. Robert Blair Kaiser of *Time* magazine suggested that "Plenty of people in the Vatican, the Pope included, were ready to shake a stern finger at the insider who put these secret papers in the press pipeline. Never in their most paranoid imagining did the Pope and his staff believe anyone would leak them, much less publish them." It soon became known, however, that the document was delivered to Hoyt from Gary MacEoin, a freelance writer in Rome.

To publish a secret papal document, especially one that contravened the preference of the pope and the dogmatic tradition of the Church, had to be the weightiest decision a Catholic editor could make. Hoyt realized the gravity of this decision and wanted his staff to know that they would take considerable heat from the upholders of the status quo. They were nervously apprehensive that they were about to "scoop" the pope himself. The report and complete documentation appeared in the issue of Saturday, April 13, 1967, and created an immediate sensation.[4] Robert Blair Kaiser was ready to call it "the biggest press story of the year, of the decade; the sort of thing *NCR*, in the best muckraking American tradition, glories in." It did indeed cause an avalanche of criticism, especially among conservative American Catholics. Bishop Charles Helmsing, who had been a patron and sometime defender of the paper, felt betrayed by the publication of the papal document. He hinted at excommunication for the editor and staff and for the board of directors. He issued an official condemnation of the paper and demanded that it stop calling itself Catholic. The bishop's friendship was never regained.

The next meeting of the board was held in Kansas City, at the law office of Jack Fallon, then chairman of the board. Halfway through the meeting, Fallon drew out a paper to read a prepared statement of resignation. Without condemning the "irregular" resistance to papal teaching in this Catholic newspaper, he expressed concern about the paper's general tone and style and also about the difficulty of exercising board responsibility for its content. We then left his office to complete the meeting at the *NCR* headquarters.

Fallon's resignation was symptomatic of something more than the content of the newspaper. It was also more complicated than a simple reaction to the bishop's displeasure. Like all of us on the board, he treasured his reputation as a loyal and faithful Catholic. While the editor accepted full responsibility for the editorial content, the public fault of the paper was also the fault of the board members. More immediately, Fallon at that time was a candidate for the University of Notre Dame board of trustees, a position of prestige. He also had a son attending the university. He was disappointed that he did not get the position, which may have been because he was said to be at odds with his own bishop.

It is likely that Fallon's resignation could be taken as a pessimistic harbinger of the decline in the subscription rate. The publication of the "forbidden" document of the birth control commission was the beginning of much dissent among the subscribers. During the remainder of 1967 and into 1968, the speculation about the pope's decision ended with the promulgation of *Humanae Vitae*. Readers of *NCR* were already aware of the consistent "liberal" ideology of the paper, which seemed to have great difficulty in accepting the papal ban on contraception.

The conservative editors of *Twin Circle* and *The Wanderer* charged *NCR* with negativism and disobedience to the Holy Father. Hoyt continued to be in disagreement with the implications of the encyclical on birth control. He authored a book *The Birth Control Debate* (the first book published by *NCR*), containing all the pertinent information as well as an objective analysis of this highly controversial topic.[5] The paper continued to present the admittedly "liberal" side—the pope was not infallible on the subject—of the American Catholic dispute about the morality of contraception. Meanwhile, by March 1969, the popularity of *NCR* had reached its peak, with over 95,000 subscriptions.

The euphoria of the Catholic liberals seemed gradually to dissipate in the aftermath of *Humanae Vitae*. Reader interest in and support of the *National Catholic Reporter* declined too, as evidenced by the sharp drop of subscriptions to 43,000 reported in March 1971. Yet board members sought broader reasons for the paper's decline. Cunneen observed that religious publications were generally losing supporters. The country, including many Catholics, entered a period of conservatism. The assassinations of Martin Luther King, Jr., and Robert F. Kennedy and the burning of the ghettos had produced a somber mood. The battle for civil rights, the massacre at Selma, Alabama, and the national dismay over the endless Vietnam conflict contributed to a rethinking of the American civic philosophy and to the student opposition to the Vietnam War itself.

Although, in retrospect, the turn for the worse seems to have been sudden, the decline of subscriptions was both gradual and continual. This was worrisome to board members. The reason for maintaining the corporation was to keep the *NCR* in existence; it must not be allowed to go under, they insisted. Our preoccupation in the board meetings following the *Humanae Vitae* discussions was how to increase the finances in order to keep the paper alive.

The financial crisis was acute enough for President Herr to call a special meeting at his Thomas More publishing office in Chicago on August 27, 1970. All the directors were there: Brennan, Burns, Cunneen, Herr, Hoyt, Marty, Thorman, and myself. Herr read a prepared statement that he wanted to include in the minutes of the meeting: "Should the *Reporter* cease to publish as of today, we would be unable to meet our legal liabilities by at least $90,000." We had assumed that if we went out of business, some other publication would take over the fulfillment of our subscriptions, "but we can no longer act on this assumption." He remarked that "if management forecasts are correct, sometime in the next twelve months the *NCR* will simply run out of cash." Without offering a solution of his own, Herr saw three alternatives: (a) discontinue; (b) reaffirm publisher and editor and continue; or (c) shake up the internal operations.

Don Thorman was convinced that one of the reasons subscribers were dropping out was because of the carping content of the editorials. People were "turned off" by the negativity of the paper, he felt, and with the discourteous attacks on authority, from civic to ecclesial. Hoyt had scolded the pope and the Vatican as well as the president and the Congress. In the current crisis climate, Thorman offered a broad five-point plan:

l) A dramatically changed editorial product;

2) A strong public relations campaign;

3) A hard-sell, fund-raising approach;

4) A rigid control of the budget; and

5) Complete control of both editorial and business policies by the publisher.

Hoyt completely disagreed with the first and the fifth points. "*NCR*," he said, "was not founded on advocacy journalism," and he saw no reason for changing the editorial thrust of the paper. Furthermore, he realized that this plan would reduce him to a simple employee subject to dismissal at any time. Herr, recognizing a personality conflict, did not want to choose between Hoyt and Thorman. He said quite bluntly that "the best thing for *NCR* is to go out of business." At this point, Herr received word that his brother had suffered a heart attack, and he had to leave the meeting, which was then "adjourned temporarily."

It was five months later, January 21, 1971, before the adjourned meeting could be reassembled. All members of the board were present at the Thomas More office in Chicago to discuss again the crisis of declining subscriptions and shaky finances. Herr opened this meeting with the statement that "there is no hope for the future of *NCR*." Martin Marty also said that he saw no chance for its survival. Bob Burns complained that the board was getting too involved in the daily running of the paper, and for this reason he resigned "from the board today." When Herr declared his resignation as president of the corporation and as member of the board of directors, Burns said he wanted the minutes to show that he was the first to resign.[6] I suggested that all resignations be postponed until the next quarterly meeting, and if the situation then proved to be hopeless, we could all resign together and close up shop. Brennan moved to accept the resignations of Herr and Burns. Marty then said that under these circumstances he also should resign.[7]

The rest of us—Brennan, Cunneen, Hoyt, Thorman, and myself—left Herr's office, went to lunch, and reconvened in Thorman's room at the Sheraton-Chicago Hotel. The simultaneous resignation of three board members required a reshifting of the board officers: Brennan was nominated to the presidency of *NCR*; Cunneen became vice-president; Thorman, treasurer; and Hoyt, secretary. In his opening remarks the new president asked for a unified front by the board but emphasized that the primary responsibility for resolving the crises must necessarily fall on the publisher and the editor. The role of the board, he cautioned, is to support their endeavors.

The discussion tended to be dispirited in the almost forlorn search for operating funds. The pressing need demanded quick cash to maintain the operation. Thorman warned that the directors would have to face the possibility of dissolving the corporation when the cash reserve went under $100,000. Brennan countered that we had to insure that adequate severance pay be available for all employees should dissolution become inevitable. The publisher and editor agreed to notify the board immediately if collapse seemed imminent, but they would maintain the paper as long as it could effectively discharge its functions. Barring such emergency, the board agreed to hold its next meeting at Kansas City in June. This was unquestionably the low point in the career of the *National Catholic Reporter.*

During the next two months I made a thorough investigation of the viability of *NCR* and came to the conclusion that the product itself, the newspaper, had to be drastically improved if it was to remain salable. I recalled the demand made at the board meeting of the previous August that a dramatic improvement had to be made in both policy and content. I studied every issue during the months following that board decision and found no notable change. My conclusion was that the editor, who was ultimately responsible for the content of the paper, was failing in his role. I outlined these conclusions in a letter to President Brennan and the directors on April 13, 1971, and requested that a meeting be called as soon as possible. The intended purpose of the meeting was to replace the editor. The special meeting was convened by Brennan on May 3, 1971, at the Crown-Sheraton Hotel in Kansas City, Missouri.

Hoyt challenged both the purpose and the meeting itself on the grounds that the board had agreed to allow the publisher and the editor to seek a resolution of the problem and that the members of the board were simply to play a supportive role in this endeavor. I replied that our supportive role was no longer adequate, and the board had the right to dismiss the editor and could wait no longer for some other solution. We could not ignore the fact that more than fifty thousand subscribers had abandoned *NCR*, and finances had reached a crisis point. The paper was failing even though the editor had received "early warning" of this probability. Thorman recalled that he had, in early 1970, urged drastic changes in the editorial product, in response to the circulation decline, and that these changes had not been forthcoming.

I agreed that the hard data in the circulation draft showed the necessity for action. I suggested that these discouraging figures had been read as a signal of our approaching end and may well have accounted for the resignations of Herr, Burns, and Marty, who apparently sensed that *NCR* could not survive much longer. The accountant's statistics, dated April 27, were introduced and discussed at length by Hoyt and Thorman, each giving his own interpretation of their significance. In my understanding, whatever financial improvement may have been affected, it was achieved by means other than the sale of the product, that is, by reduction of costs and by some success in fundraising. I argued that the continuing decline in circulation was the crucial consideration and that even a gift of $200,000 from a Texas oil millionaire would not be a solution. The fact remained that the paper was not selling.

The board discussion evolved into a heated dispute over the interpretation of facts and with a sincere effort by everybody to avoid bias and prejudice. Brennan, who had been one of the founders of *NCR*, acknowledged that the paper had not changed adequately to respond to the world situation. He felt that the board had run out of options but that a change of editors was the only remaining choice. I then moved that Robert Hoyt be asked to resign as editor of the newspaper. Thorman seconded the motion. Hoyt, however, said he would not resign. Cunneen spoke against the motion, insisting that continuing circulation decline was not inevitable and that the paper was worth saving, even at a lower rate of subscriptions.

The president then called for a vote on the motion asking for the resignation of the editor. Brennan, Thorman, and I voted affirmatively; Cunneen sided with Hoyt, who announced that, despite the board's request, he refused to resign. I then moved that the board terminate the employment of Hoyt as editor. With the same split vote the motion carried. There ensued a brief discussion about severance pay and other details concerning Hoyt's departure from the newspaper he had founded.

The press release of Hoyt's termination as editor of *NCR* elicited a strong negative reaction from Joe Noonan, a former cartoonist for the paper, who sent a letter to authors and columnists—twenty in total—who had ever appeared in *NCR*, accusing the board of "arrogance" in refusing to "disclose the facts" and asking them to boycott the paper. My former Harvard colleague, Harvey Cox, joined the boycott, but most of the others seemed satisfied with an informal telephone explanation. Another rumor circulated, insinuating that the editor's divorce and remarriage had been a prime factor in his rejection. The fact is that his private marital problems had never been mentioned in a board meeting and had made absolutely no impact on the decision. Nor were there any negative sanctions at a later date when Brennan announced his own divorce and remarriage.

Thorman then had to undertake the double role of editor and publisher. The tone of the paper softened its arrogant attitude of protest and criticism but maintained the independence to report the Catholic news honestly and objectively. While the shift in editorial policy soon became evident, there continued the nagging problem of financial instability. As publisher, Thorman had been searching for income-producing enterprises that could supplement the income from the paper itself. One of his earliest ventures was the development of the "ad random" columns that accepted advertisements not ordinarily seen in diocesan newspapers: groups such as Dignity, CORPUS, Guest House, Women's Ordination Conference, retreat houses, and renewal programs.

An attempt as a mail order medium for books and religious articles was never sufficiently lucrative and was dropped. Under the general heading of communications, Thorman introduced the production and sale of audiocassettes, which succeeded beyond expectations. Another popular innovation that became a lasting success was the publication of a liturgical service called *Celebration*. The West Coast editor of this monthly, Joe Nolan, felt that he deserved not only the agreed-upon stipend but also a "cut" of the profits. He was replaced by a woman liturgist, Megan McCarthy, who had been supplying most of the content up to then. When she withdrew, the work was taken over by Art Winter and then by longtime staff member Bill Freiburger. Meanwhile, Nolan produced a rival service, the *Good News*, but it did not seriously affect subscriptions to *Celebration*.

Thorman was imaginative and venturesome in the search for allied types of income-producing programs. One of the most successful was the introduction of a summer supplement, a pull-out section listing and describing retreats, institutes, and ecumenical gatherings throughout the country. It soon expanded into two issues each year. Other ventures were not so successful. He edited a newsletter, *Successful Marriage*, which did not pay for itself. Another newsletter, called *Link*, tried to underline the balance of urban ministry with social justice; it also folded.

During the summer months of 1971 Thorman had the loyal support of staff members Ed Brok, Art Winter, and Tom Casey and frequently consulted with President Brennan. Joe Cunneen and I were in occasional and worrisome phone contact with Kansas City, discussing several potential members to replace the four directors who were no longer with us. At the suggestion of Thorman, I interviewed businessman John Caron at his New York office. A second prospective member was Chicago monsignor, Jack Egan, a friend of many years. Negotiations were carried forward with them, and they were voted into membership of the NCR Corporation on September 17, 1971.

This special board meeting was convened by President Brennan at the New York Hilton Hotel when the remaining four directors augmented the board with the election of Caron and Egan. There were now six directors of the corporation, of which the following officers were reelected: Brennan president; Cunneen vice-president, and Thorman treasurer. I was elected secretary, a function I performed mainly by keeping detailed minutes of subsequent meetings. Thorman explained that he had formed an ad hoc National Committee for NCR, composed of ten cooperative and knowledgeable clergymen and three religious sisters, who were willing to lend their names to promotional literature.

In presenting the crucial business report, together with the auditor's report, Thorman pointed out that the subsidiary sales were slowly increasing and that the number of employees was reduced from twenty-two to sixteen. He would continue to hold down expenses, "but the heart of the *NCR* problem is to stop further decline in circulation," he remarked. He pointed out that he had acted as publisher and editor since the board meeting of May 3 and that it had been a crucial period of reorganization and redirection for the paper. He further stated that no satisfactory candidate for the editor's position had emerged and that it was easier to get someone for the business side than for the editorial side of the paper.

Consequently, Thorman assumed the official title of editor for the immediate future of six to twelve months while continuing to serve as publisher. It was further stipulated that he, in consultation with Frank Brennan, would hire a business manager. This arrangement, meant to be temporary, lasted for many years. A new addition to the board of directors was Franciscan Sister Francis Borgia Rothluebber, the first woman accepted on the board. Sister Francis had extensive experience in the administration of her religious congregation. One of the organizational principles established in the early years by Thorman was to hold all board meetings outside company headquarters. He felt that he, the CEO, should be the channel of communication—if there was any—between the directors and the employees. On several occasions, however, individual staff members were invited to present an explanation of their work at meetings of the board.

In the spring of 1974, circulation had improved and income had increased. All talk of the paper's imminent collapse and the eventual dissolution of the corporation ceased. The board then decided to buy the building that *NCR* had been renting since June 1966. An anonymous financial windfall had made possible the opening of a Washington, D.C., office under the direction of Tom Casey. Thorman noted that October 29, 1974, marked the tenth anniversary of the founding of *NCR* and suggested a special anniversary issue of the paper as well as a fundraising dinner. The anniversary was neglected because of reluctance on the part of the staff, who thought that ten years was an age too young to celebrate.

A proposition made by Brennan about changes in the managerial setup was postponed until the next meeting at the O'Hare International Towers in Chicago on September 21, 1974. Thorman anticipated that some managerial changes had to be made. He had been both publisher and editor since the departure of Hoyt, and he now anticipated hiring a new person in the capacity of editor. He had negotiated an agreement with Arthur Jones, the London bureau chief for *Forbes Magazine* to come to Kansas City. Jones had earned a solid reputation as an excellent reporter and editor. There was discussion also of adding members to the board of directors, and a series of names was proposed: Sidney Callahan, Mary McGrory, Cynthia Wedell, Mary Ann Krupsak, George Reedy, Abigail McCarthy, and Albert Outler. Thorman felt, however, that since they were not well known to the directors it was best to invite them to come aboard as a temporary committee of advisors.

In February 1975, the election of officers fulfilled the recently accepted guidelines of rearranged positions. Frank Brennan became chairman of the board, Donald Thorman president, and Joe Cunneen vice-president. Sister Francis Borgia Rothluebber took over as treasurer, and I continued in my role of secretary. No board member had the title of publisher, although Thorman continued to function in that role. For the first time, there was no seat on the board for the editor. The new editor, Arthur Jones, was introduced as an employee of the board, submitting his reports at the meetings but with no voice in its determinations.

Jones made his first appearance before the board at the May meeting after he had served five months as editor. He admitted the great effort he was making to accommodate himself to both American culture and to the Catholic Church in this country. Characteristically, Jones and his wife made it clear that they did not like living in Kansas City—they always said they considered the job at *NCR* to be a temporary position. At almost every board meeting in the next few years, Thorman told us that Jones was considering one or two attractive job offers and that we were to stay alert for a possible replacement. As a matter of fact, he did leave the paper in 1980 and move back to England. His anticipated newspaper position in London did not materialize, however, and within a year he was back in Kansas City seeking reemployment at *NCR*.

Two new board members were introduced at this meeting: Abigail McCarthy, a published columnist and the divorced wife of Minnesota Senator Eugene McCarthy; and Albert Outler, professor of theology at the Divinity School of Southern Methodist University in Dallas. McCarthy was an ardent feminist, active in Church Women United, who thought the paper should pay more attention to the so-called communal Catholic. Outler, on the other hand, had been an observer at the Second Vatican Council, commentator on *Lumen Gentium*, and a learned and affable ecumenical advisor during the lengthy considerations of the *NCR* board.[8]

At the next meeting in May 1976, at the Crown Center Hotel in Kansas City, board members were heartened by the Catholic Press Association's decision to grant high honors to *NCR*. First place awards were in the following categories: a) general excellence; b) best editorial page; c) best in-depth reporting; d) best front page; e) best regular column; and f) best in circulation promotion. One envious critic protested to the association that since *NCR* was owned and published by laypersons and did not have to adhere to the same Church guidelines imposed by bishops upon the regular diocesan publications, the paper was an "unfair" competitor and thus should be removed from the category of Catholic newspapers.

The new year promised to be a period of prosperity for *NCR*, the first time the specter of bankruptcy was completely eliminated. The veteran controller of the company, Donald Banhart, brought upbeat financial reports to board meetings. Caron recommended that the cash investment of $450,000 should be taken from savings, where it earned 5 percent interest, and be turned into five-year treasury notes, where the earnings would be almost 7 percent. Staff member Art Winter had built the audiocassette division into a consistent moneymaker for the company. His list of best sellers proved that consumers would purchase tapes about prayer and Scripture, Jesus and self-actualization, but tapes about social justice and poverty were not popular. We speculated that we were reaching two audiences: those who appreciated the paper itself for its liberal and progressive ideology and those—primarily the cassette buyers—who focused on personal piety.

Outler questioned the news analysis by *NCR* reporter Mark Winiarski of a study by American theologians on the matter of sexuality.[9] Because the bishops would undoubtedly reply to the theologians, Outler suggested that some "deep" ethical thinkers, such as Jim Gaffney, Richard McCormick, or John Noonan, be approached to give their own reflections about the problem. This was an important early approach to a topic that gradually took more and more space in *NCR* editorial and news items. In the next decade, the subject of sex was to become a central item of journalistic attention in the *National Catholic Reporter*.

The late 1970s were also a worrisome time for Donald Thorman, who came back from a journey to China with a severe case of hepatitis. He continued his duties as best he could, giving speeches and attending meetings across the country, but his colleagues and family witnessed the daily deterioration of his health. Still, he was responsible for tightening up the entire operation. The projected preliminary budget for fiscal year 1978 anticipated a net profit of $45,000. "This favorable projection," he wrote, as part of his report to the board, "was caused in part by operating efficiencies and cost controls, and in part by the price increase of *NCR* and of *Celebration*. At the same time, we regularly reviewed the continuing pressure of inflation to boost costs in all areas, especially those of printing, postage, salaries, and wages."

Thorman attended his last meeting of the board on November 17, twelve days before his sudden death. He seemed in good spirits when he reported that "the editorial department now has the highest morale it has ever had, that there is enthusiasm and cooperation within the staff who are enjoying their work." He realized that Jones intended to leave *NCR* but gave assurance that he would stay at least to the end of the fiscal year. At each meeting Thorman reminded us that Jones was receiving offers for other jobs and that radio interviews and a growing reputation on the book he wrote about Malcolm Forbes were bringing him additional exposure.

The editorial report submitted at this November meeting was highly criticized by board members because it was found to be "complacent and self-serving." Egan questioned its accuracy and its failure to focus on the direction in which *NCR* was going. This editorial complacency, he thought, was a hindrance to improvement and to a correct perspective of the editor's function. The last sentence of the report spoke of progress in the Church, but Sister Francis requested that the status of the Church be reported separately from the status of the *Reporter*. She asked that the next editorial report give some indication of the future direction, program, and plans for the paper.

This was also an appropriate time, thought Outler, for the *Reporter* to recognize and promote the transition from the old Church to the new generation. "The elders of the tribe are being listened to again, but they are gradually passing off the scene," he noted. He suggested that some of the older Roman Catholics—historians, social scientists, and well-known lay leaders—be asked to reminisce about the past forty years and to make conjectures about the next forty years of Roman Catholicism. This seemed a timely message particularly for Donald Thorman, who, by now, was in poor physical condition, had lost weight, and wore a jaundiced appearance.

On the afternoon of Wednesday, November 30, Brennan made a telephone conference call to inform us that Thorman had died that morning. We agreed to convene on Saturday for his funeral in Kansas City and for a meeting of the board at the Hilton Plaza Hotel. It was a mournful encounter. We were all very fond of Donald and concerned about the welfare of his family. Yet essential decisions had to be made about carrying on the work at the paper. We elected John Caron to take his place as president of the corporation. Jones continued as editor but was elected also to the role of publisher.

At this point, Jones joined the meeting and was told of his appointment as publisher, which meant that he was now a member of the board of directors. He said that he and Thorman had frequently discussed the prospects and programs of *NCR* and indeed had been outlining plans for the next five years. Nevertheless, he felt the need to consult outside the immediate staff and promised to make exploratory visits to each of the board members in the next six months. This special meeting of the board concluded in time to proceed to the parish Church of St. Theresa for the funeral liturgy of Donald Thorman.

During the last months of his life Thorman confided to his wife, Barbara, and to Frank Brennan that he wanted to have the first meeting of the new year—1978—in New Orleans and to combine it with a modest banquet in honor of my seventieth birthday. Arrangements were made through Jean Blake, Arthur Jones' secretary, to assemble a list of invitations. Thus, on May 31 the board meeting was held at the Pontchartrain Hotel in New Orleans, with a testimonial dinner in my honor.

Meanwhile, Jones performed the dual role of publisher and editor. He felt much more comfortable as editor and so looked for someone else to assume the job of publisher. He already had part-time help from Jason Petosa, an ex-priest with previous experience doing public relations work in his diocese. Early in 1978 his name was proposed by Jones as a likely candidate. This was acceptable and at the board meeting of February 1, 1979, held at the O'Hare Hyatt Regency, Petosa made his first report as the new publisher.

Jones was glad to be relieved of the publisher role, but he was not fully at home with the role of editor and, what's more, he was still not sure that he wanted to continue living in Kansas City. On a Sunday afternoon in January he telephoned board members with the curious suggestion that we might rehire Bob Hoyt as editor. Further, he sought board counsel on some topics he proposed to write about, such as an editorial about the new pope, John Paul II. He asked me to help him revise the piece. He was not quite comfortable with Vatican politics and with general hierarchical activities and thus modestly sought advice. Such reporting on the papacy and the analysis of Vatican affairs assumed a more professional stance when Peter Hebblethwaite became Rome correspondent. Due to his contributions, the activist and progressive interpretations of *NCR* continued without interruption, tackling the problems of racism, poverty, welfare, homelessness, pacifism, and environmentalism. New attention was paid to women's liberation, the Equal Rights Amendment, and especially to the changes occurring in the congregations of religious women.

Jones also emphasized stories that chronicled the increasing number of priests resigning from the Church. Many were having more difficulty obtaining Vatican rescripts that allowed them to marry. For the first time in the history of *NCR*, sex became a feature of news reports and editorials. Stories of questionable accuracy called attention to homosexuality in seminaries and among the clergy. Much of this was innuendo and hearsay and was especially mishandled in the review of Father Enrique Rueda's capricious and erroneous book about a "network" of gay priests. Such preoccupation with sexuality, begun by Jones, was later carried on by his successor, Tom Fox. It was a focus that eventually led to my own resignation from the board in 1986.

Tom Fox was a young but experienced newsman who had sent his first news stories to *NCR* from Vietnam, where he had been a member of the Peace Corps. Board members were interested in his professional credentials and in the depth of his Catholic social philosophy. He had married a Catholic Vietnamese woman and exhibited deep concern for all minorities, especially for the poor of the Third World and for the homeless and underprivileged of the United States. When Fox took over the editorship in July 1980, Jones was able to fulfill his long-threatened resolution to leave Kansas City. He soon made a gala departure, moving his family and his household goods back to England. His anticipated employment there in the field of journalism was unfulfilled, and within a year he was back again seeking a job at *NCR*.

There was also a kind of volatility in the relatively brief career of Jason Petosa as publisher and chief executive officer of *NCR*. He was confident of his own abilities as administrator and business manager. He felt no need for Frank Brennan's close cooperation and counsel that Donald Thorman had always utilized, for example. He also began to operate independently of the board. Without asking approval of the board of directors, he contracted with Robert Heyer to enter the book publishing business, a commitment of substantial financial subsidy. The new enterprise was called the Leaven Press. One of its earliest products was my book *The Holy Family of Father Moon*.

Ultimately and hesitantly, the board of directors accepted this contractual obligation to enter book publishing. In October 1985, we learned that Petosa had agreed to have Leaven Press take over the name and inventory of Sheed and Ward, an honorable but now defunct Catholic publishing house that had been owned by John McMeel and the late James Andrews. This too was handled by Petosa without previous consultation with the board.

In October 1985, John McMeel, who had been elected to the *NCR* board, provided a detailed financial analysis of the 1986 budget for both *NCR* and Sheed and Ward. The report reflected *NCR* as a "rather sick patient." The newspaper had a projected loss of $200,000. Three other publications of the company were also expected to lose money: *Praying, Caring Community,* and *Gathering.* This meant that the burden of providing income would have to be carried by two remaining publications—*Celebration* and *Eucharistic Minister*—and the audiocassette program. *NCR* was being revisited by the economic embarrassment that Donald Thorman had faced from the beginning.

By this time, John Caron had hoped to be relieved of the position of chairman of the board, but the company continued to have management problems as well as fiscal concerns. The controller, Bill Wells, had to be dismissed in September 1985, when he insisted on handling the book publishing department without consultation with Fox and Heyer. Caron agreed that "Bob Heyer is a very smart and knowledgeable editor. He has been very aggressive with a program of 20 books a year." The consensus of the board was that despite the financial risks involved, the Leaven Press was a worthy endeavor, even while it was a financial drain on the rest of the company. There was still time to abort, or curtail, its operations before further substantial expenses were incurred, but this was not necessary. In subsequent years, Sheed and Ward was also able to turn a profit and ceased to be a financial burden.

The problem of mismanagement by Petosa continued to bring disorganization into the day-to-day operation of the company, however. Since board members had no direct contact with the working staff of the paper in Kansas City, we tended to receive our information secondhand. Occasional complaints by women workers about employee harassment emerged, a surprising development for an organization of such moral integrity. We had prided ourselves on the high ethics of the employees and on the moral character of all concerned. From the beginning, Hoyt and Thorman had been apostles of social justice and of workers' rights.

At any rate, Petosa was dismissed by the board in July 1985, and a search began to find a proper replacement. For more than six months Fox carried the triple responsibilities of editor, publisher, and controller. A search committee was formed consisting of three board members: Joan Chittister, Jack Egan, and David O'Brien, with the assistance of three staff employees. An advertisement for publisher and chief executive officer was carried in Catholic periodicals and in the *New York Times* and the *Washington Post*. Out of a total of twenty-eight applicants, none quite met the combination of human qualities and skills required for the job. A chance meeting with an executive of the Hallmark Corporation initiated an invitation to William McSweeney to consider the position. He accepted and his appointment was confirmed at the board meeting of November 19, 1985. He took over full time on February 3, 1986.

When the search had begun, I wrote a letter of moral support to Tom Fox, repeating the words of the ad: that the publisher we are seeking had to be a highly moral and practicing Catholic with a deep love of the Catholic Church. This was the ideal of a conscientious moral employee. "I must confess," I wrote, "that over the past year or two I have detected in *NCR* occasional lapses from this ideal of conduct. I detect a kind of adolescent prurience in some of the writings in the paper, a readiness to overplay sex stories. The most blatant recently was the excessive attention paid to clerical pedophilia. Certainly this is a valid news story, but it is very bad judgment to do two long feature articles and to finance reporters to unearth the details."

The secular press reprinted from Catholic sources various stories of clergy misconduct. When Thorman had been in charge these stories were reported but not emphasized. I had always been enthusiastic about the high moral tone of *NCR*, its open support for the labor movement and the peace movement, its excellent analysis of women's liberation and the environmental movement. It was always forthright about the faults of the Church and society but also ready to praise both religious and civic virtues. After Thorman's death, however, and during the era of Jones and Fox, an unusual interest in the sexual behavior of Catholics gradually developed.

In a letter to chairman William McSweeney on April 7, 1986, I asked him to put on the agenda of the next meeting, "a discussion to raise the moral and cultural level of the newspaper's content. I am disappointed at times, at the vulgarism and the adolescent prurience of some of the writing. It seems to me that our language ought to be at least at the level of the *New Yorker*, or the *Washington Post*." The unanticipated opportunity for a moral discussion of this kind arose in the next board meeting.

A preoccupation with sexual scandals took on an almost obsessive character in the *NCR* issue of May 20, 1986, which resurrected a story that had been printed a year earlier of misconduct among the Louisiana priests of the Lafayette diocese.

The article featured a map of the diocese on the first page and simply repeated the speculations of lawyers Hebert and Simon. It was journalistic overkill of a morally distasteful subject that tended to titillate rather than inform.

I brought up this matter for discussion and for an overview of the moral values the *NCR* had always proclaimed at the meeting of the board on June 3, 1986, at the Kansas City Hyatt Regency Hotel. While the board had conscientiously refrained from interference with editorial functions, it was always assumed to have an obligation of moral and ethical control. In this case, it was not forthcoming. I then proposed a resolution: "that the *NCR* Board members express their disapproval of the article, 'Church still on trial in Pedophilia Crisis,' which appeared in the issue of May 30, 1986." Although no one seconded the motion, it aroused considerable discussion.

This was not a new conversation about a novel topic. On numerous occasions board members had criticized the editorials and reporting, but it was always done informally and with no expressed censorship to bring the matter to a head. I had made my share of complaints about the paper's handling of topics of sexuality in general and of homosexuality and clerical pedophilia in particular. At the board meeting of October 1982, I had called attention to Arthur Jones' apparent fixation on clerical celibacy and his recent undocumented report on clergy homosexuality. I had pointed out also that in reporting and analyzing such topics the paper had carelessly printed inaccuracies and innuendoes, rumors and allegations. I argued that *NCR* had to avoid the vulgarism of "yellow journalism."

The fact that no board member seconded my motion was symptomatic of the board's reticence to discuss the moral and social values for which *NCR* stood. The "oversight" of the board of directors seemed limited to concerns about circulation and finances. At any rate, I finally concluded that my moral norms for accountable publication were at a different level from theirs. This being the case, I simply declared that I had to dissociate myself from the board and from the company.

John Caron telephoned me on June 24, asking that I postpone my resignation to allow a full discussion at the next board meeting in November. He reminded me that there had not been a quorum at the June meeting; there had been six absentees who should now be allowed to consider my resolution of disapproval. It seemed reasonable that all the directors, who by then numbered eleven, should be given the opportunity to hear my complaints. On November 19, I attended the *NCR* business meeting at the Radisson Mark Plaza in Alexandria, Virginia. This time Sister Joan Chittister seconded my motion for "purposes of discussion." While the board members seemed to find the pedophilia stories distasteful and reprehensible, they were not ready to express formal disapproval of their content. The inconclusive result of the discussion confirmed my decision to withdraw from the board of directors after two decades of participation in the activities of the *National Catholic Reporter*.

10

Married Priests

✣✦✣

During 1978 the Catholic priesthood reached a turning point. One direction moved toward accepting Anglican clergy, even though married, into the Roman priesthood; the other involved Catholic priests who resigned and married against the wishes of Pope John Paul II. The signs of the times were very confusing. In 1978 the pope began to completely shut down any chance of honorable departure from the active ministry of priests who wanted to get married. Yet the same pope just two years later opened the pathway—at least slightly—for the entrance of married clergy from other churches.[1]

This papal contrast was immediately labeled a "double standard" by the leaders of CORPUS (Corps of Reserve Priests United for Service), who had been organized since 1974 as the National Association for a Married Priesthood. In response, Catholic authorities patiently pointed out that no contradiction existed. The man who resigns the active ministry and marries is disloyal to the solemn promises he had made at ordination, they explained. Even if he obtains a rescript releasing him from celibacy he is still denied the "moral right" to be restored to the ministry.

The married Episcopal priest, on the other hand, who rescinds the promises and obligations he made to his own church, is ready to embrace the full profession of faith in the Roman Catholic Church. This arrangement had to win the approval of the Vatican, even to the extent of making an exception to ordain married priests. The Holy See carefully specified that "this exception to the rule of celibacy is granted in favor of those individual persons, and should not be understood as implying any change in the Church's conviction of the value of priestly celibacy, which will remain the rule for future candidates for the priesthood for this group."

My sociological interest in this apparent dilemma of two kinds of married priests is a logical extension of the research I have conducted about priests, parishes, and Catholic institutions over several decades. Considerable excitement and a remonstrance from the Apostolic Delegate came with the publication of *America's Forgotten Priests* in 1968, my so-called celibacy study. When I revealed the fact that most priests (86 percent) discussed the problem of celibacy and that one-third entertained the thought of actually leaving in order to marry, I was accused of publicizing a topic that had been definitely "closed" by the Second Vatican Council. That was about the time when the volume of priestly resignations notably increased.

When the Second Vatican Council closed in December 1965, the formal decisions it passed were a disappointment to many American priests who wanted Vatican approval for marriage. A few had already married; others had applied for permission to marry, but many were certain that "the bishops [did] not know what the priests [were] thinking." This conviction inspired a group of diocesan clergy in St. Louis to sponsor a modest survey of their fellow priests to inform the bishops of their thoughts about clerical marriage. I had completed the first year of my term as Stillman Professor at Harvard when I received an inquiry from Robert Hoyt of the *National Catholic Reporter*, asking if I might be interested in doing another survey of diocesan priests. An aura of caution and anonymity surrounded Hoyt's inquiry. A "certain priest" had contacted him with the suggestion that *NCR* might underwrite a survey to learn the attitudes of diocesan priests about the Church's law on clerical celibacy. They felt a need for caution because the American bishops frowned on any discussion of the "sacred topic."

Hoyt's circuitous inquiry came to me in May 1966, about six months after the close of the final session of the Second Vatican Council. The council had bypassed the question of a married priesthood in the Latin rite altogether. I was willing to talk with an anonymous caller and was even ready to assemble a broad survey of priests, which would include some questions about priestly celibacy. The spokesman of the anonymous group of priests was Father Frank Matthews, a St. Louis pastor and director of the Catholic Radio and Television Apostolates. After some correspondence and several telephone conversations he came for a visit to Cambridge on Sunday, July 27, 1966. By that time, I had put together a rough draft of the questionnaire, a timetable for the research project, and a cost estimate to do the work. He agreed that the celibacy question need be only one segment of the survey and took copies of the tentative questionnaire to be "tried out" among his St. Louis colleagues.

It was not until I had completed the fifth and final version of the questionnaire that I was satisfied that it authentically reflected the opinions and concerns of the rank-and-file diocesan clergy. I had pretested the questions with groups of diocesan priests in Boston and New York while Frank Matthews and his associates sent them to similar groups in Detroit, Milwaukee, and New Orleans. I had a long conference with seven priests in Chicago and a week later with nine priests in Los Angeles, where I addressed a conference of Jesuit secondary school educators. There can be no question that this inquiry schedule adequately covered the priests' main areas of concern. It was sure to reveal "what the priests are thinking."

Although I cautiously avoided confronting the issue of celibacy head-on, I recognized this "fearful topic" as a central problem for some of the priests I interviewed. They were convinced that the old rules demanding a celibate clergy were outmoded and that the Catholic Church of the Latin rite had to change. They were sure that the survey would show many diocesan priests who shared the same conviction. But what about those who conscientiously believed they had the right to marry—and some had already done so—whether or not the rules were changed?

Because of previous experience with Church officials critical of my research work, I was more cautious and less trustful in 1966 than I had been previously. Before mailing out the questionnaires on September 7, I warned everyone with whom I consulted that they keep the project confidential. I saw no reason, as I later told the Apostolic Delegate, why I should obtain approval or "authorization" of a bishop before sending an inquiry to the priests of his diocese. I wanted no preliminary prohibition that might interfere with the subject. Since Rome ordinarily moves slowly, I estimated that it would be about three months before the inevitable *miramur* (warning) would come to me. It actually arrived three months and two days later.

The growing number of Midwestern priests who were financing this research were impatiently moving into action even before the survey results were available. During Thanksgiving weekend, a determined group of twenty-seven priests met in St. Louis to establish the National Association for Pastoral Renewal (NAPR). The reason they chose this title was primarily to distract attention away from their main focus on clerical marriage. They wanted to avoid waving a "red flag" of defiance before the bishops. They were also convinced, however, that the appointment of married priests and pastors would have to involve an overhaul of the entire institution of pastoral ministry.

Several weeks later, on December 12, 1966, the *National Catholic Reporter* published my survey results under a headline proclaiming that 62 percent of the respondents favored the option of priestly marriage. This percentage was so impressive that one of the more enthusiastic priests distributed lapel buttons carrying the simple unadorned percentage. Several days before the appearance of the *NCR* article and editorial I mailed copies of a four-page overview of the findings to every diocesan bishop in the country. The "news" was now out to the American hierarchy. Only six of these bishops acknowledged receipt of the preliminary report and its covering letter. Two of them, Bishops George Ahr of Trenton, New Jersey, and Maurice Schexnayder of Lafayette, Louisiana, sent a brief note of thanks with no further comment. Constructive criticisms were offered by Bishops Romeo Blanchette of Joliet, Illinois, and Bernard Topel of Spokane, Washington. On a negative note, Bishop John Russell of Richmond, Virginia, wanted to know what good would come from this report, either for the Church or for the vocation program.

The response from the Apostolic Delegate, Archbishop Egidio Vagnozzi, is of special interest. "I have been asked," he said, "to recommend to you that in your prudence you not publish the data of this investigation without first bringing the matter to the attention of the National Conference of Catholic Bishops and the appropriate Congregation of the Holy See." I assumed that he had read the overview I sent him on December 10 and the *NCR* story on December 14, since he was prepared for the questions of a reporter in Washington, D.C., on December 21. During the interview he did not challenge the facts. Instead, he simply belittled the priests who had supplied those facts. The survey group, he said, "was composed of older priests who had not been promoted—possibly for good reason—and of young, rather immature clerics." In effect, he was saying that I had asked the wrong priests to comment about life in the priesthood and further implied that I could have heard the true story had I sampled mature clerics who had been promoted by their bishops.[2]

Even though I had deliberately limited the number of questions about the married priesthood, this immediately became the heart of the matter. Everywhere the study was called "that celibacy survey." The widespread publicity given to the celibacy question brought charges of "sensationalism" against both me and the *National Catholic Reporter*. Archbishop Hunkeler denounced me to a Kansas City newsman as a sociologist who always aims at "sensationalism and publicity." Bishop Helmsing, in whose diocese the *NCR* is published, was disturbed about my "so-called sociological study," and he exclaimed, "God save us from surveys along the lines of the Kinsey report." The episcopal outcry seemed far out of proportion to the research findings. The subsequent book, *America's Forgotten Priests*, contained only one chapter (21 out of 254 pages) dealing with the topic of married clergy.

In spite of such episcopal strictures, NAPR proceeded to survey priests in various parts of the country with various versions of my questionnaire. Priests in dioceses from Oregon to Maine wanted the bishops to open the question for discussion. In April the National Conference of Bishops authorized an in-depth study to review the entire life and work of the typical Roman Catholic priest, including the subject of celibacy. Unexpectedly, and with apparently little input from priests and prelates, Pope Paul VI, on June 23, 1967, issued his encyclical, *Sacerdotalis Caelibatus*, reaffirming the tradition of clergy celibacy.

Meanwhile, early in March 1967, the coordinating committee of the National Association for Pastoral Renewal met in New York to plan a symposium and to elect an advisory board. I was one of these advisors, together with Petro Bilaniuk, William Birmingham, Eugene Burke, Alfred McBride, John McKenzie, Thomas Neill, and John O'Brien. There was some serious soul-searching in the early summer about holding a symposium on celibacy despite the Holy Father's pronouncement on the matter. Nevertheless, planning went forward and a contract was signed with the University of Notre Dame for the use of their Center for Continuing Education. No one at this institution of moral and intellectual Catholicism questioned the propriety of discussing mandatory celibacy in the life of the modern Church under its roof. The symposium opened on Wednesday, September 6, 1967, with 211 registered participants in attendance. An invitation to the symposium had been sent to every American bishop. None appeared, although some responded with doubts about the "sincerity" of the sponsoring group.

The paper I delivered at the symposium was later published in a book edited by George Frein, *Celibacy: The Necessary Option*. In order to look at both sides of the question I selected those priests who favored a married clergy and compared them to those who favored a celibate clergy. One group approved freedom of choice to marry both before and after ordination. They also said they would marry if the Church permitted it. The contrasting group consisted of those who were against freedom of choice to marry. They also said they would not marry if given the choice.[3]

These two groups represented polar categories; a psychologist would probably conclude that they are two distinct types of personality. The opinion that Catholic priests should be allowed to marry, or not marry, is accompanied by a series of other preferences and characteristics. The contrasting generalizations may be briefly noted:

1) The proponents of a married Catholic priesthood were the most progressive respondents to the survey. They

had a high appreciation of the spirit of Vatican II, and they were impatient that the *aggiornamento* was proceeding so slowly in their diocese;

2) The survey provided partial explanations why some men were progressive and others were conservative. Generally, the progressives were better educated; they entered the seminary at a more mature age; their talents were not fully utilized; and they lacked mature, professional relations with diocesan officials;

3) The conservative element of the professional Catholic clergy belonged to another generation, both mentally and chronologically. Curates over fifty, for example, reacted conservatively to all issues in the survey, not only on the matter of celibacy; and

4) The contemporary diocesan system is geared to the continuation of a celibate priesthood. The acceptance of a married clergy would require a substantial redesign of that system, including new methods of recruiting and training seminarians as well as assigning and reassigning priests, separate dwelling units in multistaff rectories, and many other changes unforeseen and unforeseeable.

After the Notre Dame symposium I continued my interest in the activities of the NAPR but did not have time to participate in them. I attended their second symposium the following year at St. Louis University. It was here where a new organization was born, the Society of Priests for a Free Ministry (SPFM). Their "free" ministry at first meant freedom from canonical strictures, but some emphasized ministry given freely to all. They explored an ever broader concept of the ministerial profession that would include women and other hitherto nonordained persons. In 1973 they evolved further into the Fellowship of Christian Ministry (FCM), which then included non-Catholics. Finally, the group expanded again, into the Federation of Christian Ministry, which instituted a program of professional certification for the Christian ministry.

These organized efforts seemed to be getting out of hand and were drawing the resigned priests further away from the

Church and from Catholicism. Some of the members who valued orthodoxy—such as Frank Bonnike, Terrence Dosh, Thomas Durkin, and others—constituted a kind of organizational link with the early days of CORPUS, which was clearly more conventional and less aggressive than the Federation of Christian Ministry. The founders of CORPUS had been active in the Association of Chicago Priests (ACP) and were neither radicals nor rebels. Bonnike had been president of the National Federation of Priests' Councils (NFPC). By 1974, along with Frank McGrath and Bill Nemmers, Bonnike modestly referred to themselves as "facilitators" of the new group.

The beginnings of CORPUS were quiet, subdued, and unobtrusive. The members proceeded with utmost caution. They remained anonymous and initially could be reached only through a post office box in Chicago. Nevertheless, they contracted for a Gallup poll that revealed a majority of lay Catholics willing to accept a married clergy, a "discovery" I had made a decade earlier in the often-quoted "celibacy survey." Otherwise, the group established a mailing list and distributed *CORPUS Reports* six times a year. It was deliberately low key and made no demands that might antagonize the hierarchy. It was also slow to organize. Membership was at first limited to resigned priests who insisted that ordained clergy could never really lose their priesthood.

Almost in spite of itself and its quiet development of an official position, the organization attracted many Catholic supporters who were willing to pay dues. The central goal continued to be "reinstatement to active canonical ministry in the Latin rite of the Roman Catholic Church of those non-canonical priests who are qualified and ready to serve." Over the years their ranks were expanded with the declaration that "membership in CORPUS is open to all—men and women, married and single—who share our vision and mission."[4]

The men and women who were involved in the beginnings of the National Association for Pastoral Renewal as well as those who organized CORPUS faced strong opposition from the hierarchy. There were many stories of bishops who refused to process the papers for laicization or who delayed these requests even after dismissing the priest from the diocese. In some instances, even when permission to marry had been granted from Rome, the bishops insisted that the married priest must remove himself and his wife several hundred miles away from the area where he had served. In other instances, the bishop used his influence to discourage employers from hiring the resigned priest. It became increasingly difficult to make the occupational transition to nonclerical forms of employment. Further, seminary education and training did not usually prepare a man for gainful employment outside the Church.

In those early years it was not unusual for assistance to come from concerned and cooperative laypersons who were ready to supply job information and recommendations whenever possible. Washington, D.C., seemed to be, for many, an attractive location for employment. Warren Barker, a Southern Jesuit priest who resigned and married well before the Second Vatican Council, gained a reputation as a kind of "placement counselor" for job-hunting men who had exited the priesthood. He worked for three decades in the Civil Service Commission. After his death in 1988, CORPUS established the Warren Barker Memorial Fund to assist men in transition to nonclergy employment. Of course, not everybody wanted to live and work in Washington, D.C., with the result that efforts were made in most of the big cities to organize assistance for job seekers.

One of the more active groups, WEORC, was formed in Chicago in 1975 and still publishes an employment directory also called *WEORC*. Martin Hegarty and James Wilbur edited and distributed the third edition, which includes 1,850 names of men and women formerly employed in full-time church ministry. This enterprise began with a Career Day, held at Holy Trinity parish in Chicago, where a group of resigned priests and women religious sponsored and presented a seminar for job finding by men and women who were making a transition from full-time ministry. A type of Christian collegiality has developed for participants in the Chicago area, where they enjoy occasional get-togethers such as picnics, dinner-dances, retreats, and days of recollection. They keep in contact also through an intermittent newsletter called the *Word from WEORC*.[5]

The employment directory provided an opportunity for me to survey a sample of the priests listed. This was not a scientific sample of resigned priests since the men were largely from the Midwest and particularly concerned about employment. I selected names of diocesan priests who had been ordained during the fifteen-year period from 1967 to 1982 and found that seven out of ten (72 percent) belonged to CORPUS and were willing to return to the active ministry; but only four out of ten (39 percent) thought that the Holy See would *ultimately* change the current policy and approve a married priesthood. Their marital status seems of some significance to the observer. Approximately half (52 percent) reported they are in a Catholic, Church-approved marriage. Four out of ten said that their marriage was still not validated, and about one out of five (22 percent) did not bother to even request validation.

For the most part, these resigned priests did not feel estranged from the Catholic Church. They tended to keep in touch with priest friends in the diocese who had been their classmates in the seminary. Only a handful (8 percent) broke free from the clergy. When asked how they get along with their local bishop, more than half (57 percent) reported that their bishop was quite friendly toward them. In a few instances the bishop encouraged a fraternal relationship between active and inactive clergy of the diocese. Some of them associated closely and liturgically with other resigned priests and their families, and some (29 percent) regularly celebrated Mass.

Most of the men who were involved in the organized effort to obtain employment for resigned priests were also members of CORPUS. The "paperwork" began to expand, such as the production and distribution of the bimonthly *CORPUS Reports* and correspondence with the growing volume of resigned priests. All this work was done by Chicago volunteers, including the wives of the organizers. After ten years the volume became unmanageable, and a decision was reached to set up a formal organization. A national coordinator was appointed in 1984 who began to promote membership and who soon developed a listing of 244 area representatives throughout the country. In 1988 the torch was passed from the original facilitators to an eleven-member board of directors, including president, vice-president, treasurer, and secretary. Headquarters were moved from Chicago to Minneapolis, residence of the national full-time coordinator, Terrence Dosh.

The reorganization featured a network of regional coordinators around the country and the establishment of "branches" in more than seventy cities, where efforts were made to develop friendly relations with the local bishop. Meanwhile, the movement of married priests' associations was developing in Europe. In 1985, the First International Assembly of Married Priests was held in Ariccia, Italy. A large contingent of American priests and their wives attended. Several years later, in June 1988, CORPUS held its first national conference at the American University in Washington, D.C.

This national gathering represented a kind of "new birth," a transition from a loose volunteer movement into an efficiently structured organization. Terry Dosh called it a "quantum leap" in the public consciousness of CORPUS. The second national conference was held in 1989 at Columbus, Ohio, on the campus of Capital University. The next annual conference, held in 1990 at San Jose State University in California, called attention to the problem of "priestless Sundays." A retreat conference of bishops took place at nearby Santa Clara University, which provided a base for communication between resigned priests and bishops. This meeting came to the attention of the Vatican, which issued a stern message forbidding the American bishops from holding public dialogue with the members of CORPUS.

The fourth annual national conference was held at the Vista International Hotel in New York in June 1991. Cardinal O'Connor refused an invitation to speak or to lead a prayer service and forbade CORPUS the use of St. Patrick's Cathedral for a prayer vigil. Two of the major speeches were given by Protestants: theologian Harvey Cox and sociologist Dean Hoge. A prominent Catholic speaker, Margaret Steinfels, editor of *Commonweal*, severely criticized the group for celebrating a public Eucharist and holding a demonstration in front of the cathedral. Steinfels felt that it was open to question whether the publicity surrounding this conference would "postpone rather than hasten the acceptance of a married priesthood."[6]

The rejoinder came immediately from Anthony Padovano, theologian and president of CORPUS, who pointed out that the "solemn high" Mass celebrated at the conference was a demonstration of loyalty to God and the Church. "We remain open to dialogue with the American Catholic Bishops," he declared. "We invited all bishops by personal letter to the New York conference. We sent a special invitation, after this, to thirty-one bishops in the New York City area. CORPUS affirms the papacy and the bishops, but also priests and laity. We want dialogue and have pursued it energetically for seventeen years."

The fifth national conference of CORPUS was held at the Bismarck Hotel in Chicago. While the meeting could not expect official Church approval, there were no negative pronouncements from Cardinal Bernardin or other archdiocesan personnel. The conference slogan was "A Church for Our Children." Topics included marriage relations, family life, and the new spiritual development of children. Even more so than the New York conference, the influence of wives and mothers was especially strong in Chicago, as was evidenced by the group's evolving philosophy: "The women of CORPUS have helped expand its horizons. Since women have joined us, our conferences have become family celebrations in which children play a significant role. Since women have become full members, our liturgies have become emotional and spiritual experiences which remain as unforgettable as the women who plan them and lead them."

✴✲✴✲✴✲✴✲✴✲✴

CORPUS has evolved notably since its originally stated goal: the reacceptance of married resigned priests into the active ministry. The increasing participation of spouses has added another goal: the ordination of women priests. Three wives— Linda Pinto, Anne O'Brien, and Ann Bukovchik—were elected to the organization's collegial board. Some of the more conservative members fear that the promotion of women's rights might detract from and complicate the primary goal of CORPUS. Wives are anxious that their husbands be reinstated into the active priesthood; at the same time, they fear that the chances of this happening will diminish if the shortage of male priests is met with an influx of women priests.

A new opportunity for sociological research appeared when the Holy See in 1980 decided that married priests from other churches could be admitted to the Catholic priesthood without dismissing their wives. The "Pastoral Provisions," as they were called, were contained in a letter from Franjo Cardinal Seper to Archbishop John Quinn, and were released to the public on August 21, 1980. This was quietly reported in the pages of *Origins* and explained at length the following month in *America* by former Anglican priest John Jay Hughes. The headlines in the mainstream press declared "Vatican accepts married priests," but the news media soon lost interest. In the ensuing several years I failed to find any serious "think pieces," either in the Catholic press or solemn theological treatises in the serious journals.[7]

The curiosity of the news media was not fully aroused until two years later, in June 1982, when Bishop Bernard Law acutally ordained a married Episcopal priest in the "obscure" diocese of Springfield, Missouri. Father James L. Parker, who had been incardinated in the diocese of Charleston, South Carolina, said that the intention was to have a simple, quiet ceremony in an out-of-the-way place, but *"Time* and *Life,* and the TV networks, showed up to give national publicity to my ordination and first Mass." The focus of the media was not on priestly ordination, which takes place regularly all over the country, but on the unusual fact that a married man was receiving Catholic Holy Orders. One of the less kindly comments came from a Protestant columnist, writing in the *Christian Century,* that Father Parker was "one of the renegade Anglican priests who, rebelling against his Church's decision to ordain women, broke his Anglican ordination vows. For this he was honored with Roman Catholic ordination, even though he is married and has two daughters."

Although candidates for ordination ultimately had to be approved by the Vatican Congregation for the Doctrine of the Faith, their applications were processed by Bishop Law, who had been appointed as liaison in March 1981, to supervise the transfer of Episcopal married clergy to the Catholic priesthood. He soon turned over the routine paperwork to Father Parker, who gave some initial guidance to the applicants but had no ultimate authority over them once they settled into a permanent diocese. With the exception of convening a conference for these priests and their wives in Danvers, Massachusetts, in late 1984, the Boston cardinal seems to have had little direct contact with them.

It seemed obvious to me that this was a sociological situation waiting to be researched. I was determined to track down as many of the transfer priests as I could reach, to interview them and their wives, and at the same time to learn the reactions of the authorities in both churches. The first source had to be Father Parker himself, who assured me that "no one has more information than Cardinal Law and I." He received his seminary training in Alexandria, Virginia, which was said to be a puritanical, traditional, "Black Protestant" seminary with no friendly ecumenical attitude toward Rome. His friends knew him in the seminary and early priesthood by his middle name, Luther, until he switched to his first name when he became a Catholic. He was very precise and definite in his descriptions of the transfer process and willingly expressed his own views and opinions.

Parker insisted that we must never refer to these men as "converts" to the Catholic religion. Their spiritual conversion to Christ had taken place early in life. Furthermore, he saw their decision to embrace the Roman Catholic faith as a positive development of their Anglo-Catholic beliefs, an affirmation of truth—not a negative reaction—to what was happening among the Episcopalians. Nevertheless, the ordination of women to the priesthood was an ontological impossibility. "Women do not become priests when you ordain them, any more than a man can become a mother," he insisted. He wanted to drop the word "Anglican" even from the so-called Units of Common Identity that were described as "Anglican-Use" congregations in the Catholic directory.[8]

I continued to be curious why the Catholic hierarchy seemed reluctant to give public notice to this development. When I asked Father Parker in 1986 he said that the Holy See had counseled low-key publicity. "They are not hiding anything, but they don't want to wave a red flag at the groups who are urging that we do away with celibacy." There was also a vague apprehension that the Catholic laity may not take kindly to the presence of married priests. Again, the ecumenical sensitivities of Anglicans had to be preserved in order to avoid the boast of a Catholic "victory" in the competition for converts. Whatever the reasons for silence about these married priests, the fact is that very little public attention was given to them by Catholics.

In studying this phenomenon, my research strategy was to rely on personal interviews rather than on broad survey questionnaires. During the course of three years I tape-recorded 123 interviews, which fell into several categories. By far the most numerous belonged to the priests themselves, who told of their seminary experiences, their reasons for entering the Catholic Church, their tests and delays, and the way they were confronted by Catholics. Typical were the two Episcopal priests I interviewed in Atlanta in 1987.

Father Thad Rudd, married and father of three adolescent daughters, was a graduate of Sewanee Seminary in Virginia and rector of the high Anglican Church of Our Savior in Atlanta. He expressed annoyance at the Protestant trends in the Episcopal Church. "If I change, I'll be Roman before I become Protestant," he insisted. During Christmas of 1988 he and almost fifty of his parishioners were received into the Catholic Church. At that time, he was employed in the Atlanta diocesan chancery office. He had fulfilled all the Vatican requirements, but his Roman ordination was delayed until December 1991. With the former parishioners of Our Savior Church, he has established an Anglican-use community in Dunwoody, a suburb of Atlanta.

Father David Dye, a younger priest, was curate at St. Martins-in-the-Field Church in Atlanta. He often spoke of negative trends: divorce among his fellow priests, neglect of canon law, lack of a dependable *magisterium*. His earlier experience in Brussels was as a member of the Anglican-Roman International Consultation. With his family, his French-born Catholic wife and three children, he was received into the Church at Easter of 1989 and served as campus minister at the University of Georgia. After a typical delay, he was ordained to the Catholic priesthood on May 30, 1992, by Newark auxiliary Bishop Joseph Francis, S.V.D., who was substituting for the ailing Archbishop James Lyke, O.F.M.

These two convert priests were received into the Church by Atlanta archbishop Eugene Marino, S.V.D., who had to resign shortly thereafter because of alleged sexual improprieties with a local woman. All the necessary documents preparatory to the ordinations of Fathers Rudd and Dye had been filed with the Vatican authorities. The incoming Archbishop James Lyke had already given full approval. "The papers are in order," he said, "and I do not understand why Rome is taking so long to send formal approval." Long delays were characteristic in most cases.

Among the Episcopal prelates I interviewed was a former Catholic monk, Father Mark Dyer, now the bishop of the Bethlehem, Pennsylvania, diocese, who is married to a woman priest. None of his priests had switched to the Catholic faith, he reported, but, "if a priest came to me and was of that mind, I would do all in my power to support him. There's an awful lot in the Roman Church for him to benefit from: spiritually, sacramentally, traditionally, historically. If his heart was not with us, and certainly with the Roman Church, I would have no hesitancy. He would go with my love and support."[9] Another clergyman, a retired bishop who shall remain unidentified, spoke affirmatively about three men in his diocese who turned to Rome, "with my blessing and sympathy and encouragement. They were very superior men." Then he talked about his personal feelings and remarked, "had I been younger I probably would have gone that route myself. So, I'm in complete sympathy."

Among other Episcopal informants, I had long interviews with four bishops who were very sympathetic to the Roman Church but also strongly believed in their own theological faith. Two of them are diocesan bishops much involved with the Episcopal Synod of America (ESA); the other two function as bishops in the so-called Continuing Anglican Church. This foursome—unidentified—is generally at odds with the trends of American Episcopalianism. They are opposed to the ordination of women and wish to retain the 1928 *Book of Common Prayer*, preserving the traditional Anglican liturgy.[10] They are genuinely concerned about the secular trends in marriage and family life among the Episcopalians and would not allow the appointment of a divorced priest to a pastorate. A commonly shared complaint is that "pressure" is being exerted on them by the liberal forces within the Episcopal Church.

The cooperative attitude of a few Episcopalian bishops was described by some of the transfer priests. They also noted that negotiations with the Catholic bishop were known and supported by their Ordinary. "We talked about it for more than two years, and he allowed me to stay in my parish right up to the end," noted one bishop. In another instance, Father Lawrence Lossing said that he had been a priest for twenty-one years before approaching Bishop Jean Jadot, the Apostolic Delegate in Washington, D.C. He admitted that "my

Episcopal bishop knew about this for four and a half years, while it was being discussed backstage. In fact, I told him what I was doing. I offered to resign if he felt that I would compromise my loyalty to him and to the Episcopal Church. He very graciously allowed me to stay the whole time."

Not all the Episcopal bishops took kindly to the departure of their priests. One priest who told his bishop he was attracted to Catholicism received the following answer: "You're just in a mid-life crisis. You need psychoanalysis, and I'll pay for it." In another instance a priest was ordered to move out of his parsonage within forty-eight hours. In still another case, the suffragan bishop threatened angrily to bring a church trial against the defecting priest for breach of contract, but the General Convention declined to act against him. One bishop, who was apparently more bureaucratic than his position required, ordered the priest to submit immediately "a letter renouncing your ministry." Furthermore, he added, "your stipend and medical insurance will terminate at the end of the month, as will credit toward the church pension fund. This will also deny benefits to your wife and children in the event of your death." As a special "grace note," he wrote a letter to the Catholic bishop giving an unfavorable account of this priest's ministry in the Episcopal Church.[11]

Another interviewee, a man of strong faith and openly expressed convictions, is now an elderly diocesan priest who had once been an Episcopal bishop. Father Peter Watterson was a leader among those who broke away after the 1977 St. Louis Protest Meeting of Concerned Churchmen. He was then consecrated bishop into one of the groups that formed the Continuing Anglican Church. His Episcopal diocese had consisted of parishes spread throughout the Southeast, which required almost constant travel. "It was a frustrating experience to meet so much discontent among my own clergy, and the gradual moral laxity developing in the Church," he noted. "I came to the conclusion that this was really a dead end for me. My conscience told me I had to go into the Roman Catholic Church. That had been in my heart and mind for a long time." His wife and adult children, he says proudly, "are active and faithful Catholics."

What do the Episcopal clergy think of their fellow priests who decide to "swim the Tiber?" One critical Episcopal rector thinks they are something less than high-quality men. "As a matter of fact, they are not much loss to us, and they're not much of a gain to you." He thought it was just as well that they left a church with which they were dissatisfied. "They couldn't keep up with the contemporary changes in the church. More than that, they are disloyal to their most serious commitments." Another Episcopal priest did not find fault with the "renegades," but applauded their departure because it opened opportunities in the overcrowded "job market" of the Episcopal clergy. Still another judged harshly that "most of these men are nuts and we don't understand why you all took them, because we were delighted when they left."

Critical judgments of this kind do not stand up to the rigorous investigation that the transfer priests undergo. The strength of their faith and their motivation are ascertained by their sponsoring bishop, but they are also required to have sufficient knowledge in moral, dogmatic, and ascetical theology as well as in church history, Scripture, canon law, and liturgy. It was not unusual for an individual to "retake" a failed exam in any of these disciplines. One of the priests remarked that "it took me longer than I expected, and the tests were more difficult than I had anticipated." While they successfully passed the academic examinations, it is an exaggeration to say, as John Jay Hughes boasts, that "most of these men have educational attainments beyond those of all but a small minority of Catholic priests."[12]

The general opinion widely expressed in the Church is that relatively few Catholic bishops are ready to accept former Episcopal married priests. In this matter, the Vatican does not insist on compliance to the Pastoral Provisions. Very few bishops are enthusiastic about receiving these "new" priests but generously ease the transition for them nevertheless. Others avoid making a commitment by failing to answer letters addressed to them by applicants. In most cases, however, according to the testimony of the priests themselves, "they sure don't make it easy for you to become a Catholic."

There is no satisfactory explanation why the overwhelming number of diocesan Ordinaries have not accepted these transfer priests. This is a crucial point because without their bishop's cooperation nothing can happen. The religious orders are obviously not open to married priests. All these clergymen become diocesan priests, which means that they cannot even make application or begin the process of transfer until they have found a bishop willing to present their case to the Holy See. Some bishops want nothing to do with married priests; some are cautious and hesitant and feel that their fellow Catholic priests and parishioners are "not ready" for such a novelty. The provisions prevent the assignment of these priests to parishes, and they are thus not of great help in dioceses with increasing numbers of priestless parishes.

Even when a bishop expresses willingness to accept transfer married priests, the priests themselves may be reluctant to accept the insistence on a "new" ordination. I have occasionally heard of Episcopal priests who are attracted to Rome but are unwilling to admit that their Anglican ordination was "null and void." Even if they had been willing to accept "conditional" ordination, it would have been a moot point since this too was rejected by Josef Cardinal Ratzinger when he became Prefect of the Congregation for the Doctrine of the Faith. The Vatican's continued refusal to recognize the validity of Episcopal Holy Orders is cited as a barrier to those Episcopal priests who refuse to submit to "another" ordination at the hands of a Roman bishop. The insistence that Anglican ordinations are invalid is obviously an irritant to the hierarchy of the Episcopal Church with whom the Roman bishops are trying to develop good ecumenical relations.

The presence of married priests in the Catholic Church is still a novelty for both clergy and laity. The new "job" situation also tends to be a novelty for the transfers. They are often placed in work situations for which they were not trained. As Episcopal priests they had been engaged almost exclusively in parochial ministry. Yet in the Catholic diocese the greatest shortage of priests is precisely at the parish level where these priests cannot be appointed and where they cannot have direct *cura animarum* (pastoral ministry) in the parish. Consequently, many of the transfer priests are placed in jobs for which they have no experience, and thus they have to be retrained.

They obediently accept such assignments, which are a kind of secondary ministry for them. They are chaplains in penitentiaries and hospitals, teachers in elementary and secondary schools, administrators in chanceries and Catholic charities. Nevertheless, they are regularly pressed into service to celebrate

Mass and administer the sacraments in the nearest parish. An increasing minority have been appointed administrator—not pastor—of small parishes with attached mission churches. The priest and his family, however, are not allowed to move into the parish rectory, since one or more celibate priests may also be there. Having a separate household is a distinct departure from the conventional living arrangements of Catholic clergy in this country.

The comparisons I have drawn between the two categories of married Catholic priests still leave us confused. Have they gone in separate directions, or are they on parallel roads? The process of incardinating married Episcopal priests into Roman dioceses continues slowly. The fifty-third transfer priest, Father David Dye, was ordained for the Atlanta archdiocese in May 1992. Several have been appointed as parish administrators, having satisfactorily served for five years outside the pastoral ministry. The "strangeness" of married Catholic priests is wearing off in those relatively few dioceses where they minister. In this limited sense, the "experiment" is a success.

On the other hand, the resigned priests who are active in CORPUS find themselves still out of favor with the Holy See. Even their attempts to communicate with the American bishops have been discouraged by Cardinal Antonio Innocenti, Prefect of the Vatican Congregation for the Clergy, who fears that "such encounters might lend legitimacy" to their requests for reinstatement. Nevertheless, the Association for a Married Priesthood—CORPUS—grows in numbers, distributes literature, conducts frequent regional meetings, and promotes an annual national conference. No longer treated as disreputable outcasts by the Catholic laity, married priests are gradually developing friendly relations with some bishops and many fellow clergy.

11

Wives of Catholic Clergy

✖✖

When the National Council of Catholic Women held its annual conference in New Orleans in 1973, the membership voted against the Equal Rights Amendment and thus contributed to the bill's defeat in Congress after a ten-year struggle for ratification. The ERA had no direct relation to the question of equal rights for women within the Catholic Church, but the organized Catholic laywomen probably reflected the sexist attitudes of their priests and bishops. Even while the ERA debate raged, a significant Catholic voice was heard at Detroit in 1975, with the organization of the Women's Ordination Conference (WOC). During the closing liturgy, over four hundred women rose to indicate their call to ordained priesthood.[1]

Catholic feminists, among whom I include myself, have long decried the fact that women are assigned second-class citizenship in the Catholic Church. All positions of leadership in the Church are occupied by males; further they are reserved only for males who have received Holy Orders. Years of sociological research of American Catholicism have uncovered this pattern of gender inequality. The fact that I was the first professor to offer a course on religion and women at the Harvard Divinity School was one of the reasons for establishing the Fichter Fund under the auspices of the Association for the Sociology of Religion. The income of this fund supports modest research studies about women in religion.

While no one is rash enough to predict that the Holy Father will permit women's ordination in the foreseeable future, one may suggest that being the wife of a clergyman is, if nothing else, a symbolic gesture of feminine development. Little girls growing up in the Catholic Church always had to limit their choice between two vocations: either to be a nun or to get married. The single female has no sacramental status, no divine vocation—only an ambiguous role in both Church and society. Most girls opted for marriage and family, but the religious Sisterhood was the only fully professional career in the Church open to women.

The women's liberation movement has come late to traditional hierarchical religion and even later to Roman Catholicism. Everyone knows that ministers' wives have played a permanent role in the Protestant churches since the Reformation. These wives are clearly different from the ordained women ministers in the evangelical and fundamentalist churches. It is only in the aftermath of the Second Vatican Council that one finds American Catholic women pioneering in the role and status of "clergy wife." American Catholic women had never before seen this phenomenon, which is indeed a novelty among us. We are not talking here about women priests. The Vatican has consistently denied the sacrament of Holy Orders—diaconate as well as priesthood—to females.

In the several studies I have made of deacons and priests, I have become well aware of their wives and learned a great deal about them. I have made separate surveys of three categories of women who are married to Catholic clergymen, each group distinctively different:

1) The smallest category comprises the wives of fifty-three non-Catholic clergymen (mainly Episcopalian), who transferred to the Roman Catholic Church to be ordained as priests, beginning in 1982;

2) The second group consists of the wives of permanent deacons who were ordained into the ranks of Catholic clergy since 1968. They too are a "novelty" in the Catholic population although their numbers have swelled to 10,384 in the 1992 Catholic directory; and

3) The third and largest category is formed by wives of priests who have resigned from the active ministry since the Second Vatican Council, of whom there are uncounted thousands.

In the American tradition of Latin Catholicism all three types of clergy wives are a unique innovation to both married life and clergy life, but they are not of equal status within the Church. In the language of clerical stratification it is recognized that priesthood is of higher status than diaconate, and the wives of priests may be said to rank above the wives of deacons. This kind of status differential is most obvious, of course, in the Anglican Church, where the bishop's wife is more prestigious than the pastor's wife. When we include the wives of resigned Catholic priests we encounter another status differential. Since the resigned priest has been officially "reduced" to the status of laity, his wife is probably ranked below the "valid" wives of deacons and transfer priests.

The negotiations between the National Catholic Conference of Bishops and the Holy See dealt quite secretly with the matter of accepting married Episcopal clergy into the Catholic priesthood.[2] I have been unable to obtain the specific reasons advanced by the bishops for this secrecy. The procedure was carried out with great caution because the Holy See had demanded confidentiality. Through several unofficial channels I obtained the names of some of the transfer priests and through them I compiled a nearly complete list of addresses and telephone numbers. Beginning in December 1986, I had long telephone interviews with these priests. I talked also to many of their wives.

From these discussions I compiled a short questionnaire for the wives and received a 56 percent rate of cooperative response. One of the convert priests, Father James Parker, had been appointed assistant to the ecclesiastical delegate, Bishop Bernard Law of Boston, to handle the preliminary routine of acceptance of convert priests. He wrote to the wives indicating that he was "entirely displeased" that I was "badgering" them with this confidential survey. He warned them that Father Fichter "had neither asked for, nor received, permission to write you."[3]

It is an interesting and perhaps revealing fact that the spouses themselves, whether in telephone interviews or in mailed questionnaires, saw no reason for "keeping quiet" about their shift to this "novel" Catholic marital status. Indeed, they reflected a quiet enthusiasm in telling their story. Despite occasional difficulties, misunderstandings, and vexations encountered in the process of shifting to Catholicism, none of them expressed regret for having taken this momentous step.

While all these women were new to the life of a Catholic priest's spouse, they varied in the length of years they had spent as homemaker in the Anglican parsonage. Three out of ten had been an Episcopal priest's wife for less than a decade, while in the older category one-quarter had been married more than twenty years. This means that on the average they had spent 16.2 years in a clerical marriage; their ages ranged from 32 to 61. There is a range also in their amount of education; they averaged 14.8 years of schooling. One-quarter had earned graduate degrees, while another quarter had no college at all. Their education may be relative to the point at which they married. One in four married before their husband entered the seminary, one in three while he was a seminary student, and the remaining marriages occurred after graduation and ordination.

While all of them were devout Episcopalians up to the time they converted to Catholicism, less than half had been "cradle" Episcopalians. The others, in order of frequency, had been Roman Catholics and Methodists, with a scattering of Baptists, Brethren, Lutherans, and Presbyterians, before joining their husbands in the Episcopal faith. In other words, more than half had switched religion twice since childhood. While none had a vocation to the ordained priesthood, almost half the respondents thought that marriage to a priest was a "special" kind of religious or church calling.

None of these respondents was childless. Those who were still in the child-bearing years already had an average of 3.3 children apiece, while the older wives who had "completed" their families had an average of four children. With few exceptions, the children followed their parents into the Catholic Church and, in most cases, those of elementary school age were enrolled in the local parochial school. The great majority (83 percent) think of themselves mainly as wife and homemaker, but during the course of their marriage two-thirds had been gainfully employed outside the home.

Giving up one's faith commitment in order to join another church—even when both religions are as similar as Anglicanism and Catholicism—has to be an emotionally tense experience. The Episcopal Church no longer "deposes" the resigned priest, and in about half the cases the Episcopal bishops were both cooperative and cordial. Several, however, were downright hostile and were, in the words of one wife, "glad to get rid of us." One-third of the respondents said that leaving the Episcopal Church alienated them from their family and relatives. All of them, however, still maintained good personal relations with former friends and associates. But a significant minority thought it was a good idea to make a "clean break" from the Episcopal Church itself.

Much has been made of the severe hardships and financial deprivation suffered by the clerical couple who change to the Catholic faith. Most said that the experience was "tolerable" or "not so bad," but the remaining minority reported it as a "severe" hardship. In comparison with their previous economic status in the Episcopal parsonage, six out of ten wives said that their present status was lower. The same proportion resided in a house of their own (but with a mortgage to pay). For the most part, they were uncertain what benefits would accrue to wives and children in the diocesan priests' pension plan.

The wives were more than willing to explain the differences between Catholic and Episcopal customs. Unexpectedly, only one-third of them believed that diocesan priests should be allowed optional celibacy. When I tried to follow up this matter in subsequent interviews I was told: "We want what the pope wants. If he changes his teaching on celibacy, we will agree with him." Most are sure that the Holy Father will never permit the priestly ordination of women. Only one out of six is "feminist" enough to insist on the use of "inclusive" language in the liturgy. One of the more "delicate" questions I asked concerned the establishment of Anglican-use congregations. The majority responded unfavorably but said the Church should "allow" rather than "encourage" these Units of Common Identity.[4]

Since all of these priests' wives had been raised in the Christian religion, their willingness to accept the teachings of the Catholic Church did not require a major shift of beliefs. For the most part, they were not called upon to follow the usual course of "convert instructions" for persons seeking admission to the Church. They mainly had an informal conversation rather than a formal "catechesis" with the Catholic priest designated as mentor for their husband. Their previous baptism into the Episcopal Church was sacramentally valid, and the period of preparation for the Profession of Faith, which they shared with their husband, was relatively short.

After their formal admission to the Church, the applicants, both husband and wife, were required to live as lay parishioners for at least one year before the ordination of the husband. The waiting period of the wives, however, ranged from one year in some instances to more than three years in others. Strictly speaking, this delay was irrelevant to the wife's readiness for her new role. It was her husband's "papers" that took so long to be processed by the Vatican. More than half of the wives judged this waiting period to be "too lengthy" while one-third felt it was "about right." Only a few said it was "quicker than expected."

The majority of wives called this interim period a kind of "limbo" that was fraught with tension, uncertainty, and apprehension. At this point the wife's future as the spouse of a Catholic priest did not depend upon herself. Rather it was tied to the negotiations through which her husband was requesting the rescript for ordination. Fixing the date and place of the ordination was the prerogative of the diocesan bishop, who seemed to take little interest in the wife's preparedness. I asked the wives whether they were tested, examined, or interviewed by the bishop or his delegates. More than two-thirds replied that their contact was mainly through informal conversation. Only one out of four reported in-depth interviews or psychological testing.[5]

It is quite clear that these women received no training to prepare for the role of priest's wife, which contrasts greatly with the solicitous attention paid to wives of men in formation for the diaconate. This does not mean, however, that they were completely neglected or ignored. More than half noted that since their husbands were accepted into active ministry the bishop occasionally "check[ed] up" on them. They were unanimous in calling their local bishop cordial and friendly.

I asked further whether they had experienced any resentment or unfriendliness among lay Catholics. The majority reported a congenial acceptance by the laity, but in a few instances they were treated coldly by deacons' wives, by some elderly priests, and by foreign-born clergy. The majority of the respondents felt that "some celibate priests tend to be envious" of them.

I was curious to know whether, and to what extent, these "newcomers" fit into Catholic orthodoxy, what is sometimes called "thinking with the Church." They gladly made the Profession of Faith and accepted the complete credo of Catholicism. I probed beyond conventional belief and practice by inquiring about their acceptance of pastoral letters and other public statements of the NCCB. They were, of course, unanimous in their support of the prolife movement. They were not quite so ready to agree with the bishops' dislike of the Equal Rights Amendment, however. In fact, one-third of the wives expressed approval of the ERA.

"Liberal" Catholics sometimes resent these convert Episcopalians because they are said to support the conservative element of the Catholic Church. I asked the wives whether they thought that the pastoral provision couples are social and political conservatives. Two-thirds of them thought so, but they were quick to add that this was "just a guess because we hardly know them." In probing further, I found that they were only partially supportive of the NCCB social philosophy. The majority of spouses agreed on certain social issues; they opposed capital punishment, approved low-cost housing, advocated the civil rights of minorities, and supported legislation for handgun control. On the other hand, they disagreed with the bishops on various areas, including annual guaranteed family wage, nuclear deterrence, higher social welfare payments, unionization of migrant farm workers, and the defense of illegal alien immigrants.[6]

To what extent were these women entering a "strange" life situation in the role of spouse to a Roman Catholic priest? In almost all cases the husband had been a busy parish priest, and the wife was the lady of the parsonage. In the Episcopal parish they were not expected to involve themselves in the active ministry, as was the case with many Protestant ministers' wives. In their current role in the Catholic Church, the majority did not consider themselves a partner in their husband's priesthood. At the same time, they admitted there were fewer "church demands" on their time. Thus, there were reasons to believe that they were even further removed from the heart of their husband's sacerdotal work.

When I asked if their husband works harder now than he did as an Episcopal priest, their answer was ambivalent: he was a hard worker in both situations. Most of them denied that their husband had "less time for the family." The comparison may not be clear-cut because the husband had a different set of tasks. Virtually all had been parish priests in the Episcopal Church. Now their chief ministry involved nonparochial activities, such as administration, chaplaincies, and teaching.

In well over half of the cases their residence was not in the parish where their husband was called upon for "weekend supply," that is, Sunday services. As devout and dedicated Catholics, their "church work" tended to be similar to that of any other active parishioner. According to the "provisions" set by the Vatican, the priests had to wait at least five years before being assigned to the full-time and formal *cura animarum* (parish work). Several have now reached that point and have been assigned as parish administrators, and their wives have indeed become ladies of the parsonage.

Deaconesses had been ordained in the Protestant Episcopal Church since 1920 but showed no inclination to seek transfer to the Catholic faith. Even if they had considered such a conversion there was no room for deaconesses in a Church that flourished with large numbers of religious sisters and did not even ordain married males to the diaconate until the late 1960s. My interest in the diaconate formation program was whetted by a visit to Washington, D.C., in search of information about the acceptance of Episcopal priests. Monsignor Colin MacDonald introduced me to Deacon Samuel M. Taub, staff associate of the Bishops' Committee on the Permanent Diaconate.

Deacon Taub gave me a copy of the national study of the permanent diaconate, which was inaugurated in 1978 and published in 1981. One phase of this survey was a questionnaire answered by 696 wives of deacons: "Overall, the responses indicate that the wives generally support the permanent diaconate. They feel it has had a positive effect on their own spiritual and religious development, on their relationships with their husband, and on their relationship within the Church."[7] Deacon Taub was pleased with this national report and with several diocesan and regional surveys then under way. He encouraged me to research the diaconate program in my own archdiocese.

Several key persons in the New Orleans archdiocese helped with the preparation of a survey questionnaire intended to reach the wives of the local diaconate. Father Hilton Rivet was the first archdiocesan director of the program for deacon formation and shared his experiences with me. Two other persons of influence with whom I consulted were Deacon James Swiler, director of the program, and Deacon John Williams, coordinator of the Black Catholic Office of the archdiocese. The items on the short questionnaire were pretested in telephone interviews with about a dozen wives of deacons before being distributed to a total of 126 women. The archdiocesan directory for 1990 also listed the names of unmarried or widowed, retired, those on leave, and those on duty outside the diocese.

The wives were distributed into eight ordination "classes," starting with the first group in 1974 and concluding with the last group in 1989. On the average, these wives had spent 6.1 years in a diaconal relationship in addition to several years in the formation program. They ranged in age from 39 to 79 years, with the average age at 54.3 years. With few exceptions, they were middle class, and more than half had some college education. Less than 5 percent were Hispanic, and fewer than 10 percent African-American. They differed in attitude and experience, but virtually all (93 percent) agreed that they had no desire to be ordained deaconesses. If there was a single flaw in the diaconal experience on which they almost all agreed it was the negative attitudes that the parish priests had toward them and their husbands.

The preparatory, or "training" program in which the wives were urged to participate has since become longer and more elaborate. The earliest ordination classes (1974 and 1976) completed the program in two years with no preliminary process of discernment and without a semester of clinical pastoral training. In those early years relatively few (16 percent) of wives attended all, or most, of the class meetings, as compared to half of the wives in recent years. These meetings introduced the prospective candidate and his wife to the theory and practice of the diaconate.[8]

The wives must be present at every step of the discernment. They also must be screened and are conscientiously examined for their attitudes and opinions. In this way, the number of aspirants is sharply reduced during the preliminary screening process. Some are afraid of the required academic studies and drop out. Quite regularly men withdraw because their wives object to the stipulation that widowed deacons may not remarry. A further "deselection" process continues to occur, and in some years more than two-thirds of the prospective candidates are eliminated.

According to the revised Code of Canon Law (CIC 236), the formation program must last at least three years. Some of the deacons think of this as a "mini-seminary" education. The integrated program, in which the wives participate, emphasizes not only theological knowledge but also pastoral and spiritual formation. While the bishop has not made the attendance of wives mandatory, a certain degree of social pressure is brought to bear on them. They tend to make resolutions at the beginning of the three-year formation period—and fully intend to honor them—but their attendance gradually tapers off, especially if there are young children in the family. "At the time, our youngsters were still pre-school and when I could not get to class he [the husband] taped it and we listened to it together, so I heard all the classes," remarked one wife. Some of the wives feel that a father should not apply for the diaconate program if he has children still in school. Director Deacon Swiler, however, suspects that contemporary fathers have to pay more attention to teenagers than to younger children.

The wife's required public assent to her husband's diaconal ordination had in previous years been given in the midst of the ordination ceremony itself. This testimony has now been moved to a candidacy meeting prior to the ordination Mass. The wife swears a solemn oath in the presence of witnesses, in which she says: "I do hereby give my consent to this ordination in pursuance of Canon 1050 of the Code of Canon Law. I further attest that I do so with a clear understanding of the specific obligation attached to this order and with my own free will, motivated by no consideration other than the glory of God and the service of the church of the diocese. I make this agreement under oath, as I touch the Book of Sacred Scripture."[9]

All the preparatory training culminates at the ordination Mass, usually in early December of each year, when the bishop gives a final exhortation. At the Mass, which is preceeded by a spiritual retreat and a prayer vigil, the bishop stresses the significance of mutual support and cooperation and urges the women to continue sharing in their husband's ministry. He repeats what they had often already heard: that the deacon's priorities are first to wife and family, second to gainful employment, and third to the actual ministry. One wife remarked that "he made it sound so wonderful, but that's not the way it goes. For three and a half years it was diaconate first, then job, then family." This was verified by the husband who said that "if you missed a class because of your job, the excuse was acceptable, but if it was because of some family emergency, that was not an acceptable excuse."

The ordination Mass itself is a sacred experience for married couples, but in the opinion of some wives the "revised" ceremony tends to separate rather than unite the couple. In the new code, the ordination ceremony for the married permanent deacon is exactly the same as that for the celibate transitional deacon. One of the "older" wives complained that "what is happening now is that the wife is shoved aside." She described her own earlier experience: "We walked into the cathedral with our husbands and sat in the same pew with them. They were in albs, and we held the stole and dalmatics with which we vested them. At a certain point the wives stood and gave our permission publicly as part of the ceremony. When it came time to leave we formed a procession with them."[10]

All this has been changed to bring the permanent diaconate closer to the transitional diaconate. The call from the family—traditionally the wife had to be willing to accept the terms of the ordination—has been dropped; the vesting is done by a deacon or a priest. The ordination ritual is pointed specifically at the diaconal ritual, oblivious to the fact that the primary sacrament of the deacon is matrimony. Indeed, some bishops tend to downplay the matrimonial status of the couple. Other bishops have the couple renew their marriage vows at the ordination Mass in order to emphasize the fact that marriage makes the permanent deacon significantly different from the transitional deacon.

During the years of formation and training, wives were regularly encouraged to plan for their own partnership in their husband's ministry. Except for a few complaints, the wives were generally "supportive" of their deacon husbands, but there was an essential difference between supporting the diaconal ministry and actually participating in it. The liturgical assignment "to an altar" is never given to a woman. Thus, only the deacon can commit himself to the complete service of the people of God in liturgy, in word, and in charity, not his wife. In all the preparatory ceremonies, and at the ordination itself, there has never been any suggestion that the wife function in the diaconal ministry, even as a kind of surrogate deaconess.

Virtually everyone knows that permanent deacons are not ordained to the priesthood, and their wives are not ordained to the diaconate. When I asked the women if they wanted their husbands to be ordained priests, the majority (71 percent) answered negatively. Veteran wives were less negative (48 percent) than the wives of the more recently ordained (91 percent). Only a minority (19 percent) favored the priestly ordination of women. It is probably safe to say that there are not many militant feminists among these wives.

Previous studies of the permanent diaconate have revealed that the most frustrating aspect of the diaconal experience is their unsatisfactory relationship with priests.[11] A large proportion (80 percent) of wives agreed that "some priests tend to look down on deacons." One wife told sadly of the "disappointment in my husband in not being accepted as a member of the clergy and staff." Another wife admitted that she herself felt "hurt and humiliated because some priests have no compassion for deacons."

The wives were very aware of the strained relations between their husbands and the priests, and they suspected that they themselves may have been the reason. As one wife noted, "some clergy have difficulty in accepting the role of the deacon, and it is even more rare for a priest to accept the ministry of a deacon and his wife." I probed this matter further. What are the attitudes of pastors to the wives of deacons? A fairly large minority (44 percent) were convinced that pastors "really don't know how to deal with the wives of deacons."

Three out of ten (31 percent) said that pastors "fail to utilize the talents of deacons' wives." A minority (17 percent) thought that pastors would "prefer the help of celibate deacons."

It is interesting to note that the deacons and their wives find a warmer welcome from the parishioners than from the priests. Only a small minority (16 percent) felt that the parishioners were critical of them. One wife felt that she had taken on a "new identity." They sense that they are being perceived in a new way. "People who were my friends now act as if I am a completely different person," remarked one woman. In taking on the role of the deacon's wife, she is often sought out for advice and consultation. "People think I should have the answers for everything." This is not always a complaint. One wife observes, "I get the friendship and respect of our parishioners." Another appreciates the fact that "people will come to me and talk about God and ask for help in their problems. I feel that I am in a position to guide them in the direction to meet their needs." There is no question that those who have gone through the same training as their ordained husbands are often competent to give spiritual guidance to others.

The wives of resigned and noncanonical priests attract a different kind of attention from both the laity and the hierarchy. They are not as "new" as deacons' wives or as the wives of transfer priests. There have always been some "laicized" priests, but their numbers quickly increased with the large exodus of priests after the Second Vatican Council. Even when their husbands received dispensation from the priestly vows—which now seldom happens—they were supposed to make themselves "inconspicuous." The Catholic laity had to be protected from contact with a married priest and his family. My first personal acquaintance with this type of family was during my "southern parish" research in 1948. It was a secret carefully guarded by the local pastor that two of his married parishioners had obtained a rescript of "laicization" from the Holy See.[12]

Almost two decades later, in September 1967, I again encountered wives of resigned priests. They attended a symposium at the University of Notre Dame, which was sponsored by the National Association for Pastoral Renewal. The planning committee had cautiously suggested that they stay away. "What would the bishops say if the celibacy rule is ignored even before the Symposium on Clerical Celibacy took place?" they wondered. Nevertheless a few wives quietly attended with their husbands but did not publicly participate in the meetings.[13] Subsequently, several of the priests who also attended wrote about their wives in John A. O'Brien's book *Why Priests Leave*. Research studies focused on the resigned priests rather than on their wives. Psychiatrist James Gill, for example, concluded that priests who resigned and married had little hope of marital happiness since they were all so depressed.[14] The bishops' national survey of the Catholic priesthood, published in 1972, also asked no questions of priests' wives.

It was not until 1979 that the first scientific research study was made of the wives of resigned priests. The doctoral dissertation of Maureen Hendricks involved a nonrandom sampling of 451 wives who volunteered to respond and who were contracted mainly through newspaper and magazine ads. She asked about "courtship" patterns and found that 73 percent of the wives dated and 37 percent became engaged to marry while their husbands were still in the active ministry. The education of these wives was higher than women in the general population; only 34 percent were not employed outside the home. Were these women happily married? It seems that "the marriage partners were found to have significantly greater marital happiness than marriage partners in the general population." Hendricks added that "couples in which the wife was a resigned nun had greater marital satisfaction than other resigned-priest married couples."[15]

My decision to do a research project on the wives of resigned priests was a logical extension to my study of the "Pastoral Provisions." My interest increased after an extended luncheon in New Orleans with CORPUS leaders Terry and Millie Dosh. Later, I asked Martin Hegarty in Chicago to send me the latest edition of WEORK, the employment directory he and John Wilbur have edited since 1976. I sent questionnaires only to the wives of diocesan priests who had been ordained between 1967 and 1982. Two out of five had been religious sisters—most were still in the convent when they met their future mates. The husbands had been active in the priesthood for an average of 6.4 years before resigning. A majority of the women married rather promptly, most of them (84 percent) taking marriage vows within twelve months of their husband's resignation from the ministry. Up to the time of the survey, in 1990, they had been married an average of 13.6 years.

Many of the wives appeared to be living in a kind of twilight zone, where they were not quite sure of their identity as authentic Roman Catholics. About half (48 percent) had been married in a civil ceremony or by a non-Catholic minister, and there were still some (39 percent) whose marriages had not been "validated" by the Holy See. One wife said, "we were first married in 1969, but the dispensation arrived almost twenty years later, when we were married in the Church." Another remarked that, "we were married three times—once before a judge, then at home by a friend of my husband, and finally at Mass in Church."

Whatever their "official" canonical status within the Church, they refused to allow themselves to be cut off completely from the body of the faithful. Only one out of eight confessed to feeling "estranged" from the Church, and a much smaller proportion still felt alienated from their family for having "taken" a priest from his sacred ministry. They were ambivalent too about their identity as a "priest's wife." Unless they were enthusiastically involved with the CORPUS movement, they tended to say, "I married a man, not a priest." Nevertheless, a small minority felt that marriage to a priest constituted a kind of religious "calling." In general, however, they would have liked to present themselves in the simple role of normal married Catholic laywomen.[16]

Many of the wives shared the feeling that they and their husbands were under a kind of "punitive" cloud, even when there had been an "honorable discharge" from the priesthood. The degree of frustration may be measured roughly by the manner in which the Holy See responded to the petition for dispensation. Under Pope Paul VI, the release process went more smoothly than it did after his death in 1978. When I compared the men who left the active ministry before 1975 with those who resigned later, I found that they were more than twice as likely (79 percent v. 36 percent) to have received the dispensation from the Vatican.

One of the wife respondents angrily returned her survey questionnaire, on which she had written, "I do not consider myself the 'wife of a priest' any longer (thanks to your Roman

Catholic bishops). Therefore, I'm not inclined to take part in this senseless survey." Very few wives leave the Church so completely, but some do have a feeling of being "unwanted." They have little contact with the clergy and even less with the bishop. Few are active in CORPUS or know little about it. The tendency of these wives—and their husbands—is to drop out of the existing loose network of resigned priests. Those who have no expectation that the Vatican will change the celibacy rules prefer to be "left alone." Marital anonymity, for example, is the preference of the lady who expressed dislike of "having to 'hide' knowledge of our background at times; not being able to be open about a priest-husband for fear of judgment about our right, or ability, to function within the Church."

Although the majority of the wives attend Mass "often," only a minority take part in the life of the parish community. In some instances, the local pastor does not allow such participation of either wife or husband or has been told by the bishop not to "give them communion." In other instances, especially in smaller parishes, some of the wives (24 percent) act as extraordinary ministers of the Eucharist, as lectors in the liturgy (30 percent), or as teachers in the Confraternity of Christian Doctrine (23 percent). A frustrating experience is to attend Sunday service in a "priestless" parish, where a deacon or religious sister conducts the service, gives a homily, and distributes communion.

While a small proportion of the wives admitted that they stay aloof from the local clergy, a larger minority (31 percent) insisted that the bishop wants nothing to do with them. As a matter of fact, the collective reaction of bishops has been highly inconsistent, ranging from cold exclusion and virtual ostracism in some dioceses to cordial and cooperative relations in others. "It's good to know that not all of the bishops are antagonistic," said one wife. "Our bishop invites us to an annual dinner and social evening. He is sympathetic and cooperative and hires as many married priests as he can place in the diocese." In another diocese, the bishop himself issued invitations to a discussion meeting between active and resigned priests but found few "takers" among the active priests. As the "pinch" of the clergy shortage becomes more insistent the attitudes of some bishops have begun to mellow.

When I asked the wives what they liked most and what they liked least about being married to a priest, I received mixed replies. Although most of them wanted to concentrate on this *husband* rather than on this *priest*, one enthusiastic wife said that "priests make the best husbands." Another went even further and boasted that, "if someone asked me to identify God, I would point to my husband." Marital devotion seems to be expressed more often in terms of spiritual appreciation than of romantic attachment. The husband's religious character is admired by his wife. "The best thing in being married to my husband," remarked one woman, "is that he is a kind, caring, loving, person, but his priesthood is *not* responsible for that."

On the negative side there is the rare wife with a nagging "conscience problem" when recalling the hurt she caused her pious parents by marrying a priest. None of them expressed contrition or said that what they did was the "wrong thing" to do. Yet there is the occasional twinge of guilt as a reminder that the rules have been broken and that it is sometimes better if people don't know who you are. "We found it better just to slip away from our families and friends," confessed one wife. "We were lucky to get a new start where people don't know us, and we just live day by day as ordinary Catholics." It should be reiterated that such negative reactions are expressed by only a small number of wives.

Some of the wives, however, are forthright enough to find fault with the seminary training and clerical experiences that have made marriage and family difficult for their spouse. They believed that living in an exclusively male world for so many years had blunted their husband's sensitivity to the needs of wife and children. It should be noted also that many of the wives who had been nuns for ten or fifteen years had developed characteristics that were nonmarital. That is, they had lived in the midst of a "female culture" that was in no way preparatory for marriage. Having completed the novitiate and convent training necessary for a life of virginity, they were not ready to play the role of the happily married wife.

One wife ruefully admitted that "after seventeen years of religious life it was like a shock to get married. Having three children in my thirties was the last thing I could have anticipated while in the convent." It is sometimes said that a man "never forgets" he is a priest. However, more than one married priest has said that his wife has "never forgotten that she was a nun." The behavior patterns of long years in the celibate convent do not easily wear off. The regularity of daily living, the attention to details, and the "fussiness" of the convent schedule are not the best preparation for marriage and family life.

The earlier strictures placed on married priests and their wives appear to have gradually subsided. One of the reasons may be that there are now so many who simply "refuse to disappear." Since they spend their daily lives as "practicing" Catholics, many refuse to separate themselves from the dedicated ministry. Where the diocesan personnel are friendly, it is no longer "unheard of" that a married priest is hired to teach in a Catholic college or high school or to work in diocesan institutions, even the chancery office. Their presence is felt in Catholic charities, in drug and alcohol rehabilitation programs, and in mental health and family counseling centers. Similarly, many of the wives offer their services to Catholic hospitals and in the fields of social work, child care, education, and other helping ministries. Within the Catholic Church itself, more than a third of the wives (37 percent) and almost half of the husbands (47 percent) are engaged in all varieties of the helping apostolate.

What seems potentially significant for the future of a growing ministry is the tacit approval by bishops of married priests and their wives. More than a third of the wives who answered the survey said that the bishops they knew were quietly and privately providing job opportunities for them. Now they apply for jobs that had normally been held by the clergy or by religious sisters. What had once been barely "allowed" has now become routine in the face of personnel shortages in some dioceses. Married clergy couples are supplanting the very people whose resignations had created the shortage of priests and religious in the first place.

Afterthoughts

❋❋❋

That's the end of my research stories about these good works but not the end of the good works themselves. The fact that I published the "findings" in articles and books on most of these subjects does not mean that the episodes are closed. The Catholic charismatics and the Unificationists are not slowing down in their zeal for conversions. The Jesuit educational system, struggling with secular humanism, is not slackening its efforts. Although the *National Catholic Reporter* is again down to 48,197 subscribers, it proceeds ahead in its excitable muckraking fashion.

The Stillman professorship flourishes at the Harvard Divinity School, even after the death of Father George McRae. The chair is now occupied by Elisabeth Schussler Fiorenza, an accomplished theologian. The organized movements for a married priesthood and for the priestly ordination of women are gathering strength and expanding significantly. Concern about clergy health seems to be increasing as the priest population grows older.

In a sense all of these good works are integral parts of ongoing Catholic American history, adventures about which much more will be studied and published. Each of them is a slice of social life that is open to further sociological study and interpretation but by someone else, not me. As I move quietly among the world of senior citizens, I want to look closer at holiness as exemplified by the good works of a free person of color, Henriette Delille, who founded the Sisters of the Holy Family when Louisiana was still a slave state. Her life shall be my final work, whose cause for canonization is likely to be more complicated than any of the other good works described in this volume.

Pleading a cause involves a one-sided search for facts that is designed to bolster your case and is quite different from the "value-free" search for *all* the facts. I do not intend to paint a balanced portrait of Henriette. I need not, for example, argue against any devil's advocate, such as those who in the "old days" obstructed the process of canonization. To use a religious analogy, in January 1983, Pope John Paul II dispensed with the kind of court procedures in which adversaries cross-examined each other in order to secure the reputation of being the servant of God.

Rather my intention is to search for evidence that supports my view that Henriette Delille ought to have her name enscribed on the roster of canonized saints of the Roman Catholic Church. The hypothesis I want to substantiate is that the racist hostility, bigotry, and discrimination heaped upon her and her companions constituted for them the "road to sanctity." Biographer Sister Audrey Detiege said "these Negro nuns have had to endure oppression and prejudices suffered by every other member of the black race." She added also that "the Sisters of the Holy Family, being of African descent, have been the *least* among nuns of the City of New Orleans, as they labored among God's least people, the black race."[1]

Slavery still existed in Louisiana during Henriette's lifetime (1812–62). All the sisters of the Holy Family were free women of color, but they continued to live subject to the racist discrimination of the culture, of the legal system, of the civil authorities, and of the Catholic Church itself as evidenced by the behavior of its bishops, priests, and congregations of religious sisters. They were all racists. What had to be a source of heavy and continual frustrations was the fact, amounting to a sacred doctrine, that no black girl was good enough to be a religious sister and no black boy worthy to be a seminarian.

It will not be easy to make a saint out of Henriette. The formalities of the canonization process demand proof of her living holiness, but hardly any documents exist—no letters, no notebooks, no diaries. Her *fama sanctitatis* consists of a reputation passed down in the oral history of the sisters. The second requirement is the performance of a miracle or two, which would indicate that she hears our earthly petitions and passes them on to God. You would have to believe the "prayer card" stamped with the *imprimatur* of New Orleans archbishop Francis Schulte on it as an assurance that she is in the presence of God: "We place our petition before you and earnestly request that you intervene for us with out heavenly Father."

No matter how persuasive the evidence I uncover for Henriette's canonization, the final decision has to come from the Holy Father. Only the pope can canonize someone, and he need not explain his reasons for doing so. Still, it should be time for this African-American female Creole to make the list.

Notes

Introduction

[1] Joseph H. Fichter, *One-Man Research: Reminiscences of a Catholic Sociologist* (New York: John Wiley and Sons, 1973).

[2] *Miramur* refers to a scolding or warning by Church authorities "shocked" by specific behavior.

[3] Joseph H. Fichter, *Wives of Catholic Clergy* (Kansas City, Mo.: Sheed and Ward, 1992).

[4] Catherine Clarke, *The Loyolas and the Cabots* (Boston: Ravengate, 1950).

[5] See Joseph H. Fichter, "Pastoral Ministry to the Sick, Suffering and Dying," *Pastoral Life* 27, no. 5 (May 1978): 2–8.

[6] Edward O'Connor, *The Pentecostal Movement in the Catholic Church* (South Bend, Ind.: Ave Maria Press, 1971).

[7] Joseph H. Fichter, "First Black Students at Loyola University: A Strategy to Obtain Teacher Certification," *Journal of Negro Education* (Fall 1987): 535–49.

[8] Discussed in my keynote address, "Value Outcome of Catholic Higher Education," in *Value Development in the University Classroom*, ed. Daniel Ross (Taiwan: Fu Jen University, 1992), 9–33.

[9] "Fichter Survey–Implications and Interpretations," *National Catholic Reporter*, January 11, 1967, 3 and 6.

[10] Joseph H. Fichter, "Heirs of the Kingdom?" *Commonweal*, July 12, 1991, 432–34.

Chapter 1

[1] Catherine Clarke, *The Loyolas and the Cabots* (Boston: Ravengate, 1950).

[2] Joseph H. Fichter, "Integrative Functions of Metropolitan Religion," *Harvard Divinity Bulletin* 28 (Spring 1964): 73–83.

[3] Raymond Schroth, "And Get Back A Man," *America* (October 1, 1966): 382–84.

[4] *Gaudium et Spes* was the final document issued by the Second Vatican Council, dated December 7, 1965.

[5] Joseph H. Fichter, "Catholic Professors on the Secular Campus," *America* (March 11, 1966): 318–23.

[6] PECUSA (Protestant Episcopal Church) was abandoned as the church's title at the 1979 general convention. See Joseph H. Fichter, *The Pastoral Provisions: Married Catholic Priests* (Kansas City, Mo.: Sheed and Ward, 1989), chap. 10, "Protestant Episcopal to Anglican Catholic."

[7] Mary Daly, *Beyond God the Father: Toward a Philosophy of Women's Liberation* (Boston: Beacon Press, 1985).

[8] The SDS strike was reported in detail in the *Harvard Alumni Bulletin*, vol. 27, no. 11 (April 28, 1969): 17–47.

[9] The strike of the students in OBU (Organization for Black Unity) was reported in the *Harvard Bulletin*, vol. 72, no. 6 (January 5, 1970): 13–20.

Chapter 2

[1] See Eddie Doherty, *Matt Talbot* (Milwaukee, Wis.: Bruce, 1953).

[2] John Doe (Ralph Pfau), *Prodigal Shepherd* (Indianapolis, Ind.: SMT Guild, 1958).

[3] Joseph H. Fichter, "Priests and Alcohol," *Homiletic and Pastoral Review* (August 1976): 10–21.

[4] Joseph H. Fichter, "Incidence of Clergy Alcoholism," in *Rehabilitation of Clergy Alcoholics: Ardent Spirits Subdued* (New York: Human Sciences Press, 1982), 23–26.

[5] Joseph H. Fichter, "Alcohol Addiction: Priests and Prelates," *America* (October 22, 1977): 258–60.

[6] Bishops' Committee on Priestly Life and Ministry, *Recommendations and an Enquiry about Alcoholism among Catholic Clergy*, Washington, D.C.: U. S. Catholic Conference, 1978.

[7] A description of "the Incomparable Sister Ignatia" appears in *Alcoholics Anonymous Comes of Age* (New York: A.A. World Services, 1957), 7, 8, 143, 206. See also Mary C. Darrah, *Sister Ignatia: Angel of Alcoholics Anonymous* (Chicago: Loyola University Press, 1992).

[8] See chap. 9, "Liberal Catholic Journalism."

[9] Joseph H. Fichter, "Spirituality, Religiosity and Alcoholism," *America* (May 21, 1977): 458–61.

[10] The A.A. Fifth Step is to admit humbly to another person "the exact nature of his faults." See *Twelve Steps and Twelve Traditions* (New York: A.A. World Series, 1952).

Chapter 3

[1] This is attributed to Warren Farrell in *The Liberated Man* (New York: Random House, 1975).

[2] This "Afterword," pp. 77–84, should be read as a complete refutation of the unsubstantiated "Preface" that appears on pp. 3–7.

[3] For comparable data, see Ronald Wilson and Jack Elinson, "National Survey of Personal Health Practices and Consequences," *Public Health Reports*, vol. 96, no. 3 (May–June 1981): 218–25.

[4] Compare the earlier study by Haitung King and John Bailar, "The Health of the Clergy: A Review of Demographic Literature," *Demography*, vol. 6, no. 1 (February 1969): 27–43.

[5] Compare Joseph H. Fichter, "Incidence of Clergy Alcoholism," in *Rehabilitation of Clergy Alcoholics: Ardent Spirits Subdued* (New York: Human Sciences Press, 1982), 23–26.

[6] See Joseph H. Fichter, "The Myth of Clergy Burnout," *Sociological Analysis*, vol. 45, no. 4 (Winter 1964): 373–82.

[7] Joseph H. Fichter, "Candidates for Burnout," in *The Health of American Catholic Priests* (Washington, D.C.: U.S. Catholic

Conference, 1985), 52–56. See also Joseph H. Fichter, "Life Style and Health Status of American Catholic Priests," *Social Compass*, vol. 34 (1987): 539–48.

[8] Joseph H. Fichter, "Cranky Old Priests," *Church* (Fall 1986): 34–35.

[9] Joseph H. Fichter, "The Dilemma of Priest Retirement," *Journal for the Scientific Study of Religion*, vol. 24, no. 1 (March 1985): 101–104.

[10] *Christus Dominus*, the council document on the Office of Bishops, notes that bishops "should offer their resignation" (art. 21) and accept the resignation of pastors (art. 31) when unable to do their work.

Chapter 4

[1] Joseph H. Fichter, *Rehabilitation of Clergy Alcoholics: Ardent Spirits Subdued* (New York: Human Sciences Press, 1982).

[2] Joseph H. Fichter, *Religion and Pain: The Spiritual Dimensions of Health Care* (New York: Crossroad, 1981).

[3] Joseph H. Fichter, *Healing Ministries: Conversations on the Spiritual Dimensions of Health Care* (Mahwah, N.J.: Paulist Press, 1986).

[4] The most frequent complaint concerned management reluctance to recognize union organization of nurses and nonprofessional workers.

[5] The sisters also operate Our Lady of the Lakes University in San Antonio, Texas.

[6] Joseph H. Fichter, "Pastoral Care in Catholic Hospitals," *Homiletic and Pastoral Review* (April 1980): 32, 50–56.

[7] Joseph H. Fichter, "Youth in Search of the Sacred," in *The Social Impact of New Religious Movements*, ed. Bryan Wilson (New York: Rose of Sharon, 1981), 21–42.

[8] Dennis E. Saylor, *And You Visited Me* (Medford, Mass.: Morse Press, 1979).

[9] Joseph H. Fichter, *The Holy Family of Father Moon* (Kansas City, Mo.: Leaven Press, 1985).

[10] Elsewhere in Maine, the Catholic Church operates three hospitals: Mercy Hospital in Portland, St. Joseph's in Bangor, and St. Mary's Medical Center in Lewiston.

Chapter 5

[1] Mary Jo Nietz, *Charisma and Community* (New Brunswick, N.J.: Transactions, 1987).

[2] Joseph H. Fichter, "Parallel Conversions: Charismatics and Recovered Alcoholics," *Christian Century*, vol. 93 (February 18, 1976): 148–50.

[3] Joseph H. Fichter, *Autobiographies of Conversion* (Lewiston, N.Y.: Mellen Press, 1987), 5.

[4] See Patti Mansfield, *As By A New Pentecost, The Dramatic Beginning of the Catholic Charismatic Renewal* (Steubenville, Ohio: Franciscan University Press, 1992).

[5] Killian McDonnell, in *New Covenant* (September 1973): 12.

[6] Reference is to the council document *Lumen Gentium* (art. 9).

[7] Joseph H. Fichter, "Liberal and Conservative Catholic Pentecostals," *Social Compass*, vol. 21 (Spring 1974): 303–10.

[8] Joseph H. Fichter, "The Catholic Laity and the Charismatic Renewal, Is This the Reformation?" *Thought* (September 1976): 123–34.

[9] See Joseph H. Fichter, "Women in Charismatic Renewal," *National Catholic Reporter*, February 13, 1973, 9 and 11–13.

[10] David Wilkerson, "Ministration or Ministry," *New Covenant* (August 1973): 14–15.

[11] J. Massingberd Ford, *The Pentecostal Experience* (Paramus, N.J.: Paulist Press, 1970).

Chapter 6

[1] Joseph H. Fichter, "First Black Students at Loyola University: A Strategy to Obtain Teaching Certification," *Journal of Negro Education* (Fall 1987): 535–49.

[2] Joseph H. Fichter, "Shelter for the Elderly Poor," *America* (February 1, 1986): 68–71.

[3] Sister Francis Borgia Hart, *Violets in the King's Garden* (New Orleans: Privately published, 1976), 122, describes the work of the sisters after Hurricane Betsy.

[4] Sister Sienna Marie Braxton, "Lafon Child Development Center," in *The Greatest Gift of All*, ed. Peter Clark (New Orleans: Foundation Press, 1992), 106f.

[5] Sister M. Boniface Adams, "The Gift of Religious Leadership: Henriette Delille and the Foundation of the Holy Family Sisters," in *Cross, Crozier and Crucible*, ed. Glenn Conrad (New Orleans: Archdiocese of New Orleans, 1993), 360–74.

[6] Father Cyprian Davis was professor of church history at St. Meinrad School of Theology, Jasper, Indiana.

[7] *Placage* refers to an illegal and nonsacramental agreement to live together.

[8] Joseph H. Fichter, "A Saintly Person of Color," *America* (February 29, 1992): 156f.

[9] H. E. Sterkx, *The Free Negro in Antebellum Louisiana* (Rutherford, N.J.: Fairleigh-Dickinson University, 1972), 69f.

[10] E. Franklin Frazier, *The Free Negro Family* (Nashville, Tenn.: Fisk University Press, 1932).

[11] See "Foreign Missions," in Peter Clark, ed., *The Greatest Gift of All*, 82f.

Chapter 7

[1] Paul Montgomery, *New York Times*, August 1, 1982.

2 John Lofland, *Doomsday Cult: A Study of Conversion, Proselytization, and Maintenance of Faith* (Englewood Cliffs, N.J.: Prentice Hall, 1984). Although not identified as such by Lofland, the Doomsday Cult was the first Unification group in the United States.

3 Joseph H. Fichter, *Autobiographies of Conversion* (Lewiston, N.Y.: Mellen Press, 1987).

4 Douglas Lenz, "Twenty-two Months as a Moonie," *LCA Partners* (February 1982): 12–15.

5 Joseph H. Fichter, ed., *Alternatives to American Mainline Churches* (New York: Rose of Sharon Press, 1983).

6 For an explanation of the ecclesial structure of the Unification Church, see chap. 6, "The Family of God," in Joseph H. Fichter, *The Holy Family of Father Moon* (Kansas City, Mo.: Leaven Press, 1985), 93–110.

7 Andrew Wilson, ed., *The Future of the World: Scholars View the Thought of Reverend Moon* (New York: International Cultural Foundation, 1987).

8 See chap. 7, "Social Factors of Ecumenism," in Joseph H. Fichter, *A Sociologist Looks at Religion* (Wilmington, Del.: Michael Glazier, 1988), 123–37.

9 Joseph H. Fichter, "Married Priests and Ecumenism," *The Ecumenist* (January–February 1988): 26–30.

10 See chap. 12, "Catholic Sisterhoods: Tradition and Modernity," in Joseph H. Fichter, *A Sociologist Looks at Religion* (Wilmington, Del.: Michael Glazier), 210–22.

11 Carleton Sherwood, *Inquisition: The Persecution and Prosecution of the Rev. Sun Myung Moon* (Washington, D.C.: Regnery Gateway, 1991), 3.

12 Ibid., 378.

13 Susan Elan, "Jesuit in the Moonlight," *Fairfield County Advocate*, August 20, 1992, 7.

[14] *Moonwatch*, May 31, 1993, vol. 1, no. 2, 1.

Chapter 8

[1] Compare chap. 6, "The Education of Character," in John W. Donohue, *Jesuit Education* (New York: Fordham University Press, 1963), 159–85.

[2] Joseph H. Fichter, *Graduates of Predominantly Negro Colleges: Class of 1964* (Washington, D.C.: U.S. Government Printing Office, 1967).

[3] See chap. 1, "The Quest for Facts," in Joseph H. Fichter, *Send Us A Boy—Get Back A Man* (Washington, D.C.: Jesuit Educational Association, 1966), 1–19.

[4] The Donohue study stayed on the level of exhortation without questioning the students about their moral and ethical values; see Donohue, *Jesuit Education*, 168–75.

[5] See chap. 6, "Making Better Christians," in Joseph H. Fichter, *Jesuit High Schools Revisited* (Washington, D.C.: Jesuit Educational Association, 1969), 89–107.

[6] Raymond Schroth, "And Get Back a Man," *Commonweal*, January 30, 1970, 32–33.

[7] See "Introduction," in Joseph H. Fichter, *Loyola Students and Their Values* (New Orleans: Loyola University, 1984), 1–7.

[8] Dean R. Hoge, *Commitment on Campus: Changes in Religion and Values Over Five Decades* (Philadelphia: Westminster, 1974).

[9] Daniel Ross, "Development of Values in Asian Universities," in *Value Development in the University Classroom*, ed. Daniel Ross (Taiwan: Fu Jen University, 1992), 104–117.

[10] Ibid., "Values Outcome of Catholic Higher Education," 9–33.

[11] Ibid., "Where Do We Go From Here?" 461–71.

Chapter 9

[1] Joseph H. Fichter, *America's Forgotten Priests: What They Are Saying* (New York: Harper and Row, 1968). They were so named

by Bishop Stephen Leven, who observed that the Second Vatican Council completely ignored curates.

[2] Ibid., chap. 3, "The Priest-Bishop Relationship," 52–70.

[3] See "That Celibacy Survey," *America* (January 21, 1967): 92–94.

[4] This was a preliminary to the publication of the encyclical *Humanae Vitae*, which instituted continuing arguments about contraception.

[5] Robert Hoyt, ed., *The Birth Control Debate* (Kansas City, Mo.: NCR Publication, 1969).

[6] Robert Burns is the successful long-term publisher of the magazine *U. S. Catholic*.

[7] Martin Marty, professor of history at the University of Chicago, was the Lutheran "ecumenical" member of the NCR board.

[8] Albert Outler's "response" to the *Dogmatic Consitution of the Church (Lumen Gentium)* appears in Walter Abbott, ed., *The Documents of Vatican II* (New York: America Press, 1966), 102–106.

[9] Notice had been taken by Charles Westoff and Larry Bumpass, "Revolution in Birth Control Practices of United States Roman Catholics," *Science*, vol. 179 (January 1973): 41–44.

Chapter 10

[1] Joseph H. Fichter, *The Pastoral Provisions: Married Catholic Priests* (Kansas City, Mo.: Sheed and Ward, 1989).

[2] Archbishop Egidio Vagnozzi made these remarks at a Washington, D.C., press conference on December 21, 1966.

[3] Joseph H. Fichter, "Sociology and Clerical Celibacy," in George H. Frein, ed., *Celibacy: The Necessary Option* (New York: Herder and Herder, 1968), 102–122.

[4] *CORPUS Directory*, edited by national coordinator Terrence Dosh, was published June 1990. It lists members and their wives and children.

[5] Joseph H. Fichter, *Wives of Catholic Clergy* (Kansas City, Mo.: Sheed and Ward, 1992), 114–32.

[6] Margaret Steinfels, "Are Politics of Change Fracturing the Church?" *Origins* (July 18, 1991): 137–43. Reply by Anthony Padovano, "Married Priests and Eucharistic Celebrations," 143–44, appears in the same issue.

[7] James Parker, "A Married Catholic Priest?" in Dan O'Neill, ed., *The New Catholics* (New York: Crossroad, 1987).

[8] There are two distinct provisions: the first refers to acceptance and ordination of individual Anglican priests; the second to a special privilege granted to groups that are allowed to retain their Anglican liturgy and customs. See Joseph H. Fichter, "Parishes for Anglican-Usage," *America* (November 14, 1987): 354–57.

[9] See Fichter, *Pastoral Provisions*, 61.

[10] Joseph H. Fichter, "Blaming Women Priests: A Note on the Anglican Split," *Church* (Winter 1987).

[11] See Mary V. Dally, *Married to a Catholic Priest: A Journey in Faith* (Chicago: Loyola University Press, 1988), 92.

[12] For questions regarding their tests of "academic readiness," see Fichter, *Pastoral Provisions*, 72f.

Chapter 11

[1] For this new role, see Ruth A. Wallace, *They Call Her Pastor* (Albany, N.Y.: State University Press, 1992).

[2] Joseph H. Fichter, "Rome Welcomes Married Priests," *Commonweal,* March 25, 1988, 177–80.

[3] Joseph H. Fichter, *Wives of Catholic Clergy* (Kansas City, Mo.: Sheed and Ward, 1992), *xi*.

[4] Joseph H. Fichter, "Parishes for Anglican-Usage," *America* (November 14, 1987): 354–57. Reprinted in *Catholic Digest* (May 1988): 94–97.

[5] Joseph H. Fichter, *The Pastoral Provisions: Married Catholic Priests* (Kansas City, Mo.: Sheed and Ward, 1989), 64–66.

[6] Ibid., 58–60.

[7] *Permanent Deacons in the United States* (Washington, D.C.: United States Catholic Conference, 1985).

[8] Marie Garon, "New Role for Women—Deacon's Wife," *Diaconate Magazine* (September–October 1985): 9–11.

[9] Fichter, *Wives of Catholic Clergy*, 81.

[10] Ibid., 82.

[11] U.S. Bishops, "Partners in the Mystery of Redemption," *Origins* (April 21, 1988): para. 122.

[12] Joseph H. Fichter, *Southern Parish: Dynamics of a City Church* (1951; New York: Arno Press, 1978).

[13] George H. Frein, ed., *Celibacy the Necessary Option* (New York: Herder and Herder, 1968).

[14] James Gill, "Despondence: Why We See It in Priests," *Medical Insight* (December 1969): 31–32.

[15] Maureen Hendricks, *A Study of the Marriages and Marital Adjustment of Resigned Roman Catholic Priests and Their Wives*, unpublished doctoral dissertation (Greeley, Colo.: University of Northern Colorado, 1979).

[16] See Fichter, chap. 7, "Wives of Resigned Priests," in *Wives of Catholic Clergy*, 114–32.

Afterthoughts

[1] Sister Audrey Detiege, *Henriette Delille: Free Woman of Color* (New Orleans: Privately published, 1976).

Bibliography

Abbott, Walter, ed. *The Documents of Vatican II*. New York: America Press, 1966.

Bishops' Committee on Priestly Life and Ministry. *Recommendations and an Enquiry about Alcoholism among Catholic Clergy*. Washington, D.C.: U.S. Catholic Conference, 1978.

Clark, Peter, ed. *The Greatest Gift of All*. New Orleans: Foundation Press, 1992.

Clarke, Catherine. *The Loyolas and the Cabots*. Boston: Ravengate, 1950.

Conrad, Glenn, ed. *Cross, Crozier and Crucible*. New Orleans: Archdiocese of New Orleans, 1993.

Dally, Mary V. *Married to a Catholic Priest: A Journey in Faith*. Chicago: Loyola University Press, 1988.

Daly, Mary. *Beyond God the Father: Toward a Philosophy of Women's Liberation*. Boston: Beacon Press, 1985.

————. *The Church and the Second Sex: Including the Feminist Postchristian*. Boston: Beacon Press, 1985.

D'Antonio, William, and Joan Aldous, eds. *Families and Religion, Conflict and Change in Modern Society*. Beverly Hills, Calif.: Sage, 1983.

Darrah, Mary C. *Sister Ignatia: Angel of Alcoholics Anonymous*. Chicago: Loyola University Press, 1992.

Detiege, Sister Audrey. *Henriette Delille: Free Woman of Color*. New Orleans: Privately published, 1976.

Doe, John (Ralph Pfau). *Prodigal Shepherd*. Indianapolis, Ind.: SMT Guild, 1958.

Doherty, Eddie. *Matt Talbot*. Milwaukee, Wis.: Bruce, 1953.

Donohue, John W. *Jesuit Education.* New York: Fordham University Press, 1963.

Farrell, Warren. *The Liberated Man.* New York: Random House, 1975.

Fichter, Joseph H., ed. *Alternatives to American Mainline Churches.* New York: Rose of Sharon Press, 1983.

Fichter, Joseph H. *Social Relations in the Urban Parish.* Chicago: University of Chicago Press, 1954.

———. *Parochial School.* South Bend, Ind.: University of Notre Dame Press, 1958.

———. *Religion as an Occupation.* South Bend, Ind.: University of Notre Dame Press, 1961.

———. *Priest and People.* New York: Sheed and Ward, 1965.

———. *Send Us a Boy—Get Back a Man.* Washington, D.C.: Jesuit Educational Association, 1966.

———. *Graduates of Predominantly Negro Colleges: Class of 1964.* Washington, D.C.: U.S. Government Printing Office, 1967.

———. *America's Forgotten Priests: What They Are Saying.* New York: Harper and Row, 1968.

———. *Jesuit High Schools Revisited.* Washington, D.C.: Jesuit Educational Association, 1969.

———. *Sociology.* 2nd ed. Chicago: University of Chicago Press, 1971.

———. *One-Man Research: Reminiscences of a Catholic Sociologist.* New York: John Wiley and Sons, 1973.

———. *Organization Man in the Church.* Cambridge, Mass.: Schenkman, 1974.

———. *The Catholic Cult of the Paraclete.* New York: Sheed and Ward, 1975.

———. *Southern Parish: Dynamics of a City Church.* Rev. ed. New York: Arno Press, 1978.

———. *Religion and Pain: The Spiritual Dimensions of Health Care.* New York: Crossroad, 1981.

———. *Rehabilitation of Clergy Alcoholics: Ardent Spirits Subdued.* New York: Human Sciences Press, 1982.

———. *Loyola Students and their Values.* New Orleans: Loyola University, 1984.

———. *The Health of American Catholic Priests.* Washington, D.C.: U. S. Catholic Conference, 1985.

———. *The Holy Family of Father Moon.* Kansas City, Mo.: Leaven Press, 1985.

———. *Healing Ministries: Conversations on the Spiritual Dimensions of Health Care.* Mahwah, N.J.: Paulist Press, 1986.

———. *Autobiographies of Conversion.* Lewiston, N.Y.: Mellen Press, 1987.

———. *A Sociologist Looks at Religion.* Wilmington, Del.: Michael Glazier, 1988.

———. *The Pastoral Provisions: Married Catholic Priests.* Kansas City, Mo.: Sheed and Ward, 1989.

———. *Wives of Catholic Clergy.* Kansas City, Mo.: Sheed and Ward, 1992.

Ford, J. Massingberd. *The Pentecostal Experience.* Paramus, N.J.: Paulist Press, 1970.

Frazier, E. Franklin. *The Free Negro Family.* Nashville, Tenn.: Fisk University Press, 1932.

Frein, George, H., ed. *Celibacy: The Necessary Option.* New York: Herder and Herder, 1968.

Hart, Sister Francis Borgia. *Violets in the King's Garden.* New Orleans: Privately published, 1976.

Hoge, Dean R. *Commitment on Campus: Changes in Religion and Values Over Five Decades.* Philadelphia: Westminster, 1974.

Hoyt, Robert, ed. *The Birth Control Debate.* Kansas City, Mo.: NCR Publication, 1969.

Lofland, John. *Doomsday Cult: A Study of Conversion, Proselytization, and Maintenance of Faith.* Rev. ed. Englewood Cliffs, N.J.: Prentice Hall, 1984.

Mansfield, Patti. *As By A New Pentecost: The Dramatic Beginning of the Catholic Charismatic Renewal.* Steubenville, Ohio: Franciscan University Press, 1992.

Moon, Sun Myung. *The Divine Principle.* New York: HSA Publications, 1973.

Nietz, Mary Jo. *Charisma and Community.* New Brunswick, N.J.: Transactions, 1987.

O'Brien, John A. *Why Priests Leave.* New York: Hawthorn, 1969.

O'Connor, Edward. *The Pentecostal Movement in the Catholic Church.* South Bend, Ind.: Ave Maria Press, 1971.

O'Neill, Dan, ed. *The New Catholics.* New York: Crossroad, 1987.

Ross, Daniel, ed. *Value Development in the University Classroom.* Taiwan: Fu Jen University, 1992.

Saylor, Dennis E. *And You Visited Me.* Medford, Mass.: Morse Press, 1979.

Sherwood, Carleton. *Inquisition: The Persecution and Prosecution of the Rev. Sun Myung Moon.* Washington, D.C.: Regnery Gateway, 1991.

Sontag, Frederick. *Sun Myung Moon and the Unification Church.* Nashville, Tenn.: Abingdon Press, 1977.

Sterkx, H.E. *The Free Negro in Antebellum Louisiana.* Rutherford, N.J.: Fairleigh-Dickinson University, 1972.

Wallace, Ruth A. *They Call Her Pastor*. Albany, N.Y.: State University Press, 1992.

Wilson, Andrew, ed. *The Future of the World: Scholars View the Thought of Reverend Moon*. New York: International Cultural Foundation, 1987.

Wilson, Bryan, ed. *The Social Impact of New Religious Movements*. New York: Rose of Sharon, 1981.

Index